TO KILL
RASPUTIN
THE LIFE AND DEATH OF GRIGORI RASPUTIN

ABOUT THE AUTHOR

Andrew Cook worked for many years as a foreign affairs and defence specialist, and the contacts he made enabled him to navigate and gain access to classified intelligence services archives. He is only the fifth historian to be given special permission under the 1992 'Waldegrave Initiative' by the Cabinet Office to examine closed MI5 documents that will never be released. He was the historical consultant for the recent BBC *Timewatch* documentary on Rasputin, but the key discoveries came after the screening and appear for the first time in *To Kill Rasputin*. He is author of critically acclaimed *Prince Eddy: The King Britain Never Had, Ace of Spies: The True Story of Sidney Reilly* and *M: MI5's First Spymaster*. He is a regular contributor on espionage history to *The Guardian*, *The Times* and *History Today*. He lives in Bedfordshire.

TO KILL
RASPUTIN

THE LIFE AND DEATH OF GRIGORI RASPUTIN

ANDREW COOK

TEMPUS

Cover illustration: ~~...~~ *Rasputin* ~~...~~ al
History, St ~~...~~

Spine illustration: Autopsy photograph of Rasputin, never before published. Courtesy of the Museum of Political History, St Petersburg.

Back cover illustration: Russian police crime scene photograph of the frozen body of Rasputin. Petrovsky Bridge, where he was thrown into the Neva River, is in the background. Courtesy of the Museum of Political History, St Petersburg.

This edition first published 2006

Tempus Publishing Limited
The Mill, Brimscombe Port,
Stroud, Gloucestershire, GL5 2QG
www.tempus-publishing.com

© Andrew Cook, 2005, 2006

The right of Andrew Cook to be identified as the Author
of this work has been asserted in accordance with the
Copyrights, Designs and Patents Act 1988.

British Library Cataloguing in Publication Data.
A catalogue record for this book is available from the British Library.

ISBN 0 7524 3906 5

Typesetting and origination by Tempus Publishing Limited
Printed and bound in Great Britain

Contents

Acknowledgements

I would like to thank the following people for their invaluable help:

In particular I am indebted to Betty Aikenhead and Muriel Harding-Newman (the daughters of John Scale); Edward Harding-Newman (John Scale's grandson); Sandra Noble (Stephen Alley's granddaughter); Michael Alley (Stephen Alley's second cousin); Dr John Alley (from the American branch of the Alley family); Charles Alley (from the South African branch of the Alley family); Gordon Rayner (Oswald Rayner's nephew); Caroline Rayner (Oswald Rayner's daughter); Myra Whelch (Oswald Rayner's first cousin once removed); Michael Winwood (Oswald Rayner's first cousin twice removed); Dmitri Kennaway (stepson of Joyce Frankel, Oswald Rayner's sister); Laurence Huot-Soloviev (great-granddaughter of Grigori Rasputin); 3rd Earl Lloyd George of Dwyfor (grandson of David Lloyd George); Mark Lane (grandson of William Compton); Svetlana Hodakovskaya (Senior Scientist, Museum of Political History, St

Petersburg); Professor Derrick Pounder (Senior Home Office Forensic Pathologist and Head of Forensic Medicine, University of Dundee); Professor Vladimir V. Zharov (Senior Forensic Pathologist, Ministry of Health of the Russian Federation, Moscow) and to HM Government. As a result of an approach to the Cabinet Office, the Government agreed to provide me with a briefing on the British Intelligence Mission in Petrograd for the purpose of this book.

John Francis and John Power of Francis & Francis Investigations have played a key role in tracing the surviving relatives and associates of the British officers involved in the plot and indeed many other key individuals whose parents, grandparents and great-grandparents played a part in the story.

I am also grateful to Bill Adams; Professor Christopher Andrew (Corpus Christi College, Cambridge); Dr Michael Attias; Jordan Auslander; Dmitri Belanovski; Vanessa Bell (Assistant Archivist, News International Ltd); Gill Bennett (Chief Historian, Foreign & Commonwealth Office); Robin Darwall-Smith (University College Archivist, Oxford); Howard Davies (The National Archives); Corinne Fawcett (University of Nottingham Archives); Susheel Gill; Stephen Griffith; Dr Nicholas Hiley (University of Kent); Rachel Hosker (Archivist, University of Glasgow); Professor A.V. Hoffbrand (Royal Free Hospital, London); Igor Kozyrin (Military Medical Archive, St Petersburg); Professor Christine Lee (Royal Free Hospital, London); Alexi Litvin (State Archive of the Russian Federation, GARF, Moscow); Natasha Nikolaeva; David Penn FSA (Keeper of the Department of Exhibits & Firearms, Imperial War Museum, London); Sarah Prescott (Archives Assistant, King's College, London); Kevin Proffitt (Senior Archivist, American Jewish Archives); Clare Rider (Inner Temple Archives); Michael Rosetti (Archives of the New York State Supreme Court); Graham Salt; Laura Scannel (Bar Council Archive); Simon Sebag Montefiore; Professor Robert Service (St Antony's College, Oxford); Oleg

Shishkin; Galina Sveshnikova (Yusupov Palace, St Petersburg); Mari Takayanagi (Archivist, House of Lords Record Office) and John Wells (Department of Manuscripts, Cambridge University Library).

Furthermore, I would like to thank Bill Locke at Lion Television (Executive Producer of the BBC Timewatch film *Who Killed Rasputin?*) whose unstinting support and encouragement enabled me to take this project forward. I am also indebted to John Farren (Editor of the BBC Timewatch series) for commissioning this story and thus enabling the new evidence surrounding Rasputin's murder to be presented to a wider public. Thanks must also go to all those involved in the production of *Who Killed Rasputin?*, in particular to Michael Wadding, Lisa Charles and Richard Cullen, for their part in making it such a powerful and thought-provoking film.

A special thank you also goes to Margaret Ashby; Sophie Bradshaw; Alison Cook; Julia Dvinskaya; Elaine Enstone; Monica Finch; Carolyn Jardine; Denise Khan; Ingrid Lock; Patrick Ooi; Janie New; Hannah Renier; Beryl Rook; Bob Sheth; Andy Watts; Caroline Zahen; and to RP Translate who facilitated the translation of source material into English. Finally, my thanks go to my publisher Jonathan Reeve for his support throughout this project.

NOTE ON DATES

The New Style (Gregorian) calendar, which had been in use in continental Europe and in Britain since 1582, did not replace the Old Style (Julian) calendar in Russia until 1918, when thirteen days were omitted. In this book, dates are given in Old Style in respect of events before 1918 and in New Style for events afterwards. However, British diplomats and officials in Russia used New Style before the change. When two systems are running concurrently in respect to documentary sources, confusion can gain the upper hand. In order to assist the reader, dual dates have therefore been used in certain parts of this book.

PREFACE

When the idea of writing a revised second edition of my biography of 'Ace of Spies' Sidney Reilly was first suggested to me by my publisher Jonathan Reeve, I saw it as an ideal opportunity to follow up several unresolved lines of enquiry that were still outstanding at the time the first edition went to press in 2002.

One of these concerned John Scale, the man who had recruited Reilly to the Secret Intelligence Service, and whose hidden hand had guided his first mission in Russia in April 1918. I knew that Scale had died in 1949, but had so far been unable to trace his family. I was convinced that he was the key not only to Sidney Reilly's Russian mission but to a host of other espionage conundrums that followed the Russian Revolution.

Eventually, in early 2003, after much painstaking research, his daughter Muriel Harding-Newman was located in Scotland. Meeting her persuaded me that the murder of Grigori Rasputin in 1916 was not quite as straightforward as it at first seemed. The traditional account, as told in the 1927 book *Rasputin* by his self-confessed assassin Prince Felix Yusupov, reads like an over-dramatised gothic horror story. Rasputin is first poisoned, then shot and finally drowned in the River Neva by five disaffected aristocrats, led by Yusupov. The conspirators' motives are, according to this account, driven by concern about Rasputin's influence over Tsar Nicholas II and his wife Alexandra. Although this account has been questioned over the years by historians, credible alternative theories had thus far been thin on the ground.

However, according to Muriel Harding-Newman, her father had been instrumental in the murder plot. She also had in her possession an Aladdin's Cave of intelligence material that had belonged to him, including a list of all British intelligence officers who were stationed in Petrograd at the time of Rasputin's death. Once back at home I took the time to read again my copy of Yusupov's book. Over the next few months I managed to trace the families of a number of other British intelligence officers on Scale's list and read the diplomatic and intelligence reports that were being exchanged between London and Petrograd in 1916. These made stark reading, and reminded me just how close Britain came to defeat at this, the darkest hour of the war, haunted by the spectre that Russia was about to conclude a separate peace with Germany and withdraw from the conflict. Time and again the name of Rasputin cropped up in the reports.

In Russia, archive records indicated that three investigations into his death had been inconclusive due to the fact that they had never been completed and, as a consequence, no one had ever been charged or faced cross-examination in a court of law. Two investigations at the time of his death were run concurrently by the Ministry of the Interior and the Ministry of Justice. These had been halted when it became evident that members of the Tsar's own family were involved in the plot. After the fall of the monarchy in March 1917, the new Provisional Government set up an 'Extraordinary Commission of Inquiry for the Investigation of Illegal Acts by Ministers and Other Responsible Persons'. Among the many issues it sought to investigate were

Rasputin's influence and the circumstances surrounding his death. This was to be the responsibility of the Commission's Thirteenth Section. The enquiry was still ongoing when the Bolsheviks seized power and closed down the Commission.

Rasputin's dramatic death has, to a great degree, obscured other questions about his life. Why, for example, does the story about a peasant from a distant Siberian village becoming the all-powerful favourite of the last Russian Emperor excite us more than almost any other episode in Russian history? Why are there more lies and concealment than truth in the story of his murder? What is hidden under the contradictions of his life that have been woven from the real facts, rumours, mysticism, myths and pure invention? Was Rasputin a victim or an immoral charlatan? An evil demon that brought down the royal family, or somebody who could have been its saviour?

These were some of the questions foremost in my mind when I set out to reinvestigate the circumstances behind his death. The results of that search eventually led to the commissioning of the BBC Timewatch film *Who Killed Rasputin?*, for which I acted as Historical Consultant, and ultimately to the publication of this book, which draws on significant new discoveries made since the film was broadcast.

Principal Characters

Stephen Alley	Member of the British Intelligence Mission in Petrograd.
Alexander Balk	Governor of Petrograd.
Sir George Buchanan	British Ambassador to Petrograd.
Byzhinski	Prince Yusupov's butler.
Mansfield Cumming	Known as 'C', Head of MI1c, the British Secret Service.
Grand Duchess Elizaveta Fyodorovna	Grand Duke Dmitri Pavlovich's surrogate mother.
David Lloyd George	Britain's Secretary of State for War after Kitchener's death in June 1916.

Maria (Mounya) Golovina	Mutual friend of Rasputin and Prince Yusupov.
Sir Samuel Hoare	Head of the British Intelligence Mission in Petrograd.
Bishop Iliodor	See Sergei Trufanov.
Lord Kitchener	Britain's Secretary of State for War 1914–16.
Vera Koralli	Celebrated Russian ballerina and mistress of Grand Duke Dmitri Pavlovich.
Professor Kossorotov	Russian pathologist who undertook the original post mortem of Rasputin's body.
Stanislaus Lazovert	The medical doctor of Purish-kevich's military detachment, recruited by Purishkevich to drive on the night of Rasputin's murder.
Robert H. Bruce Lockhart	British consular officer in Moscow.
A.A. Makarov	Minister of Justice, formerly Minister of the Interior.
Ivan Manasevich Manuilov	Jewish journalist, spy and double agent, 'secretary' to Rasputin.
Grand Duke Alexander Mikhailovich	Princess Irina Yusupova's father and Prince Yusupov's

	father-in-law. Also a relative of Dmitri Pavlovich.
Ivan Nefedov	Prince Yusupov's batman.
Grand Duke Nikolai Nikolaivich	Tsar Nicholas's uncle and Supreme Commander of the Russian Armies until relieved of his post.
Grand Duke Dmitri Pavlovich	Tsar Nicholas's second cousin and one-time protégé; friend of Prince Yusupov who was present at the murder of Rasputin.
Lt-Col. Popel	Officer of the Detached Gendarme Corps and General Popov's right-hand man.
General Popov	Commander-in-Chief of the Corps of Gendarmes and chief investigator of Rasputin's disappearance.
Alexander Protopopov	Russian Minister of the Interior.
Vladimir Purishkevich	Monarchist and well-known Member of the Duma. An enemy of Rasputin and present at his murder.
Maria Rasputina	Rasputin's elder daughter.

Varvara Rasputina	Rasputin's younger daughter.
Oswald Rayner	Member of the British Intelligence Mission in Petrograd.
Mikhail Rodzyanko	Speaker of the Third and Fourth Dumas.
John Scale	Member of the British Intelligence Mission in Petrograd.
Aron Simanovich	Rasputin's close friend, secretary and agent.
Hon. Albert Stopford	British businessman and diplomat.
Sergei Sukhotin	Military lieutenant and friend of Yusupov. Present on the night of the murder.
Sergei Trufanov	Also known as Bishop Iliodor. Notorious Orthodox preacher, anti-Semite and former friend of Rasputin who stole letters from the monk's home in Siberia.
Alexis Vasiliev	Chief of Police in Petrograd.
Anna Vyrubova	Lady-in-waiting and close friend of the Tsarina.
Robert Wilton	The *Times*'s correspondent in Petrograd at the time of the murder.

Grand Duchess Xenia	Princess Irina Yusupova's mother and Prince Yusupov's mother-in-law.
Prince Felix Yusupov	Also Count Sumarokov-Elston, Russian aristocrat and self-confessed assassin of Rasputin.
Princess Irina Yusupova	Prince Yusupov's wife.

ONE

MANHUNT

Gorokhovaya Street was a sober sort of place – indeed, a household name for high-minded respectability because of its police station; the regulation coat worn by plain-clothes men was popularly called a *gorokhovayo*.[1] It was only a mile from the private palaces and vast public spaces of the fashionable centre of Petrograd (Russia's capital city St Petersburg, until the war made German-sounding names anathema). If you lived there you were prosperous enough. The residential block at number 64, a warren of high-ceilinged apartments with a huge carriage entrance, was well supplied with heat and light, which was more than could be said for a lot of dwellings in Petrograd in the freezing winter of 1916. The war at this stage had left even the middle classes short of essential supplies and most heads of household were struggling to provide their families with coal, lamp oil, food and clothing.

The head of the household at Apartment 20, 64 Gorokhovaya Street was Grigori Yefimovich Rasputin, the tall, bearded spiritual advisor to Her Majesty the Tsarina, and he was a good provider. The flat was solidly furnished and even had a telephone. Rasputin himself had a motor car at his command. Wherever he went he was received with awe, and his supporters (though not his opponents) were convinced that he was a *starets* or holy man. Early on this Saturday morning, 17 December 1916, with the city still dark and blanketed with snow, the maid Katya Petyorkina was already up, had lit the lamps and was busying herself with the stove and the samovar when somebody knocked at the door.

The two visitors were officers of the Okhrana, the political police. The Okhrana was just one of nine separate forces working for the Tsar through Minister of the Interior Alexander Protopopov and Chief of Police Alexis Vasiliev, but it was the most feared. The Tsar, and the Tsarina in particular, insisted that the *starets* be protected, for they clung to him for emotional support as they struggled with their young son's bouts of illness. The boy had haemophilia, an incurable disease inherited through the female line by some of the descendants of Britain's Queen Victoria. The Tsarina, who was Victoria's granddaughter, had acted as a carrier of the disease, and now lived in superstitious dread that if anything befell Rasputin her son's life would be at risk.

All the same, Katya Petyorkina, Rasputin's two teenage daughters, Maria and Varvara, and his niece Anya who also lived in the apartment, knew they should mind what they said around these people. Everything got back to the Tsar in the end and there were things he was better off not knowing.

The two agents wanted to talk to Rasputin; they didn't say why. But when Katya went to Rasputin's bedroom to wake him up she found that he had not yet come home. This was unusual.

Maria, Varvara and Anya rose hurriedly and dressed. One of the Okhrana men went off to find whoever had been in charge of the block overnight, and got hold of the yard superintendent. He confirmed that a big car with a canvas hood had rolled up after midnight. He had spoken to its passenger, had seen this passenger being welcomed by Rasputin himself at the back door, and later he had seen both Rasputin and the visitor leave in the car towards the city centre.[2]

Back in the flat, the Okhrana men heard whispering and murmuring between the girls and the maid. When they questioned Katya, a woman of twenty-nine, she admitted that somebody had called at the kitchen door at the back of the flat at around half-past twelve the previous night, and Rasputin had gone out with whoever it was. She slept in a curtained-off corner of the kitchen, and she had heard voices. That was all she had to say.

The girls volunteered no more. They were worried. The two taciturn snoopers remained on the premises, and one of them muttered into the telephone. Other people would start turning up soon. People came every day to see Rasputin and hear him talk. These days he was at his best in the morning, before he'd had a drink.

Maria, at nineteen the elder daughter and already engaged to be married, knew her father had expected to go out with Prince Felix Yusupov (known to his friends as 'the Little One') to the Yusupov Palace in the middle of the night. He had told her so and she wouldn't forget something like that – she knew what the inside of a palace was like, having been privately presented to the Tsarina, and she had heard that Yusupov's houses were as splendid as the Winter Palace itself. She had even walked past the endless yellow and white frontage of the one on the Moika. She knew Yusupov only by sight; he was a tall, slender, epicene young man.

At about eight o'clock, Rasputin's niece Anya, a smart and resourceful girl, telephoned to Maria (Mounya) Golovina – most likely out of the hearing of the Okhrana men. Mounya was the friend who had originally introduced Rasputin to Yusupov, but Rasputin had specifically instructed his daughters not to tell Mounya where he was going the previous night because Yusupov didn't want her tagging along uninvited.[3] Mounya was older, about thirty like Yusupov, and an educated woman who drank in everything Rasputin said. She had a pale, tight little face and was forever at the flat. A good many of Rasputin's hangers-on

were well-off women like her, who wore furs and smart hats with
aigrettes and well-cut, tailored suits, even in wartime. But Mounya
was a good sort.

Anya asked Mounya to call the Little One and find out what
was going on; she thought he might have been going out with
her uncle last night. Mounya confirmed that Rasputin had said
that he was going somewhere special, but she said that if he had
gone out with Felix Yusupov they'd probably have gone to the
gypsies. That meant going out to the Islands and dancing and
drinking all night, so they would still be asleep, and there was
nothing to worry about. He would be home soon. She would
be over later.[4]

Rasputin's close friends, Aron Simanovich and Father Isodor,
arrived a little later. They were already concerned because
Rasputin had told them where he was going and promised to
telephone to say he was safe, but he had not done so. Out of
consideration for the girls' feelings, they did not add that they
had already made enquiries at the police station at 61 Moika and
had heard rumours of trouble at the Yusupov Palace opposite.[5]
Ivan Manasevich Manuilov, another man whom the girls knew,
came in, and then some ladies – it was normal for a crowd to
gather at Rasputin's home. The samovar was kept steaming and
conversation wandered, while anxiety increasingly nagged at
Rasputin's two daughters; Simanovich was obviously on edge,
and nobody would tell them why. The sisters knew their father
had become important in this city. It wasn't everyone who got
phone calls from the Tsarina herself. He was the peasant who
consorted with royalty. Often he was called to the royal residence at Tsarskoye Selo several times in a week. At school there
were girls who sneered at them behind their back for having
come from Siberia and being the daughters of an unlettered
muzhik (peasant), but their father had influence, and those girls
were somehow wary of the Rasputina sisters.

They wished he would turn up; it was mortifying. All these
women – they only hoped he would be sober when he did. The
Okhrana men asked a lot of questions but nobody could tell

them anything. Having made their first communication back to headquarters the two officers remained on the premises, waiting.

Fifteen miles from the city centre Her Majesty the Tsarina Alexandra was at home with her four daughters at the Alexander Palace at Tsarskoye Selo. It was one of many mansions on the royal estate, one of which belonged to her great friend, Anna Vyrubova, a portly woman who looked older than her thirty years.

It was Vyrubova who got a call from Mounya Golovina that Saturday morning. She learned that Rasputin, 'Our Friend' as he was known to the imperial couple, had gone out the night before and failed to return home. It is possible that something was also said about Yusupov.

Vyrubova herself had received death threats in the past. Rasputin's enemies thought that he, Vyrubova and the Tsarina made up a malevolent triumvirate of power behind the Tsar. At this time she was spending her days in her own home but sleeping at the Alexander Palace, to which the Tsarina had invited her for her own protection.[6] Vyrubova made the Tsarina aware that Rasputin's absence was giving cause for concern.

Back in the city, the Minister of the Interior, Alexander Protopopov, had received an early-morning tip-off from the Governor of Petrograd, Alexander Balk, that Rasputin was rumoured to have been shot at the Yusupov Palace in the early hours. As a result, Protopopov made an incognito visit to Rasputin's apartment and discovered that he had not returned home.

Later that morning Protopopov signed Decree No. 573 initiating an immediate and secret investigation into the 'disappearance of Grigori Yefimovich Rasputin'. As chief investigator, Protopopov appointed General P.K. Popov, the Commander-in-Chief of the Corps of Gendarmes. Popov was an energetic and dedicated investigator who specialised in political enquiry. Prior to 1914 he had been head of the city's Okhrana Department. His first move was to descend on the policemen who had been called out to the Yusupov Palace and the officers stationed on the opposite side of the canal and take statements. Viewed from the police station, all arrivals and departures at the tall central doors of the palace across the canal were illuminated as on a distant stage. And how sound carries across water. Last night something had been going on all right, specifically in the courtyard in front of a house that adjoined the palace. That house was less imposing than the main building and set back from the road, but it too belonged to the Yusupovs.

Soon, a carefully worded telegram was sent to the Tsar at the Stavka, the wartime Army Command Headquarters at Moghilev several hundred miles south of Petrograd, stating that, on the night of Friday 16 December,

> by house 94 on the Moika owned by Prince Yusupov, a police-man on duty heard a few revolver shots and was soon invited to the study of Prince Yusupov, where he himself was and the unknown person who introduced himself as Purishkevich. The latter said 'I am Purishkevich. Rasputin is dead. If you love the Tsar and the homeland, you'll keep your mouth shut.' The police-man reported this to his superior. The investigation conducted this morning has established that one of Yusupov's guests, about 3.00a.m., was shooting in the courtyard adjacent to building 94 that has an entrance leading directly to the Prince's study. A human cry was heard and the sound of a departing motor-car. The shooter was in a field uniform. The immediate examination of the snow revealed blood spots. When questioned at the City Governor's Office, the young prince stated that he'd had a party that night, but Rasputin was not there.
>
> Enquiries at Rasputin's flat at Gorokhovaya 64 revealed that on the 16th December at 9.00p.m. Rasputin, as he always did, left the bodyguards attached to his flat and the motor-car, telling them he would not be going out that night and to get some sleep. The interrogation of domestic servants and the yard man estab-lished that at 12.30a.m. a big canvas-covered motor approached, in which sat an unknown person and the driver. The unknown person went through the back door to Rasputin's flat, where the latter appeared to be expecting him, since he greeted him as an

old acquaintance and went out with him through the same back door. They got in the car and drove down Gorokhovaya Street towards Morskaya Street.

Rasputin has not returned home and efforts to find him have so far proved unsuccessful. There are strong grounds to assume that he was shot in Yusupov's courtyard, his body taken out of town and hidden away.[7]

This Okhrana briefing went directly to the Tsar in person. The idea that Rasputin might have been murdered would appal him. The scenes the Tsarina would make; the blame, the resentment, the hysteria. On the other hand, he might now regain some authority in his own household...

The naming of Vladimir Purishkevich, a well-known member of the Duma (parliament) and monarchist loudly opposed to Rasputin, would have dismayed Tsar Nicholas, but not as much as the mention of Prince Felix Yusupov, who was married to his niece. He must also have been concerned to learn that his second cousin and one-time protégé, Grand Duke Dmitri Pavlovich, had also been present at the Yusupov Palace that Friday night. But Dmitri had always been close – too close – to Felix.[8]

That afternoon the Tsarina – German by birth, but brought up in England – scribbled a frantic note to the Tsar at the Stavka in her sometimes incoherent Russian.

We are sitting together – can imagine our feelings – thoughts – our Friend has disappeared. Yesterday A[nna Vyrubova] saw him and he said Felix asked him to come in the night, a motor wld fetch him to see Irina...

This night big scandal at Yusupov's house – big meeting, Dmitri [Pavlovich], Purishkevich etc. all drunk, Police heard shots, Purishkevich ran out screaming to the police that our Friend was killed.

Police searching...

Felix wished to leave tonight for Crimea, [I] begged Kalinin [Protopopov] to stop him...

Felix claims He never came to the house and never asked him.
Seems like quite a paw [a trap]. I still trust in God's mercy that
one has only driven Him off somewhere…

I cannot and won't believe he has been killed. God have
mercy…

…come quickly – nobody will dare to touch her [Anna
Vyrubova] or do anything when you are here.

Felix often came to him here…[9]

Protopopov sent a memo to the head of the Palace Guard,
General Voikov. Voikov was not at Tsarskoye Selo this weekend.
Protopopov's note contained more information about what
Rasputin had been wearing – 'an expensive shirt and a fur coat'
– and added that a party had taken place at the Yusupov Palace
the night before and the Gendarmerie had now begun a full
investigation.

For my part I have directed that the investigation is to be conducted according to martial law in order to have all the circumstances of the case elucidated thoroughly and without delay. In
accordance with Her Majesty's orders kindly go on Monday
directly to Tsarskoye Selo without calling at Petrograd on your
way.[10]

Mounya Golovina had rung Yusupov as she promised. She knew
he was staying at the palace of his father-in-law Grand Duke
Alexander Mikhailovich, further along the Moika, while his
own set of apartments at the Yusupov Palace was refurbished.
The servants told her 'they' were still asleep; which supported
her theory that Yusupov and Rasputin had been out at the gypsy
encampment.

When she arrived at Rasputin's apartment on Gorokhovaya
Street it was full of people, some looking concerned yet reluc-
tant to voice fears that might distress Rasputin's daughters. The
girls were very tense. Mounya made some excuse to take Maria
out with her to order more refreshments, and together they

made their way past snow piles down the salt-strewn street to a local fruit shop, which had a telephone. Mounya made the call, but this time the servants told her Yusupov had gone out. She left a message. They went back to the flat, hoping that he would soon ring her back.

A couple of miles north, across the wide River Neva separating fashionable Petrograd from the St Peter and St Paul Fortress and the well-wooded Islands, a bridge guard called Fyodor Kyzmin began his shift at midday. The Little Neva here separated Petrovski Island from Kristovski Island. Kyzmin had to trudge across the long, wide bridge every hour.[11] It was covered in thick snow and any trace of recent crime would be visible. At about one o'clock, he was completing his usual round under a lowering grey sky in a temperature a couple of degrees below zero when some passing workmen told him that further back there was blood on the bridge, its barrier and its support, and a shoe lay on the ice below. He went to check and found that they were right. He hadn't noticed this before. He went to fetch a policeman, who, having checked, also found that they were right, and went to fetch an inspector, Asonov. They all came back and the inspector took measurements, made notes, and induced Kyzmin to fish about with a boat-hook and retrieve 'a man's galosh and a worn brown shoe, Size 10, manufactured by Treygolnik'.

Not wanting to stir up trouble, Inspector Asonov put in a report early in the afternoon.

The search of the water space opposite the location mentioned in the statement, where the ice had not yet covered the water and pools of water had formed, was conducted and did not reveal anything suspicious. Removed galosh and shoe were handed to the guard Fedor Kyzmin until further instructions are given.[12]

However, there were no divers in the Gendarmerie; the River Police had to provide those, and the system was slow to crank into action. It seems unlikely that any divers inspected the

Petrovski Bridge on Saturday. Nobody came to ask Kyzmin, in
his hut, about any shoe, or galosh, that had been found.

At last, at lunchtime Yusupov telephoned the apartment on
Gorokhovaya Street and asked to speak to Mounya Golovina.
She took the phone and – aware that the Okhrana were listen-
ing – spoke in English. She looked agitated. Shortly afterwards
she left, telling Maria that she would be back but that she must
speak to Yusupov alone, at the home she shared with her mother
on the Moika. Maria and the others noticed that she seemed
agitated. And when Mounya got home it is possible that, before
he arrived, Anna Vyrubova called to tell her what the Okhrana
suspected about Yusupov's involvement, because according to
him Mounya:

> …rushed up and said in a stifled voice: 'What have you done
> with him? They say he was murdered at your house and that it
> was you who killed him.'[13]

Yusupov tried to reassure her. He told her that policemen had
been crawling all over the place this morning – he had held a
small house-warming party last night and things had got rather
out of hand; his closest friend Dmitri, Grand Duke Dmitri
Pavlovich, had shot one of the yard dogs by accident. There
had been a great fuss – there was a police station just across
the canal beside the Ministry of the Interior, so of course they
had heard the gun – and then Purishkevich had said something
stupid to a policeman about shooting Rasputin, and at the
crack of dawn a couple of examining magistrates had turned
up asking about Rasputin and looking at the dog's bloodstains
in the snow in the yard. But Rasputin hadn't been near the
place! As it happened he'd rung up in the middle of the house-
warming to ask Yusupov to make up a party and come out to
the gypsies, but Yusupov had made his excuses because he'd got
guests. He'd actually gone back into the dinner party and told
them all what Rasputin had said. Anyway, he had been badly
shaken by the examining magistrates and then this morning, at

his father-in-law's place where he was trying to get some sleep, he was woken up by a policeman called Grigoriev and had to go through the whole thing again. He had fully explained the situation. It was all cleared up now.

Mounya was not quite so sure.

> 'It's all too horrible,' she said. 'The Empress and Anna [Vyrubova] are convinced that you murdered him last night at your house.'
>
> 'Will you telephone to Tsarskoye Selo and ask if the Empress will receive me? I'll explain the whole thing to her, but be quick.'
>
> [Mounya] telephoned to Tsarskoye Selo and was told that Her Majesty was expecting me. As I was leaving, she took me by the arm: 'Don't go to Tsarskoye Selo, I beseech you,' she said. 'Something dreadful will happen to you if you do; they'll never believe you are innocent...'[14]

Yusupov was spared 'something dreadful' when Anna Vyrubova rang and said the Tsarina had collapsed in a faint, and didn't want Yusupov to come to the Alexander Palace but demanded that he write down what had happened. He promised to do so and left.

Later that afternoon Mounya returned to Rasputin's apartment with her mother, hoping that Yusupov was telling the truth. He would probably figure in a list of suspects, if the police were making a list of people bearing a grudge against Rasputin. On the other hand, a list like that would be very long indeed. And back in the apartment that evening they were thinking exactly that, and were beginning to fear the worst, and Mounya and her mother had begun to cry a little when they heard a loud knock at the door.

The visitors wore uniform. General Popov and Lt-Col. Popel of the Detached Gendarme Corps explained that they were there to conduct certain enquiries on behalf of the Ministry of the Interior.

Popov had already spoken to Yusupov's batman Ivan Nefedev at the Yusupov Palace, and had realised that he was going to get

precious little change out of any of the servants there. According
to Nefedev, on the night of Friday 16 December,

> I did not hear any gunshots either in the dining room or outside
> in the streets. About 4.00a.m. I heard the bell and entered the
> Prince's study. The guests were already gone. The Prince told me
> to go outside to the yard and have a look at what had happened
> there. I went out through the side entrance to the yard of house
> number 92, however, by that time there was nobody there and
> I did not notice anything unusual. I reported this to the Prince.
> He rung the bell again a few minutes later and ordered me to
> have a look in the yard again because there was a dead dog. I
> went through the side door to the yard of house number 92
> and this time noticed a dog lying by the fence… the dead dog
> was a mongrel which used to live in the Yusupov's house. I have
> nothing more to say on the matter.

Mounya Golovina was interviewed on the Saturday. The rest
had to wait until the following morning, which was fortunate
for the investigators, as the women's attitude to the police would
change overnight. That evening, however, Mounya told Popov
that, on Friday 16 December,

> I arrived at Grigori Efimovich Rasputin's apartment at around 12
> noon and stayed there until 10.00p.m. On the night of that day
> Grigori Efimovich was not going to go anywhere, although in
> the morning while slightly excited he said that, 'I'm going to go
> out tonight', but he did not say where to. When I asked him to let
> me know if he would go, he responded that he would not tell me.
> I told him I would sense it anyway. Grigori Efimovich then said,
> 'you would sense but you would not find me'. We had this con-
> versation as a joke therefore I did not attach any importance to it.
> I went home around 10.00p.m. Grigori Efimovich used to call his
> male visitors 'dear'. I used to call Prince Felix Felixovich Yusupov
> 'the little one'… Prince Yusupov was first introduced to Rasputin
> about five years ago at my apartment, later they met once or

twice again at our apartment. This year, 1916, Prince Yusupov saw Rasputin at our apartment, and according to the Prince, Rasputin made a better impression on him than in previous years. The Prince complained of chest pains and I advised him to visit Rasputin's apartment. Prince Yusupov visited Rasputin with me twice in late November and at the beginning of December 1916 – he stayed less than an hour at Rasputin's apartment on both occasions. Once Rasputin asked Prince Yusupov to take him to the gypsies. That is why when on the morning of [Saturday] 17th December Rasputin's daughters told me on the telephone that Grigori Efimovich left the night before with 'the little one', meaning Prince Yusupov, I reassured them saying that there was nothing to worry about. I assumed that perhaps they went to the gypsies, he even wanted to pre-warn the place they were going to visit. On the afternoon of 17th December Prince Yusupov visited me and told me that Grigori Efimovich telephoned him on the night of [Friday] 16th December and suggested visiting the gypsies. However, the Prince told Rasputin that he had guests and could not go that evening. When Prince Yusupov returned to his guests after that telephone conversation he told them: 'do you know who called me? Rasputin suggested we visit the gypsies together'. As Prince Yusupov stated, he did not see Rasputin during the evening and night of 16th December.[15]

In fact, Yusupov had spent a busy morning firefighting – dashing from point to point in his chauffeured car. He knew Rasputin was dead; he had been intimately involved in arranging his murder. Now he set about covering his tracks. He made a statement to the city's Governor, Alexander Balk. Then he was whisked from the Prefecture back to the palace on the Moika to check for bloodstains in daylight, and directed the servants to clean up wherever he found anything incriminating, before racing over to Mounya Golovina's to act the innocent. He left Mounya's house, which was also on the Moika, in order to visit Dmitri Pavlovich at his own apartment in the Sergei Palace on the Nevski Prospekt.

Dmitri Pavlovich, a sallow man with moody Greek eyes, was a few years younger than Felix Yusupov. Over a late lunch he was able to reveal to Yusupov what exactly had happened early that morning after he and the other murderers drove off with Rasputin's body, and roughly where it had been dumped. Lt Sergei Sukhotin, who had been with them throughout the previous night and had assisted in the murder, came in and was sent off to fetch Vladimir Purishkevich, the idea being that they would all get their stories in line. This was particularly impor-tant because Felix Yusupov now had to compose a letter to the Tsarina.

Purishkevich, whose loose talk had contributed so much to the mess they were in, was maintaining his usual high profile. He was an odd-looking character, bald with pebble glasses, and excitable. Having previously arranged for any member of the Duma who wished – there were about 400 of them – to visit his hospital train from nine o'clock in the morning onwards on Saturday 17 December, he had spent a busy morning show-ing parties around. Medical aid and expertise were carried to Russian soldiers at the front by around 300 private hospital trains like his; many rich individuals sponsored locomotives and staff and beautifully fitted carriages, but few regularly trav-elled with them as he did. He had made more than one trip to Romania in recent months, during the ignominious retreat in which Romanian and Russian troops had been beaten back by Germans. On his latest return, just six weeks before, he had personally reported to the Tsar at the Stavka on the situation in Rena, Braila and Galati. He had chosen this particular Saturday on which to depart once more on a mission of mercy.[16]

He and his wife and two sons were already installed in their private carriage and the train was ready to leave Petrograd's Warsaw Station that evening on its long journey across the snowy wastes of Russia and Ukraine. His wife was a qualified nurse and his sons would act as orderlies. Purishkevich would support them and was sincere in his wish to assist. There was no doubt that his humanitarian efforts were valuable, albeit probably funded, at least, by the sinister Black Hundreds, a pro-German secret society of Russian autocrats. Purishkevich is said to have been 'a major conduit' for finance to this and other similar organisations for years; they paid for pogroms against the Jewish population.[17]

Purishkevich had slept in his clothes, spent the morning of Saturday 17 December conducting guests around his train, and in the afternoon had run errands and paid visits. He had arranged the train's departure and was about to take a final meal before leaving when Sukhotin arrived to drag him off to the Sergei Palace for the final conspiratorial debriefing. He later recalled that:

> At the palace I found both my host and Yusupov. They were both extremely agitated, and were drinking cup after cup of black coffee with brandy. They declared that they had not slept at all last night, and could not have had a more disturbing day, for the Empress Alexandra Feodorovna [the Tsarina] had already been informed of the disappearance and even the death of Rasputin and had named us as his murderers.[18]

All the conspirators contributed to Yusupov's letter. Unctuous deference and injured innocence were laid on with a trowel...

> Your Imperial Majesty,
> I hasten to obey the commands of Your Majesty and to report what occurred in my house last night...
> I had arranged a little supper as a house-warming in my new quarters and invited my friends, a few ladies and the Grand Duke Dmitri Pavlovich. About midnight I was rung up by Grigori Yefimovich, who invited me to go with him and see the gypsies. I declined, giving as my excuse the party in my own house, and I asked him where he was speaking from, for a great many voices could be heard coming over the wire. But he answered 'You want to know too much' and with that he rang off. That is all I heard from Grigori Yefimovich during the night...

> About three o'clock most of my guests took their departure,
> and after I had said good-bye to the Grand Duke and two ladies
> I retired with the others to my study.[19]

It was a masterly picture. Behold the considerate host, enjoying a
final nightcap with his guests before a roaring fire.

> Suddenly I had the impression that a shot had been fired close by.
> I called my man and ordered him to see what had happened. He
> came back almost at once with the report that a shot had been
> heard, but no-one knew where it had come from…

There was a good deal more along similar lines. The Tsarina
does not seem to have been convinced.

Yusupov was going to leave that Saturday evening to join his
wife, who was unwell, and their child in the Crimea and spend
the Christmas holiday. Grand Duke Dmitri Pavlovich, a serving
officer, was due to return to the Tsar's headquarters, the Stavka,
on Sunday.

Today, Saturday, was 17 December in Petrograd, where the old
Julian calendar was still in use. In Western Europe and North
America it was 30 December. So for thirty-six-year-old newcomer Sir Samuel Hoare, Head of the British Intelligence
Mission in Petrograd,[20] it was the last working day of 1916.
Tomorrow he and his wife would celebrate New Year's Eve quietly. They were not yet so well integrated in the Petrograd social
scene as some other officers of the Mission. A fair-haired, open-
faced fellow, on this Saturday afternoon he was at the Restriction
of Enemy Supplies Committee meeting – a Duma committee
meeting which was taking place despite the sudden prorogation
of the Duma the previous day. The point under discussion was
how to keep goods from the Central Powers – Germany, Turkey,
and Italy – out of Russia.

The meeting dragged on with the usual Russian disregard for
time. Hoare remembered that:

Several times during the sitting individual members left the room
and returned with whispered messages to their neighbours. At
the time I paid no attention to these interruptions of business.
When the Committee broke up, I went with the Chairman and
the Secretary to another room for the purpose of discussing various points connected with the publication of the Russian Black
List. Before we could go far with our discussion, a well-known
official of the Ministry of Commerce entered with the news
that Rasputin had been murdered that morning by the Grand
Duke Dmitri Pavlovich and Prince Yusupov. Professor Struve,
Chairman of the Committee, at once sent out for an evening
paper. In a few minutes the *Bourse Gazette* was brought in with
the news actually published in it. The *Bourse Gazette* is always a
paper of headlines. In this case the first heavy type was devoted
to the peace proposals, the second to the fighting in Romania.
Then came a headline: *Death Of Grigori Rasputin In Petrograd*. In
the body of the paper there was little more than a single line and
that on the second page. The announcement ran as follows: *At
six o'clock this morning Grigori Rasputin Novich died after a party in
one of the most aristocratic houses in the centre of Petrograd.*

To one who has only been in Russia a few months the news
was almost overwhelming. To Russian public men like Professor
Struve, a man whose name has for a generation been in the
forefront of Russian political and economic life, the news
seemed almost incredible. As I had no wish to appear to meddle
in Russian internal affairs, I did not attempt to discuss the situation; nor needless to say could our prosaic conversation about
the Black List continue.[21]

'I did not attempt to discuss the situation'. A strange remark for
the head of the British Intelligence Mission to make; but then
spying, at its untrustworthy end, was not Hoare's speciality.

The following Sunday morning he set about drafting a report
for despatch to London. By then he had 'been in touch with
various people representing different classes and sections of
opinion' and concluded that Yusupov had held 'a ball' on the

Friday night which was attended by several Grand Dukes. He had heard more than one version of what happened but 'the generally accepted story is that he was shot as he was leaving the house in a motor. The motor is supposed to have taken the body to the Islands where it was thrown into the sea or one of the rivers.'

Hoare felt confident enough to write all this down on Sunday and send it, amended, on Monday. But others in the British military and diplomatic community had heard about Rasputin's disappearance even before the Saturday evening paper appeared.[22] Many members of the British Intelligence Mission occupied rooms at the Hotel Astoria, opposite St Isaac's Cathedral, more or less permanently, and nothing is known of what they had heard or whether, indeed, they spent Saturday sleeping off an eventful Friday night. But the Hon. Albert Stopford, a businessman and diplomat, a frequent visitor from England who was particularly well connected and always stayed at the Hotel d'Europe on the Nevski, had certainly been royally entertained on the night of Friday 16 December, so the next day,

> about 5p.m. was asleep when Seymour came. A friend in the police whom he met in the street told him Rasputin had been shot three times by Felix Yusupov. He did not know if Rasputin was dead. I telephoned to the Embassy but Lady Georgina was out. She rang me up at 5.40 [p.m.] to say she had just heard the report.... In the hotel the rumour was generally known by 7.15 [p.m.].[23]

Lady Georgina's husband, the British Ambassador Sir George Buchanan, telephoned his friend Grand Duke Nikolai Mikhailovich, a relative of Dmitri Pavlovich, at half-past five on Saturday 17 December and told him the news. Stopford set off for the theatre, where he saw 'Grand Duke Boris [Vladimirovich], Grand Duke Dmitri [Pavlovich] and a cousin of Felix Yusupov's' but nobody knew anything definite. The 'cousin of Yusupov's' was probably Vera Koralli, a ballerina who was Dmitri Pavlovich's lover at the time. She was briefly staying in Petrograd while engaged to perform with the Moscow Imperial Theatre.[24]

Stopford was shocked but not at all surprised that Rasputin had been done away with. He had heard ten days before, apparently from Dmitri Pavlovich himself, that what he coyly described in his diary as a 'tragic dénouement' might be on the cards.

By now the diligently lying Felix Yusupov had (according to his own later account) visited A.A. Makarov, the Minister of Justice, who seemed pretty well satisfied with the shot-dog story,[25] and Mikhail Rodzyanko, the Speaker of the Duma, who was a distant relation, and who 'applauded my conduct in a voice of thunder' for he knew that Yusupov had intended to kill Rasputin. As Yusupov nipped about town in his small brown motor car he might have been less sanguine had he known that the Okhrana were sceptical of everything he said and preferred to listen to the police witnesses and officials who had searched the yard at his palace on 94 Moika.

Dmitri Pavlovich, having rested that Saturday morning before his late lunch with Yusupov, was now running on adrenalin. He dined that evening at the Yacht Club. There he was seen by his father's cousin Nikolai Mikhailovich, who had heard of the scandal, and of Felix's involvement, from Sir George Buchanan at half-past five.[26] Dmitri Pavlovich left the theatre early in order to avoid ovations.[27] He had given orders for a party to be held in his apartment, and when his guests left theatres and restaurants, they began to arrive.

Yusupov returned to dine early at the palace of his father-in-law Alexander Mikhailovich, where he was staying. Afterwards he was due at the station to catch his train out of town. As he entered the hall a porter told him that a lady was waiting. She had claimed that she had an appointment with him at seven. He had made no such arrangement and when he heard her description – 'she was dressed in black, but he could not make out her features as she was wearing a thick veil' – he was understandably suspicious and took a surreptitious peep at the waiting visitor. She was 'one of Rasputin's most fervent admirers', so he told the porter to tell her he would be back very late, and hurried off to pack.[28] And then, in Yusupov's own account,

> The whole town believed that I was responsible for Rasputin's disappearance. Directors of factories and representatives of various businesses rang up to tell me that their workmen had decided to form a bodyguard to protect me if the need arose.[29]

Prince Felix Yusupov was having a long day, and it had not ended yet. He had just retired to his room to discuss events with Prince Fyodor Romanov, one of his brothers-in-law, when Nikolai Mikhailovich bustled in to see him. Nikolai Mikhailovich was about sixty, liberal in his views, and a very good friend of Sir George Buchanan, the British Ambassador.[30] He had called much earlier in the evening and had been put off; but he was certainly persistent.

The others left, and Nikolai Mikhailovich tried to bluff Yusupov into telling the truth. He failed; he left; and at last Yusupov got some sleep.[31]

Purishkevich, the eccentric member of the Duma, steamed out of the city at ten o'clock that Saturday night on his hospital train. It was he who had first boasted of Rasputin's murder to a policeman, yet, according to extant records, nobody had questioned him further.

At midnight, a couple of miles away across the icy Neva and the woods of Petrovski Island, Fyodor Kyzmin was to due to finish his shift at midnight. The beat policeman he'd seen in the morning came over to his hut shortly beforehand, and as soon as he had handed over to the night guard, Kyzmin and the policeman set off together through the snow to the police station with the boot. (From now on, most accounts refer to it as a single, brown boot).

A police inspector took it, at three o'clock in the morning on Sunday, to 64 Gorokhovaya Street. Most of the household were still up and Rasputin's friend Aron Simanovich was with the girls. The boot was identified by Simanovich, Maria and Varvara Rasputina, two Okhrana agents and the lady *dvornik*, or concierge, of the block, as belonging to the missing Grigori Rasputin.

Dmitri Pavlovich's party in the Sergei Palace reportedly continued until half-past seven on Sunday morning, and was 'of a most riotous description'.[32]

TWO

FINGER OF SUSPICION

Prince Felix Yusupov was interviewed by General Popov of the Gendarmerie. The date on his statement is Sunday 18 December, and it seems likely that this interview took place early, because by the end of the morning Yusupov, by his own account, had moved out of the palace where he had been ordered to remain.

Yusupov began by explaining how he and Rasputin had become acquainted:

I had first met Grigori Efimovich Rasputin about 5 years ago at Mournya Evgenievna Golovina's house. During the following years I saw him a couple of times at Golovina's house. This year, 1916, I saw him in November also at Golovina's house and he made a better impression on me than during previous years. I suffer from chest pains and my medical treatment does not help substantially. I discussed this with Mournya Evgenievna Golovina and she advised me to go to Rasputin's apartment and talk to him about it. He had cured many people and could be of help to me. At the end of November I went to Rasputin accompanied by Golovina. Rasputin did his passes and I thought that my condition had improved slightly. During my last visits Rasputin told me 'we will cure you completely, but we still need to go to the gypsies, you'll see good women there and your illness will completely disappear'. These words made an unpleasant impression on me.

Questioning then apparently turned to Rasputin's alleged visit to the Yusupov Palace on the night of Friday 16 December. Having had the best part of a day to concoct and perfect his version of events, Yusupov was clearly at pains to explain the circumstances surrounding the rumours:

Around 10th December Rasputin telephoned me and suggested we went to the gypsies. I refused and gave him an excuse that I had to sit exams the next day. During our meetings Rasputin initiated conversations about my wife, where and how we live. He said that he wished to meet my wife. I evasively responded that a meeting could be arranged when she returned from the Crimea. However, I did not want to introduce Rasputin to my household.

Having emphasised his reluctance to invite Rasputin to the Yusupov Palace, Yusupov was now pressed to give his account of the night of 16 December:

I'd had the rooms of my Moika house refurbished and Grand Duke Dmitri Pavlovich suggested I have a house warming party. It was decided to invite Vladimir Mitrofanovich Purishkevich, several officers and society ladies to the party. Given the obvious reasons I do not want to name the ladies who attended the party. I also do not want to name the officers who were at the party because this may create rumours and damage the careers of these innocent people. The party was planned for 16th December. In order not to embarrass the ladies, I ordered my servants to serve the tea and dinner in advance and not to enter the room later. The majority of guests were supposed to arrive not at the front entrance of the building at 94 Moika, but to the side entrance at number 92. I kept the key to that entrance on me. I arrived home at around 10.00p.m. I think that I entered the apartment through the side entrance at number 92, although I can't be certain. Everything was ready for the guests in the dining room and the study. Grand Duke Dmitri Pavlovich arrived at around 11.30p.m.; he came through the front entrance, then the other guests started to arrive as well. All the ladies without doubt arrived at the side entrance at number 92. I can't remember where the male guests arrived. The guests had tea, played the grand piano, danced and had dinner.

Yusupov continued to maintain that Rasputin had never visited the palace that night, although he had indeed spoken with him:

> At around 12.30–1.00am I went upstairs to my study in the same building and heard a telephone ring. It turned out to be Rasputin who invited me to visit the gypsies with him. I replied that I was not able to come because I had guests. Rasputin suggested that I should leave the guests and come with him, but I refused. I asked Rasputin where he was calling from, but he refused to answer. I asked Rasputin this question because on the telephone I could hear voices, some noise and even female squeals, therefore I came to the conclusion that Rasputin was not calling from home, but from a restaurant or from the gypsies. Following that conversation I went downstairs into the dining room and said to my guests; 'Gentlemen, Rasputin spoke to me a minute ago and invited me to the gypsies'. The guests cracked jokes and laughed, suggesting that we go, but everyone stayed and continued with the dinner.

Popov was clearly already familiar with the shot-dog story, which he must have heard anecdotally, and did not accept it as uncritically as Balk and the Minister of Justice, Makarov, had done. The Prince was asked to be specific. Who had fired the shot? Where and when? Yusupov said:

> At around 2.30–3.00a.m. two ladies decided to go home and left through the side entrance. The Grand Duke Dmitri Pavlovich left with them. When they went out I heard a gunshot in the yard, so I rang the bell and ordered one of the attendants to go out and have a look. The servant returned and reported that everyone had left and there was nothing in the yard. Then I went out to the yard myself and noticed a dead dog by the fence. When I came out to the yard a person hurriedly walked away from the dog. He was wearing a grey shirt, similar to a military uniform, he was slim, but I could not see him well because it was dark. When I came back to the apartment I ordered the servant to remove the dog from the yard. I called the Grand Duke Dmitri Pavlovich straight away and told him about the dead dog. His Imperial Highness told me that he had killed the dog. I remonstrated that there had been no need to do that, as it had created a noise and the police would be coming and the fact that I had a party with ladies in attendance would become public. Dmitri Pavlovich replied that it was nothing wrong and there was no need to worry. I then ordered to call a policeman from the street and told him that if there were to be enquiries about the gunshots, he was to say that my friend had killed a dog.[1]

Yusupov's account of the murder night is a mixture of truth, fabrication and omission that others later contradicted with different truths and more fabrication and omission. Whilst not central to the account of the night's events, some have questioned the basis on which Yusupov claimed he initially re-established contact with Rasputin, namely to seek relief from chest pains. Although his story was corroborated by family friend Mounya Golovina when questioned by Popov, Rasputin's family and associates have subsequently denied this. Both his daughter Maria and his secretary Aron Simanovich have maintained that

Yusupov sought Rasputin's help to cure him of his homosexual desires.[2]

By Sunday lunchtime he had been driven to the Sergei Palace on the Nevski Prospekt to stay in a room provided by Dmitri Pavlovich. At least Dmitri, as a Grand Duke, would not be bothered by policemen. And a move would also take the heat off Yusupov's parents-in-law and especially his wife's young brothers. As Romanovs, the family had nothing to fear from the law, but Grand Duke Alexander Mikhailovich and Grand Duchess Xenia would prefer to avoid incurring the Tsar's displeasure by harbouring a suspect.

The Sergei Palace was an imposing stone building on a prominent corner of the Nevski Prospekt, Petrograd's busiest thoroughfare. It overlooked the Anichkov Bridge over the Fontanka Canal, and was opposite the palace of Maria Fyodorovna, the Tsar's mother. Above its lower floors there rose a tall *piano nobile* or ballroom floor adorned on the outside with pilasters. The upper levels were occupied by the Anglo-Russian Hospital, one of many such charitably funded hospitals founded to deal with casualties brought back from the front. Dmitri Pavlovich had donated the space and a 200-bed hospital was installed in 1915. Its staff and equipment were a 'gift from Britain to Russia', having been funded by public subscription and promoted by the Foreign Office and the British Red Cross. Lady Muriel Paget and Lady Sybil Grey ran the hospital with the help of British doctors and nurses and a small complement of Russian Red Cross officials. Dmitri was glad to do something to help – *noblesse oblige,* and all that – and besides, his butler had hanged himself in the building so he did not want to be rattling around, when on leave, in a great shell of a place that had felt spooky ever since. The hospital had moved in during the winter of 1915, when plumbing and baths, sadly lacking before, had been installed. Family retainers ('swarms' of them, according to the exasperated Lady Grey) continued to occupy the attics. Dmitri's apartment was accessible by a door from the main entrance hall and by a concealed staircase which led up to the doctor's rooms.

As a Romanov, Dmitri could be constrained only by the Tsar himself. Yusupov must have felt relatively safe. The two young men had plenty to discuss, not least the detention in her own home of Madame Marianna Derfelden, the stepdaughter of Dmitri's father. She was one of their own circle and, it was said, a former lover of Dmitri's. Somebody must have told the investigators that she had been among the women present at the Yusupov Palace. She loathed Rasputin's influence over the Tsarina but was the sister of one of his leading supporters. Her detention, as it turned out, did not cause her great hardship. Her mother wrote later:

> When we arrived at 8 Theatre Square, where Marianna lived, we were stopped by two soldiers who let us through only after taking down our names. All the highest society was at Marianna's! Some ladies she barely knew arrived in order to express their sympathy with her. Officers came up to kiss her hand.[3]

Another hot topic was Dmitri's telephone call to the Tsarina before the party the previous Saturday night. He had heard that she suspected him of involvement, and had rung Tsarskoye Selo and asked to see her. She refused. This was serious, for the imperial family had taken Dmitri under their wing when he was a boy, treated him fairly and knew him well. For the Tsarina to snub him like this, she must be sure that he and Felix Yusupov had something to hide.

And worse was to come. At lunchtime, a telephone call from an aide-de-camp at Tsarskoye Selo informed Grand Duke Dmitri Pavlovich that the Tsarina ordered him to remain at the Sergei Palace under house arrest. He was furious, knowing that only the Tsar could legally issue such an order. The Tsarina had married into the royal family over twenty years ago and had never fitted in; the Romanovs, Yusupovs, Obolenskis and Galitzines – the aristocrats of Russia – had never liked her; she was prissy and boring and dull. But Tsar Nicholas, everyone knew, did exactly what the Tsarina told him to, and he was an autocrat who could do anything. Dmitri accepted her command. What else could he do?

Visitors started to appear. And among them all afternoon – indeed for days afterwards – the British Ambassador's friend Nikolai Mikhailovich made a trying companion.

> The Grand Duke Nikolai Mikhailovich came several times a day, or telephoned the wildest, most improbable news, couched in such mysterious terms that we never really knew what it was all about. He always tried to bluff us that he knew all about the conspiracy, hoping by this means to worm our secret out of us.
>
>   He took an active part in the search for Rasputin's body. He warned us that the Tsarina, convinced of our complicity in Rasputin's assassination, demanded that we be shot at once...[4]

The Grand Duke Nikolai Mikhailovich was known to loathe Rasputin. But he was not usually so curious, and had probably been asked to probe as deeply as possible. Sir George Buchanan wanted to know what had really happened because he had his own suspicions. Perhaps he also wanted to know whether Yusupov and Dmitri, a couple of social butterflies, were capable of sticking to their story. Because by now, London had heard something.

General Popov and Lt-Col. Popel got into their stride. Having yesterday had time to interview only Yusupov's servants at the Moika, and Mounya Golovina, they now descended on several locations in swift succession. Popov interviewed Maria and Varvara Rasputina, and Katya their maid, at 64 Gorokhovaya Street. Popel took statements from Anya, the niece, and the building attendants at 64, and then headed uptown for the Moika, where there were police witnesses. After that he went out to the Islands and saw the bridge guard.

Rasputin's daughters, having identified their father's footwear, were desperately worried and willing to tell Popov anything they knew that might help. Maria, the elder girl, admitted that her father had been expecting to see Yusupov 'the Little One' late on Friday night, and that Mounya Golovina had seemed concerned yesterday after she had spoken to the Prince on the telephone.

> I saw Prince Yusupov at our apartment only once – about five or six days ago, that must be around the 12th December this year. The prince has the following distinctive features: taller than average, skinny, pale, long face, large circles under the eyes, brown hair. I can't remember whether he has a moustache or a beard.

Varvara, who was sixteen, had nothing much to add. Popel's interrogation of Anya, the niece, confirmed what Maria had said but brought another visitor into the frame.

> Around 1.00p.m. on 16th December my uncle Grigori Efimovich returned from the bath house and went to sleep. During that day my uncle had many visitors who had also visited him previously. Around 10.00p.m. a plump blonde called Sister Maria arrived, she was called Sister although she wasn't a nurse. Shortly after midnight my uncle lay down on the bed fully clothed. Katya who lives with us and myself came up to my uncle and asked him why he did not get undressed. My uncle replied that 'today I am going to visit the Little One.' Later I went to sleep and did not hear when my uncle left or who with.

Katya the maid confirmed what Rasputin had said, as he rested 'fully clothed and in his boots'.

> When I asked him who [he would be visiting] Rasputin replied 'the Little One, he is going to pick me up' and ordered me to go to bed… I went into the kitchen but did not fall asleep. Rasputin had put on a silk shirt embroidered with basilisks but could not do up all the collar buttons. He came into the kitchen and I did

up his buttons. At the time somebody rang the back entrance bell. Rasputin opened the door himself. The visitor asked 'Is nobody here?' Grigori Efimovich replied 'Nobody and the children are asleep. Come in dear'. Both of them went through the kitchen past me into the rooms. At the time I was behind the kitchen partition for the maid. I moved aside the curtain and saw that the visitor was the Little One, known to me as Irina Alexandrovna's husband... I recognised his face. I can't tell whether the collar of his coat was up. A short time later Rasputin went through the kitchen. I was in bed by that time. Grigori Efimovich said in a low voice that he had locked the front door and was going to leave by the back entrance, and that he would come back through that entrance, and ordered me to lock the door behind him. I replied 'Yes' to all these orders while still in bed and locked the door when they went out. I have not seen Grigori Efimovich since.[5]

Mounya Golovina had told her that Yusupov denied having been there, but when Katya heard this she had insisted that she was not mistaken; the person she saw had been 'the Little One'.

After that Maria Evgenievna Golovina has not visited us. The distinctive features of the Little One are the following: quite tall, slim, slim face, straight nose, dark hair, no moustache and no beard, blue circles under the eyes.

Popel then questioned the *dvornik*, the concierge, who would have been in the pay of the Okhrana. She was a woman of twenty-eight, illiterate, and held no great opinion of the tenant of number 64.

On 16th December I saw Grigori Rasputin only once, at about 3.00p.m. when he returned from the bath-house, when he went through the back entrance. He had not received any visitors in the morning because he was very drunk.[6] Even when he came back from the bath-house he was not quite sober. He had not more than seven visitors between 3.00p.m. and midnight; they used to visit him previously as well. Only at around 10.00p.m. a lady I had never seen before arrived and stayed with Rasputin until 11.00p.m., when she left. The lady had the following distinctive features: blonde hair, about 25 years of age, medium height, medium build. She was wearing a flared dark brown coat and same colour, only slightly darker, boots and a black hat with no veil. When I locked the front door at midnight Grigori Rasputin was home. I don't know when he left the house or with whom because he left through the back door.[7]

The yardkeeper who had been on duty at the apartment block that night said he had been outside, near the gates, when

...soon after 1.00a.m. a large car arrived at the gates. The car was khaki in colour, had a canvas top and safety glass windows; there was a spare tyre on the back. The car had come from the Fontanka direction. It reversed and stopped. A person unknown to me came out of the car and came straight to the wicket gate. I asked who he was visiting and he responded 'Rasputin.' I opened the gate and told him 'Here is the front door' but the stranger said he was going to go in through the back entrance. He swiftly went straight to that entrance. It was obvious that the person was familiar with the layout of the building. About 30 minutes later the stranger came out with G.E. Rasputin. They got into the car and drove off towards Fontanka... The driver looked slightly older than the stranger, about 35 years of age, had black medium-sized moustache, no beard, was wearing a black coat with lambskin collar, fur hat and red long gloves. Having left, Rasputin did not return home.[8]

Popel set off for Morskaya Street. There he interviewed Efimov, the policeman who had been on sentry duty outside the Ministry of the Interior, across the canal from the Yusupov Palace at 94 Moika and its adjoining house, number 92, on the night of the disappearance.

I was on my post at Morskaya Street building number 61. At
2.30a.m. I heard a gunshot and 3 to 5 seconds later three more
shots followed fast one after another. The sound of gunshots came
from Moika Street in the region of building number 92. The first
gunshot was followed by a low scream as if it was a woman's;
there was no noise. In 20 to 30 minutes after the shot no car or
carriage went along Moika Street. Only half an hour later a car
drove along Moika from the Blue Bridge towards Potselyev. It did
not stop anywhere. I reported the shots by telephone to the 3rd
Kazan Police Station and went towards the place of shooting.[9]

Reluctantly, perhaps. Officer Efimov was fifty-nine and hardly
looking for trouble. A moment later he saw the beat policeman,
Vlasuk, coming across the Pochamski Bridge over the canal
from the Moika side. He too had heard shots but he thought
they were fired somewhere near the German church on the
Moika. But Efimov insisted the bangs had come from number
92. Vlasuk, ten years younger but probably no more keen than
Efimov to hunt down a gunman in the middle of the night,
turned back to investigate.

Questioned by Popel, Vlasuk confirmed that there had been
'three or four gunshots one after another'. The yardkeeper at
number 92 hadn't heard a thing, he said, but then Vlasuk looked
through the fence and saw 'two people wearing tunics and no
hats'.

When they approached us I recognised them. It was Prince
Yusupov and his butler Byzhinski. I asked the latter who had
fired the shots. Byzhinski replied that he had not heard any shots.
However it was possible that somebody could have fired a toy
pistol for fun. I think the Prince also said that he had not heard
the shots.

They left. Vlasuk claims that he stayed there, looked through the
fence, and saw nothing suspicious in the yard or the street. Then
he went back to his post, not bothering to report the incident

'because I often heard similar sounds being made by burst car tyres'. Fifteen or twenty minutes later Byzhinski came, saying that Prince Yusupov would like to see him. There followed the interview in which Purishkevich allegedly said to Vlasuk:

'Are you Christian Orthodox?'

'Yes.'

'Do you know me?'

I replied that I didn't.

'Have you heard of Purishkevich?'

'Yes.'

'I am Purishkevich. Have you heard of Rasputin and do you know him?'

I replied that I did not know Rasputin but had heard of him. The stranger then told me that he – Rasputin – had perished.

'And if you love the Tsar and the Fatherland, you are to keep quiet about it and not tell anything to anybody.'

'Yes, Sir.'

'Now you may go.'

I turned around and went back to my post. It was very quiet in the house and I did not see anybody apart from the Prince, the stranger and Byzhinski… I checked the street and yard again, but everything was still quiet and I did not see anybody. About 20 minutes later Inspector Kalyadich approached me at my post and I told him about the incident. Then Kalyadich and I went to the front entrance of building number 94 [the Yusupov Palace]. We saw a car ready to go at the front entrance. We asked the driver who the car was waiting for. He replied that it was for the Prince. Kalyadich ordered me to stay there and watch who was going to use the car… Prince Yusupov alone came out of the front door and drove away towards the Potselyev Bridge… I waited by the door of that building for some time. I did not notice anyone else and returned to my post. It was shortly past 5.00a.m. Kalyadich returned from his rounds after ten or fifteen minutes… The car belonged to the Prince. He always used it. I know this car well. It is small and brown in colour. I had not noticed any signs of a murder and explained the conversation with the stranger in the study as some kind of test of my knowledge of my responsibilities. Meaning a test of my actions following such an announcement...[10]

Popel interviewed one other person, who had somehow been left out of the interrogations at the Yusupov Palace the day before. This was a young man called Bobkov, the palace watchman. He too had heard shots – two of them, not very loud; he thought they had come from some nearby street, but then, he had been some way away at the time – outside building number 96 – and 'I did not pay any attention to the sounds assuming they were the sounds of frost or drain pipes'. He had heard no scream. He had seen nothing suspicious. He had seen no cars coming or going. And 'my eyesight is extremely poor due to my war injury'. Lucky to get the job as a watchman, then.

The nineteen-year-old yard man at number 92 Moika, the three-storey Yusupov house next door in whose yard the crime appeared to have taken place, who claimed to have been sweeping the pavement outside it from two o'clock in the morning onwards, was sure that the gunshots he had faintly heard had come from a nearby street.

Yusupov spent the Sunday afternoon in the Anglo-Russian Hospital upstairs from Dmitri Pavlovich's having a fish-bone removed from his throat. He and Dmitri

...were sought by the supporters of Rasputin on the pretext of visiting some wounded patients. Lady Sybil Grey confronted them [the Rasputinists] and refused them admission to *her hospital*. Like everyone else in Petrograd she was well aware that Yusupov was the murderer and wrote 'there was an uproar of excitement and thankfulness, workers toasting him, nuns blessing him.' Only the Tsarina dissented.[11]

Dmitri's mood was not improved by receiving a telegram of congratulation from his aunt, the Grand Duchess Elizaveta

Fyodorovna. She had been a widow for over a decade, had become a nun, and was at present far from the city. Yusupov wrote:

> Aware of the ties of friendship between us, and not suspecting that he himself had taken an active part in the destruction of the *starets*, the Grand Duchess requested him to tell me that she was praying for me and blessed my patriotic action.[12]

The Grand Duchess happened to be the Tsarina's elder sister, and from her self-imposed exile exercised quite an influence on the two young men, who regarded her with awe. It is indicative of her unworldliness that she would send such a message, which compromised them both. The Okhrana were watching the suspects closely. They were so obviously heroes that they might, should they move fast and get the smart regiments behind them, be able to engineer a coup. Elizaveta Fyodorovna's telegram was intercepted by the Okhrana and a copy sent to Protopopov, the Minister of the Interior. He was close to both Rasputin and the Tsarina and showed it to the Tsarina, 'who immediately concluded that the Grand Duchess Elizaveta Fyodorovna was in the plot'.

She may well have been. Yusupov and Dmitri Pavlovich were in awe of her and in her time she had learned about politically motivated violence. Her husband, Grand Duke Sergei, had been assassinated in 1905. As a Mother Superior, she could perfectly well present a beatific countenance to the world while privately fomenting anger.

Albert Stopford ate an early lunch with a set of Grand Dukes and Grand Duchesses and set off at sixteen minutes past one on foot for the embassy in 'glorious weather: -20 Fahrenheit'.

> …brilliant sunshine, in which the red Embassy was glowing. I found the Ambassador, Lady Georgina, Miss Meriel, General Hanbury-Williams, and Colonel Burn, who had brought the

bag. I told them all I had heard about Rasputin's disappearance. I also told the General that I had written home ten days ago that the political situation would end in a tragic dénouement. Whilst we were talking, there was brought in a copy of the Police Report with the different arrivals, departures, and police calls at the Yusupov Palace that night.[13]

General Hanbury-Williams was in charge of British military matters in Russia as the Ambassador was responsible for political action. The Police Report drawn up the previous day appears to have been shown to some journalists, as well as the embassy, on the Sunday afternoon. Statements came mainly from officers who had been on night duty in the police station across the canal.[14] There were too many of these to ignore. Something that the suspects wanted to keep quiet had taken place in the early hours of the morning.

The document was eagerly scanned by all who could read Russian. Another document – a 'Memorandum, privately circulated' – had just appeared in English and was read with just as much avidity. This summarised what was being said socially. Rasputin, the gossip said, had been shot in a basement room of the Yusupov Palace; Yusupov, Dmitri Pavlovich, Fyodor and Nikita (Yusupov's two young brothers-in-law) were all in the palace and knew about it. 'Conjointly with other Princes of the Blood, including the sons of the late Grand Duke Konstantin, they had decided some time previously to "remove" Rasputin, because they regarded him as the cause of a dangerous scandal affecting the Dynasty and the Empire.'[15] The plot was well known, but action did not become imperative until the Duma was summarily prorogued last Friday. Lots were drawn and an assassin chosen; the unlucky one – a son of Grand Duke Konstantin – withdrew, leaving Yusupov to do the deed. The conspirators often met Rasputin at the palace and on this occasion the invitees included 'some of Rasputin's lady friends' to entice him. The report continued:

> A revolver was placed in [Rasputin's] hand, but he flatly
> declined to commit suicide and discharged the weapon some-
> where in the direction of Grand Duke Dmitri. The bullet
> smashed a pane of glass, and the sound attracted the atten-
> tion of the police outside. Subsequently he was killed and
> his body removed to a place unknown, presumably Tsarskoye
> Selo.[16]

Stopford took a look at both reports (it is even probable that he
wrote the 'Memorandum privately circulated') and left to do
some networking.

Versions of the Police Report were already being written up
for publication in tomorrow's newspaper. Quite how the *Times*'s
correspondent in Petrograd, Robert Wilton, got hold of it is
unknown, but he had it long enough to translate it and cable a
copy to his London office, where it never arrived.

Head of British Intelligence Samuel Hoare, who did not
share Stopford's talent for being in the right place at the right
time, was meanwhile compiling his own report for his boss
in London, as best he could. Later that day he scribbled a telegram. In his autobiography he emphasises the significance of
this.

> On New Year's Eve, 1916, I sent to London an urgent wire, coded
> for greater secrecy by Lady Maud, that on the previous morning,
> Rasputin had been killed in Petrograd in a private house. Mine
> was the first news of the assassination that reached the west, and
> I was the first non-Russian to hear afterwards of the finding of
> the corpse.[17]

In England this Sunday was, indeed, New Year's Eve. But there
is more to this, for Hoare's telegram, retrieved from the archive,
reads as follows:

Decode of Telegram
Dec. 18/31 Urgent. Private for C:-

> News correct that Rasputin was killed in Petrograd in private
> house early morning of Dec 30.[18]

Why 'News correct that'? His autobiography states that his was
the first message 'C' got, yet the telegram implies that he is writing in response to a query. In his eyrie in Whitehall Court, this
wintry London Sunday, the workaholic 'C', Mansfield Cumming,
Head of MI1c, the Secret Intelligence Service, must have heard
something. If so he would have wondered why Hoare – who
was after all in charge of the British Intelligence Mission – had
not been the first to tell him about it.

Hoare was desperate for reliable information. Typed out on
Monday before despatch, his report – corrected later in ink –
alleges that Rasputin had last been seen on Thursday (not Friday)
night; that Rasputin's flat was on the English Prospekt, which it
was not; that 'several' Grand Dukes were present at the shooting.
He amended this document again, slightly, when reprinting it in
his autobiography. However, it goes on to state something that
does have the ring of truth.

> I am informed that the Grand Duke Dmitri Pavlovich and Count
> Elston [Prince Yusupov was also Count Sumarokov-Elston] were
> together all the afternoon of December 31st and when asked,
> they make no secret of the fact that Rasputin has been killed.

Hoare had not so many friends in well-informed circles that he
could have got it from anywhere else. He padded his report with
quotations from Sunday's (and later Monday's) Petrograd papers,
at least one of which printed extracts from the Police Report of
the previous day that Stopford had seen. It also included a passage about galoshes and the following, in Hoare's translation:

> A freshly made hole in the ice was discovered and footsteps pass-
> ing backwards and forwards from it in different directions. Divers
> were given the duty of examining the bed of the river.

The divers did not necessarily understand the importance of their task. The body must absolutely be found, and identified by the imperial couple. A Rasputin who had been killed would polarise opinion in circles that mattered, but a Rasputin who might have escaped 'thanks to the Grace of God' would be the object of superstitious wonder. The Tsarina's faith in his powers of precognition and healing had never wavered. In his life-time she had almost worshipped him. Should he never be seen again, she and Vyrubova and the coven of middle-class witches who had followed Rasputin in life would believe in him as the second Messiah. Not only this, but a wave of 'false Rasputins' might arise, claiming his identity. At this rate any beardie with a crucifix might gain a following among the impressionable and isolated.

While Hoare cobbled together all he knew, a young woman, with a companion and a maid, was gliding unchallenged away from the city. Her departure had been noted, the reception book of the hotel where she had stayed in Petrograd had been examined, and the staff had been questioned.

Report, December, 1916

To Director of the Department of Police.

A dancer of the Moscow Imperial Theatres Vera Alexeyevna KORALLI, 27 years of age, of the Orthodox faith, arrived in the capital from Moscow, checked in at the Hotel Medved (Koniushennaya ul.) and occupied rooms 103 and 115. At the reception she produced her passport issued by the Moscow Imperial Theatres Office on 16th August, 1914, No 2071, for five years. She is accompanied by her maidservant, a peasant woman, Wilkomir Uezd, Zhmudkaya Volost, and Veronika Osipovna Kuhto, 25 years of age, Catholic, passport issued by the constable of the 2nd police station, Tverskoi district, the Moscow City Police on the 16th June, 1915 No 203, for five years.

19th December, on a train departing at 7.20p.m., the above left for Moscow. The tickets were delivered to them by a lackey in court uniform. During the time of her residence in the capital, KORALLI was visited by: His Imperial Highness the Grand Duke DMITRI PAVLOVICH, escorted by unknown officer, and adjutant of His Imperial Highness MIKHAIL ALEXANDROVICH.

KORALLI also met with another occupant of the hotel, assistant attorney Alexandre Afanasyevich KAZANTSEV, 27 years of age, Orthodox, passport issued by the constable of the 1st police station, Prechistenka district, the Moscow City Police on the 16th July, 1915 No 2038, for five years.

Over the time of her stay in the capital, KORALLI spent every night at the hotel and was not seen leaving the hotel on the night of 16/17 December this year.

Nothing is known to the prejudice of any the above by the department I am in charge of.

Signed: the Chief of Department, Maj.-General Globachev.[19]

The Okhrana had been told to back off. Vera Koralli, Dmitri Pavlovich's mistress, was believed to have been at the Yusupov Palace on Friday night but she was allowed to leave town unhindered. This could only be because her lover was a Romanov.

Had he known this, the Hon. Albert Stopford would have drawn comfort from the intelligence. As it was, that Sunday he was out picking up the gen as best he could. He had heard at the embassy that Prince Yusupov had been at the Anglo-Russian Hospital that afternoon, having a fish-bone removed. Stopford, who knew both Dmitri Pavlovich and Felix Yusupov well, had until now assumed that the wanted Prince was serenely en route to the Crimea. The Yusupov Palace had been assuring callers that Prince Felix had gone there. The second, and much more worrying, piece of news came from his friend the Grand Duchess Vladimir, to whom, with Sir George's permission, he had shown the Police Report. The Grand Duchess told him that Grand Duke Dmitri Pavlovich had been placed under house arrest.:

…an unheard-of thing, for since the murder of the Emperor
Paul (1801) no grand Duke has ever been put under arrest on a
grave charge, and on that occasion the Emperor Paul lost his life
for only threatening it.[20]

This was bad enough. But later that evening she had heard
from Dmitri Pavlovich himself that it was the Empress who had
ordered him to be detained. In other words, *the Tsarina had not
acted within her rights, yet her orders had been carried out.* What the
British most feared was a palace coup engineered by the Tsarina;
and here, *de facto,* was the first sign of it.

Over dinner with the Grand Duchess, Stopford discovered that Dmitri Pavlovich had spoken to the Grand Duchess
Vladimir and sworn that he had left Yusupov's party at four
o'clock on Saturday morning and was innocent.

> We were all petrified by the Grand Duke Dmitri's denying all
> knowledge of the affair, and saying that, although he had been
> to supper there, he had left before four.

He was 'petrified'. The implication is that Dmitri had been
expected to take the rap. Nobody else would do, because
nobody else was fully a Romanov, with a cast-iron excuse to get
away with murder. If Dmitri refused to take blame, then Yusupov
might be accused and put on trial for his life. Yusupov's position
was by no means as secure as Dmitri's and he knew it; with the
prospect of a firing squad in sight, he would crack.

And if he did, what might he reveal?

But maybe Dmitri was just being careful. After all, telephones
were not secure. Comforting himself with this thought, Stopford
walked rapidly to the embassy rather than ring with the news.

> There were lights on the Embassy staircase, so I asked if I could
> see Lady Georgina, and was shown up to the Ambassador's bed-
> room; he was just going to undress. I told him of the Grand Duke

Dmitri's absolute denial of any share in the murder – which, after
all, is only natural, though he swore it on his own icon. If all the
conspirators acknowledged their complicity on the telephone
to their friends and relations it might be disastrous to the actual
perpetrator or to the whole lot.

I found the Ambassador very much perturbed and tired. He
walked up and down the room; I sat by the fire.[21]

Sir George Buchanan was not a young man. He cut a strange
figure, and with his spare frame, red face, shock of white hair and
droopy white moustache was a dream for caricaturists. Dmitri's
denial was clearly unexpected.

In Hoare's flat across town, it was getting late, and he had to
finish his report to get it typed up for despatch tomorrow.

The feeling in Petrograd is most remarkable. All classes speak and
act as if some great weight had been taken from their shoulders.
Servants, *isvostchiks*, working men, all freely discuss the event…

Servants and cab-drivers were the only people he would have
had the opportunity to ask. Nonetheless, he felt compelled to
finish on a predictive note, so he took a wild guess.

What effect it will have in Government circles is difficult to say.
My own view is that it will lead to the immediate dismissal of
Protopopov and of various directors of the Secret Police, whilst in
the course of the next few weeks the most notorious of Rasputin's
clientele will gradually retire into private life. I would suggest for
instance that careful attention should be paid to any changes that
take place in the Department of the Interior and the Holy Synod,
where Rasputin's influence was always strongest.[22]

He turned out to be completely wrong.

In the embassy, having wished Buchanan goodnight, Stopford
went to sit with Lady Georgina. At half-past ten she got a phone
call from the Reuters man, Pierre Beringer, to say that the police

of the district where Rasputin lived had 'seen an automobile go to his house at about 4a.m., fetch him and take him away'. Yet there was still no proof that he was dead. Who knew what to believe?

THREE

Body of Evidence

The scene is monochrome: the wide, snow-covered bridge, a heavy, whitish morning sky, a shuffle of black-clad onlookers, snow and ice stretching east to the gracious range of lemon-and-white Petrograd palaces, and west to dark woods with the Gulf of Finland far beyond.

Not far from the bank of the wide, frozen channel, policemen are looking for something.

Some say it was on the Sunday afternoon that somebody – a policeman? a diver? – identified a shape, the length of a man, beneath the glassy crust of the Little Neva. But the divers, who had been told to search under ice inches thick, hauled nothing from the river. They waited until the following morning, being 'not at all anxious to work'[1] because of the bitter cold; so while excitement, and in some cases fear, mounted in the city on that Sunday evening, only one fact seemed certain. The police now believed they were about to find Rasputin.

The body was retrieved at twenty to nine on the morning of Monday 19 December, or on Monday, New Year's Day of

1917, London time. Or slightly later than twenty to nine, if you believe the dubious source that has Constable Andreev sweeping the ice at that time, discovering a frozen sable collar, reporting it, and the body being retrieved from under ice broken with crowbars.[2]

Planks were laid on the frozen surface. With the aid of grappling hooks, and watched by an unhelpful twitter of examining judges and journalists who had been herded to a vantage point on the bridge, men hauled the corpse, frozen stiff, out of the groaning, creaking ice and onto a raft of boards.

There was no mistaking the man. A fit-looking, bearded fellow in the loose blouse of a *muzhik* which had ridden up at the back, where his frigid flesh arched defensively away from the cold surface. A peasant with good hair and teeth in the prime of life, the legs below the thighs still tied in a sack. The face blackened and eyes and nose swollen, and the arms flung upward and bent at the elbows, the hands petrified as if clawing the air.

A police photographer shuffled gingerly along the planks and placed a ruler in shot before focusing carefully.

On the bridge, observers peered at the distant form, and glimpsed a flash of blue silk stained dark red. A sodden, frosted fur was heaped up next to it like a faithful dog.

An urgent telephone call brought out the bigwigs: the district Chief of Police, the Head of the Okhrana, an investigator from the Ministry of Justice called Zavadskis, General Popov and others.

The body would take a day to thaw out, so no immediate examination would be possible. But Petrograd could breathe again. Rasputin was well and truly dead.

The rigid form was loaded into the back of a motor lorry for despatch to the Vyborg Military Hospital. The journalists raced back to town to file their copy and the rest of the party drove to luncheon at a restaurant.

That Rasputin's body was found by the police and pulled out of the Little Neva on that particular day is not in dispute. Most of the other 'facts' tend to be replaced by new 'facts' with each account that one reads. This is more than a problem of translation. There are different versions of almost everything that happened to Rasputin from the moment he left his apartment until his remains went up in smoke months later.

There is, for instance, the galosh. Or overshoe. Or pair of galoshes. Whether there was one or a pair, some kind of footwear was found and taken to Rasputin's apartment where his daughters confirmed that it was his. Whether there was a sinister bloodstain on the galosh, or galoshes, varies according to who tells the story. Kyzmin the bridge guard described blood spots in the snow. There is a photograph purporting to show blood spots on the snowy struts projecting below the bridge, but since the picture is in black and white it is hard to be certain what the smudges are. There are no photographs showing footprints to and from the gap in the ice, yet there is an account of such footprints. One writer alleges that a hole had been carefully cut in the ice for disposal of the body; another (Hoare) that Makarov, the Minister of Justice, claimed to have received an anonymous phone call on the Saturday morning, telling him to search in the Islands.

The hidden agenda in all this, and of the message Hoare 'received in strict confidence from the Chief of the Department of Military Police in the General Staff' and would dutifully pass on to London, is the agenda of the searchers. The Okhrana, under Protopopov, the Minister of the Interior, was stressing in all public statements that 'it was the intention of the murderers that the body should be discovered'. They had to make it clear that a group of people opposed to Rasputin, that is, opposed to the Tsar's current policies as advised by Rasputin, *wanted* his death to be indisputable, so they had left clues. In other words, he had not died accidentally in some drunken brawl and been tossed into the Baltic never to be seen again, but must have been murdered and left in a place where he would be found, in a treasonable bid to clear the field for a change of policy or even a change of power. By inference, this was a political crime. So pleas of innocence from the likes of Prince Yusupov were not going to wash.

Once the body was found, there are still more contradictory accounts. One has it being hauled immediately to the riverbank before being driven to a nearby police station for investigation by a police surgeon. 'The greater part of the shirt was drenched in blood, which had started to decompose spreading a noxious smell around the investigation room.' Three bullet-holes were found, and a 'vast wound on the head'. Then Simanovich and Isodor arrived and made the first official identification.

The early detection of the bullet-holes certainly took place. The police were releasing information to the press, and Robert Wilton, the *Times*'s correspondent, was able to cable London as early as Tuesday 2 January 'it is stated that there were three bullet wounds in Rasputin's body, in the head, chest, and side'.[3] The source for the information about the bullet-holes was probably also the police. Yusupov has another account, which he says is from the 'official report':[4] the police believed the boot to be a size 11, not a size 10; the 'nearby police station' has become a shed; the police believed the murder had taken place on the bridge; the sable collar was a sable sleeve; the first identification was by a domestic servant, and later by Rasputin's two daughters and Maria Rasputina's Cossack fiancé. And so on. The devil is certainly in the detail.

The Tsar had returned that Monday morning to Tsarskoye Selo.

> Those in attendance upon him said that on receiving the news of Rasputin's death his mood was more cheerful than since the outbreak of war. He... evidently felt and believed that the disappearance of the *starets* had freed him from those heavy fetters which he had lacked the strength to cast off. But with his return to Tsarskoye Selo his mood abruptly changed, and once again he fell under the influence of those who surrounded him.[5]

The Tsarina was horrified when she heard that the body had been found and identified. Until now she had kept hope alive.

Her faith in the charismatic peasant had been complete, her adoration of him beyond all reason. The Tsarevich's tutor wrote:

> Her grief was inconsolable. Her idol had been shattered. He who alone could save her son had been slain.[6]

As the corpse defrosted, news of its retrieval was nimbly set in lead type for the evening papers, and all Petrograd buzzed with excitement. This time Hoare got the electrifying intelligence from a source he trusted. He sent another telegram.

> Private
> CTG.89. PETROGRAD. 1st January 1917, sent at 4.15p.m.
> URGENT
> Private for C:
> Following is official and absolutely reliable but given me in strict confidence:-
> Body of Rasputin has been found under ice in water near Petrovski Island Petrograd. Evidence shows that it was the intention of the murderers that body should be discovered. HOARE.[7]

He had not long finished adding versions of Saturday's Police Report to what he had written yesterday, and now there was this. His pages had already been removed from the typewriter. A fresh sheet was begun.

> Since writing the above memorandum I have received definite information that the body of Rasputin has been discovered in the River Neva, near the Petrovski Bridge. I received this information in strict confidence from the Chief of the Department of Military Police in the General Staff. I understand that he himself saw the body. It appears that traces were purposely left about the hole in the ice into which the body was thrown in order that it should be discovered... A rough map has already been published in the *Evening Times* under the heading of MYSTERIOUS MURDER.

It is also certain that Rasputin was actually killed in Count Elston's [Yusupov's] house and not in the motor. During the evening there seems to have been a certain amount of promiscuous shooting in which a dog was killed in the courtyard and a window broken. Early in the morning six men appeared in the courtyard with a body dressed in a *shuba* [full-length fur coat] which they put in a motor that was waiting. I understand that these facts are stated in detail in the report of the four secret police who were waiting for Rasputin in the courtyard. A very well-known Russian told me that one of his friends had seen this report in which were stated all the details of the arrivals and departures to and from Count Elston's house during the evening.

…I am also informed, upon absolutely reliable authority, that the Empress was informed of the crime either late on Saturday night or early on Sunday morning. As late as six o'clock on Saturday afternoon, when the news had already been published in the *Bourse Gazette,* she appears to have known nothing of what happened…[8]

Hoare was doing his best to keep up, but it was now Monday, nearly twenty-four hours after Stopford, Buchanan and Robert Wilton of the *Times* had seen the Police Report he refers to.

He claims in his autobiography that he was immediately invited to a macabre viewing.

On the morning that the body was found… the Colonel representing the Corps of Gendarmes in the General Staff came into my office and announced that in view of our friendly relationship he was ready to confer a great favour upon me.

'They have just found Rasputin's corpse. No one of importance has yet seen it. Would you like to go with me, and be the only foreigner to see it?' It was one of those black and cruel Petrograd mornings and I was just recovering from a serious chill. Was I therefore very cowardly and unenterprising when, after thanking him for his kindness, I declined the offer that he had made to me? I fear that I seemed to him sadly lacking in nerve and that my stock fell heavily in his estimation.[9]

Whether out of cowardice or common sense, he had done the right thing. Already the British were being mentioned in connection with the murder.

In London, meanwhile, it was New Year's Day, when little political news was generally reported. The *Times*'s Night Editor rifled through everything that had come in and suddenly found an astonishing message from Reuters in Petrograd:

> The body of the notorious monk Rasputin was found on the bank of one of the branches of the Neva this morning.

He printed the bare sentence and Wickham Steed, the famous Foreign Editor, added some obituary to pad it out ('…[Rasputin] described in unblushing detail the amazing attentions he had extorted from and paid to women of all classes. His actions gave rise to much scandal…'). If an obituary can be salacious, this was. There had been nothing at all from Wilton, their own correspondent, and a sharp query was sent.

Rasputin, even in death, perhaps especially in death, might cause scenes ugly enough to rattle the Tsar. The body had to be got away from the Petrovski Bridge for a rapid autopsy and immediate burial. Yet as usual, nobody in this bumbling government could work out how to get from intention to action. Samuel Hoare's report was written one month later (British date 5 February). He had heard a convincing version of what happened:

> The body was put into a motor lorry and ordered to be taken to the Vyborg Military Hospital. The whole party, examining judges, police, and the rest, then went off to have luncheon with a German Jew who is now known as Artmanov. They had not begun luncheon when they received a telephone message from

Protopopov saying that on no account must the body be taken to the Vyborg side, because it was a workman's quarter and there might be demonstrations. They replied that it had already been sent there but Protopopov said that it must be stopped. They asked how it could be stopped. He said that he did not mind how, but stopped it must be. Accordingly they informed all the police at the street corners along the route through which it was to pass that they were to stop the lorry when they saw it approaching. The lorry was finally stopped, and was ordered to proceed instead to the Tchesminskis Almshouse, a desolate institution on the road to Tsarskoye.[10]

According to Hoare, Protopopov insisted that the body must be returned to Rasputin's family by eight o'clock the next morning and he didn't care if it was impossible, it was necessary. The whole party then wanted to know how they were to examine a body out in the back of beyond when they didn't have transport. A motor car would cost 200 roubles and it wasn't in the budget. Protopopov told them the cost would be taken care of and one of the examining magistrates went off to find the pathologist Professor Kossorotov and take him out there in a car.

This account has the authentically chaotic ring of Protopopov, carrying out the unreasonable demands of an autocratic Tsarina, challenged by a group of underlings fortified by a lunchtime drink and community of feeling. However, Hoare had not seen the Autopsy Report, which shows the body was in fact examined a day later. The post mortem was not signed off by Professor Kossorotov until ten o'clock on the night of Tuesday 20 December/2 January. Kossorotov himself said, in an interview the following year, that he expected to perform the autopsy on Wednesday morning. But at seven o'clock on Tuesday evening, not long after his arrival at a professional dinner being held in his honour, he was called to the telephone and Protopopov told him to go and perform the autopsy now, or else.[11]

Whenever the autopsy took place, according to Hoare:

Although the almshouse was lighted with electric light, there was no light at all when they arrived and no means of lighting it. The three *gorodovois* [watchmen] who were there said that no light was necessary as 'dead men need no light'. The judge and the surgeon declared that they must have some light. Accordingly they sent out and obtained two small lamps to hang upon the wall, while one of the *gorodovois* held a lantern. After a while the *gorodovoi* declared that he felt ill and could not hold the lantern any more. The judge and the surgeon therefore were left alone in the partially lighted room.[12]

The Autopsy Report appears competently done, given such circumstances. Professor Kossorotov wrote:

The body is that of a man of 50 years of age, of above average height, dressed in a blue embroidered smock over a white shirt. His legs, in high goatskin boots, were bound with a cord, and the same cord was used to bind his wrists. His light chestnut coloured hair, moustache and beard were long, dishevelled, and soaked in blood. His mouth was half-open, teeth clenched. The upper part of his face was covered in blood. His shirt was also blood-stained.

Three bullet wounds can be identified.

The first penetrated the left-hand side of his chest and passed through his stomach and liver.

The second entered the right-hand part of his back and passed through his kidneys.

The third hit the victim on the forehead and penetrated the brain.

Ballistic analysis
The first two bullets hit the victim when he was standing
The third bullet hit the victim when he was lying on the ground.

The bullets came from revolvers of various calibres.

Examination of the brain
The cerebral matter exudes a strong smell of alcohol.

Examination of stomach

The stomach contains an amount corresponding to approximately 20 soup-spoonsful of a brownish, alcohol-smelling liquid. Examination reveals no trace of poison.

Examination of the lungs

The lungs contain water (which prompts the assumption that the victim was still breathing when he was thrown into the river).

Wounds

The left-hand side has a gaping wound inflicted by some sharp object or possibly a spur.

The right eye has come out of its orbital cavity and fallen on to the face. At the corner of the right eye the skin is torn.

The right ear is torn and partially detached.

The neck has a wound caused by a blunt object.

The victim's face and body bear the signs of blows inflicted by some flexible but hard object.

The genitals have been crushed due to the effect of a similar object.

Cause of death

The victim must rapidly have been weakened by haemorrhagia arising from a wound to the liver and a wound to the right-hand kidney. Death would then have been inevitable within 10 to 20 minutes. At the moment of death the deceased was in a drunken state. The first bullet passed through the stomach and liver. This mortal wound was inflicted by a shot from a range of 20cm. The wound to the right-hand side, inflicted almost simultaneously with the first, would also have been lethal; it passed through the right-hand kidney. At the time of the attack the victim was standing and not wearing a cloak. The body was already on the ground when the frontal wound was inflicted.

Objects found on the body

A heavy gold chain.

A small gold cross on which are engraved the following words:
Save and Protect.

A gold and platinum bracelet with a clasp bearing the letter N
and the Imperial Russian crown with the two-headed eagle.

These two objects [presumably the bracelet and the cross] and
the blue silk flowers [flowered smock] and white shirt worn by
the deceased were reclaimed by the Imperial Palace on 28th
December. After medical/legal examination and autopsy, the
body of Grigori Efimovich Rasputin was transported to the
chapel of Tchesma Hospital.[13]

In one account, the Tsarina and Vyrubova arrived in a carriage
early on Wednesday morning, disguised as nurses, to claim the
body. In another they turned up at the almshouse in the middle
of the autopsy and demanded to see it. On being told that this
was impossible, they asked for the clothes. It is said that 'a couple
of days later' a surgeon performing a routine operation on the
Tsarevich's knee (at Tsarskoye Selo) saw Rasputin's blue silk shirt
embroidered with yellow flowers under the operating table.[14]
Yet according to the paragraph at the end of the post mortem,
it would be a week before the shirt – a gift from the Empress
– was taken to Tsarskoye Selo.

As Kossorotov began his grisly work that Tuesday, Wickham
Steed, the Foreign Editor of the *Times,* was scratching his head
over a wire dated Petrograd, 1 January. It was both alarming and
puzzling. It began:

> The body of Rasputin was recovered this morning by divers from
> the bottom of an ice-hole in the Neva near Petrovski Bridge,
> which crosses one of the lesser arms of the river north of the
> city.
>
> According to this morning's newspapers, the tragedy to which
> this discovery points appears to have been enacted on Saturday
> morning at the Yusupov Palace on the Moika canal. But none of
> the names of participants is mentioned.

Meaning murder. Prince Yusupov had been a well-known figure in London society before he married. There were cuttings… This was obviously big news, too big to spike, but it was just as obviously chapter two of a story. Where on earth was chapter one? Something was missing. By the time Steed had rummaged for anything from Petrograd correspondent Wilton that might have come in earlier and slipped behind the desk, it was the middle of the night in Russia. In London, the *Times* must also be put to bed, so late on Tuesday under the headlines RASPUTIN DEAD — BODY RECOVERED IN THE NEVA — SUSPICION OF MURDER, Steed composed the following lead-in, to appear in italics:

> Telegrams received from Petrograd allege that the notorious monk Rasputin, whose body has just been recovered from the Neva, was murdered. The messages so far to hand from our Petrograd Correspondent make no direct reference to this and other material points. His narrative must therefore be regarded as still incomplete.[15]

Wilton's story appeared below this paragraph on Wednesday. His wire of Saturday had never arrived. He received a baffled enquiry from London that Tuesday, wrote a full report of the Rasputin affair and sent it back with the only explanation for the lost message that he could think of.

> I send you my notes of the Rasputin affair written on the day after he was killed. [Sunday 31 December.] A full message was cabled, but probably never reached you… any delay in messages sent from here is due entirely to the censorship which invariably gives preference to Agency telegrams.

His notes show that he had been ahead of all the news agencies in that he saw the Police Report on Sunday, just as Stopford did. Wilton was well connected in Petrograd, and in a position to see what had been going on since he worked out of an office in Gorokhovaya Street.

For a Head of the British Intelligence Mission, Hoare was comparatively ill-informed. He knew Purishkevich, and had been told well in advance by the man himself that there was to be an attempt to 'liquidate the affair of Rasputin'. He had, however, taken no notice at all, thinking Purishkevich's tone 'so casual that I thought his words were symptomatic of what everyone was thinking and saying rather than an expression of a definitely thought out plan'. Now, presumably cursing his own lack of judgement, he kept quiet about Purishkevich's warning in his despatches to London.[16] Stopford did not confide in him. Nor, for reasons we shall discover later, did certain members of his own team.

Stopford wrote on Tuesday morning to the Marchioness of Ripon, a society hostess of his own age.[17] She was a remarkable woman; Prince Yusupov had been a great friend of hers, despite the difference in their ages, in London before the war, when she had been responsible for bringing Diaghilev and Nijinskis to London. Stopford, knowing that she could be relied upon to pass information to people in government who mattered, sent regular letters to her or her daughter Lady Juliet Duff, a Russophile and fluent Russian speaker who also knew Yusupov well.[18]

> I have got such awful rheumatism in both arms and both hands I can hardly hold a pen…
>
> All the Imperial Family are off their heads at the Grand Duke Dmitri's arrest, for even the Emperor has not the right to arrest his family. It has never been done since Peter the Great had his son Alexei Petrovich arrested, and it was for threatening to arrest the Tsarevich (Alexander I) that the Emperor Paul was killed.[19]

In England people told each other that those Russians were quite mad. Things had changed in the last century or so, and it seemed unlikely that any present-day Romanovs would actually kill the Tsar. On the other hand, if Felix Yusupov, of all people, could murder that ghastly monk, who knew what was possible?

Rasputin was buried in a quiet private ceremony at Tsarskoye Selo at half-past eight in the morning of Wednesday 21 December, less than forty-eight hours after his body was found. Eye-witness accounts of the funeral are in the files of the Extraordinary Commission set up by the Provisional Government six months later to examine the circumstances of Rasputin's death. A grave had been dug beneath the nave of a still unfinished church, endowed by Anna Vyrubova, at Tsarskoye Selo. The mourn-ers were Tsar Nicholas II, the Tsarina Alexandra, the four royal daughters and the Tsarevich, Vyrubova, Lili Dehn the actress, who was also a close friend of the Tsarina, and the nurse Akilina Laptinskaya. She had been close to Rasputin for a decade, and had brought the body in a car overnight from the Tchesma Infirmary. Regarding them from a respectful distance were the usual unnoticed smattering of retainers and personal maids, the architect, another priest, and the man in charge of construction. Numerous Okhrana officers lurked in the surrounding woods. Colonel Loman, whose wife and daughter were followers of Rasputin but whose own devotion to the dead mystic was in doubt, watched from behind a bush.

The metal casket was lowered into the grave. An icy church smelling of fresh-sawn planks and builders' sand was a bizarre resting place for a person who might have expected to take his leave in a candle-lit cathedral amid clouds of incense, weeping women and priests intoning a doleful lament. But the ten-minute service was conducted by Father Vasiliev, the imperial family's confessor, specially brought from Petrograd, and by nine o'clock the mourners were turning away. When they had gone, Okhrana men emerged from the woods and shovelled earth over the coffin.

News of the funeral did not immediately reach Petrograd. The following Saturday 24 December, 6 January in the British calendar, Albert Stopford wrote again to Lady Ripon:

Here we are all expecting anything may happen. I won't write you all the gossip, mostly founded on lies, some on antiquated truths. Dmitri Pavlovich and Felix are kept under arrest, and when the Grand Duke Paul [Dmitri's father] asked on Monday last for his son to be allowed to come and stay in his palace at Tsarskoye Selo the Emperor replied: 'The Empress cannot allow it for the present'!

The Empress-Mother is still at Kiev; she ought to be here, as her son still fears her a little (not very much). The Allied Embassies would like her back in Petrograd.

Unluckily the bag goes out this afternoon, and I shall only have all the news at dinner as it is the Russian Christmas Eve and I dine at the Grand Duchess's [Grand Duchess Vladimir]. Tomorrow I shall go to the Emperor's church at Tsarskoye Selo to see how they are all getting on down there.

Until the unexpected arrest of Dmitri Pavlovich, the whole tribe of Romanovs, along with almost every other aristocrat, had believed that, with Rasputin out of the way, the Tsar would somehow regain control. They still hoped that, with the passage of time, he would. Stopford would learn that night that Grand Duke Dmitri was already under escort – in a train without a restaurant car – to Kasmin, on the Persian front, one of the hardest postings of the war. Felix Yusupov had been banished to Archangelskoye, the legendary family palace outside Moscow. A few days later Stopford wrote:

He is so clever he will always get all he wants, whereas the other boy is always helpless and desolate; he had *une crise de nerfs*, and completely broke down in the train next day in his famished condition.

The British were waiting for great developments of a different kind. Hoare was not the only one who saw in Rasputin's murder the coming of a new dawn. Sir George Buchanan was convinced that the Duma would take advantage of the situation and push the Tsarina into the background, clearing the way for the Tsar to listen to sensible advice from a pro-Ally perspective.

The very day before Rasputin's death, the Duma's proceedings had been summarily halted by imperial command because so many parliamentarians had spoken up against Rasputin and the politicians and churchmen he had put in place. Now that he was gone, and there was such visible public support on every side for his supposed assassins, the British expected the liberals in Parliament to rally their forces and reconstitute the Duma as an effective force firmly behind the Allies in the war, instead of the limp assembly it had become.

Buchanan and the others miscalculated badly. The pro-Ally members of the Duma had neither influence nor ability, nor sufficient drive to take action.

On the morning of Friday 31 December/12 January, Sir George Buchanan had an audience with the Tsar. He was realistic about the desperately precarious state of political order in Russia and knew he must speak frankly; no one else would. He asked the Foreign Office for permission to say his piece on behalf of the King, but London replied that the King was out of town. Sir George would have to make it clear to the Tsar that his views were purely personal.

> On all previous occasions His Majesty had received me informally in his study, and after asking me to sit down, had produced his cigarette case and asked me to smoke. I was, therefore, disagreeably surprised at being ushered this time into the audience chamber and at finding His Majesty awaiting me there, standing in the middle of the room. I at once realized that he had divined the object of my audience… My heart, I confess, sank within me… The Emperor of all the Russias was then an autocrat, whose slightest wish was law; and I was about not only to disregard the hint which he had so plainly given me but to put myself in the wrong by overstepping the bounds of an Ambassador's sphere of action.[20]

The forthcoming Allied Mission – a deputation from England and France, due to arrive in less than three weeks – was to see people of influence and set up links to enable Russia to get in step with the other two Allied powers. Buchanan explained that it was difficult for the English and French visitors to have any faith in this process when one hardly knew which Minister would be in power from one week to the next. It was important to allow good people to make their own decisions about the team they wanted to work with. And on this topic, he felt he must warn His Majesty (again) that the Tsarina must not be used as a tool of the German propaganda machine by those around her. He tried to tell him (again) how important it was to work *with* the people of Russia. Warming to his theme, Sir George suggested that the Tsar had come to the parting of the ways.

> If I were to see a friend walking through a wood on a dark night along a path which I knew ended in a precipice, would it not be my duty, sir, to warn him of his danger? And is it not equally my duty to warn Your Majesty of the abyss that lies ahead of you?[21]

The Tsar thanked him but told him not to exaggerate Russia's problems. If they were in any way as severe as he implied, he could in any case rely on his army to defend him from an uprising.

According to Stopford, who met him bounding up the embassy stairs, Sir George came back from the audience looking rather chipper. However, at some point the following day, his mood was to change to one of concern and trepidation. Quite how or when it reached him is not clear, but his own diary leaves us in little doubt that Buchanan received news of the most unwelcome kind – news that could have catastrophic diplomatic consequences for Britain. Rather than wait to see if he would be summoned, Buchanan decided to take the bull by the horns and raise the matter directly with the Tsar himself at the Russian New Year's Reception.

The stunning news Buchanan had heard on the grapevine was to the effect that evidence had recently come into the possession of the Tsar that led him to suspect 'a certain British subject' of being Rasputin's killer. According to Buchanan:

> I took the opportunity of assuring him that the suspicion was absolutely groundless. His Majesty thanked me and said that he was very glad to hear this.[22]

Whether or not the Tsar believed Buchanan's assurance and indeed how assured Buchanan himself actually was that no British subject was in anyway involved is equally unclear. It would seem that Buchanan had contacted Hoare for his reaction, but then again, Hoare was not necessarily aware of what his own men were up to a good deal of the time.

Who then was this nameless mystery man who had come to the Tsar's attention and who had caused Buchanan at least one night's troubled sleep? The Tsar had supported the Allies in the first place in order to get foreign debt written off and access to Constantinople as a reward when they won, so he did not want to offend them. But he, the Okhrana and Rasputin's friends had been asking themselves exactly who had had an *interest* in murdering Rasputin, and had drawn certain conclusions.

FOUR

THE SPIES WHO CAME INTO THE COLD

R obert H. Bruce Lockhart was a handsome rugger player with a weakness for dangerous love affairs. He was also a British consular officer with a better understanding of Russia's troubles than most. He had been in Russia since 1912 and had learned to be wary of the political judgement of his compatriots. In particular, he wrote in 1932,

> ...my experiences of the war and of the Russian revolution have left me with a very poor opinion of secret service work. Doubtless it has its uses and its functions, but political work is not its strong point. The buying of information puts a premium on manufactured news. But even manufactured news is less dangerous than the honest reports of men who, however brave and however gifted as linguists, are frequently incapable of forming a reliable political judgement.[1]

The extreme revolutionary surge in Russia by the end of 1916 was unstoppable, but very few of the British had yet recognised that Russia's imperial system was too far gone to save. Part of the problem was the company they kept. Bruce Lockhart was pretty well alone among the British in taking the progressive intelligentsia seriously as a political force, and he was stationed in Moscow. He was also a Foreign Office employee. In Petrograd, the capital, the Ambassador and Consul worked for the Foreign Office; the Military Attaché worked for the War Office; and the British Intelligence Mission was ostensibly part of the War Office, paid for out of Foreign Office funds. While the functions of all three were different, all must keep a close eye on their particular spheres of interest.

In Petrograd, both diplomats and Secret Service men felt it necessary to cultivate contacts in the Duma but also, importantly, among the aristocracy. As newcomers, Sir Samuel Hoare and his wife were completely out of the social loop, and had a dull time of it in consequence. The Hon. Albert Stopford knew the conspirators and brought Dmitri Pavlovich and Buchanan together. But Stopford and Buchanan were older men, on a different wavelength to Dmitri and Yusupov.

> During the war years a junior lieutenant in the British Military
> Censor's office probably went to more parties in high places than
> all the members of the Embassy staff put together.[2]

Bruce Lockhart was referring to Lt Oswald Rayner, whose job disguised his intelligence function. Rayner, a good-looking young man, was a Smethwick draper's son, the least likely recipient, one might suppose, of the glittering favours that Prince Yusupov could bestow. Yet at twenty-seven he had been taken up by the inner circle of gilded youth. He had reached this position by his own intellect, industry, charm and great good fortune.

He had been born in November 1888 into modest circumstances, and would in due course have five younger brothers and sisters. At eleven he obtained a scholarship to King Edward's School, then located in New Street, Birmingham.[3] The boy absorbed education like blotting paper, but the son of a draper

with six children could go only so far before lack of money
would dictate that he go out in the world and obtain employment; and we know from correspondence that the family was in
financial difficulties in the early years of the century.[4] Rayner
was good at languages, and when he left school he was fortunate
enough to obtain a position as an English teacher at an establishment run by a Mr Ölquist in Helsinki. In Finland (which was
then annexed to Russia) he would meet a Finnish couple whose
generosity would change his life forever. In February 1907, when
he was eighteen, he wrote home delightedly:

Dear Mother and Father,

I am writing to you in order to lay before you such a romance
as you would scarce expect to find anywhere outside the bounds
of fiction.

As you already know, people have been very kind and hospi-
table to me in Finland. Amongst those who have been kindest, I
believe I have already mentioned Mr and Mrs Uno Donner. Mr
and Mrs Donner have very often invited me to spend evenings
with them at their flat. I have always enjoyed these visits more
than any others; for from the first, I could be perfectly natural
there. At all other places I have been obliged, more or less, to
pose as a good deal older than I really am, in order to apologise
as it were for my position as English Teacher in the Institute…
To make a long story short, they have asked me if I would like
to put myself under their charge and continue my studies at
Oxford! They broached the subject just after dinner one evening
a few days ago. Naturally I was quite overcome with astonishment and returned home dazed, expecting every moment to
wake up from a more than usually vivid dream. I promised to
give them a definite answer the following day at 12 o'clock. I
was brooding over the matter during the night, and came to the
conclusion that provided you agreed to the proposal, this strange
turn of my fortunes would open out new roads for my future,
and provide me with my highest aspiration realised – an Oxford
University career.[5]

Thanks to this kind couple, Oswald Rayner was already soaring away from Smethwick. By April he had moved into the home of Mrs Sinebrichov, whom he described simply as a widow, and 'Mrs Donner's mother'. The Sinebrichov family had been providing Helsinki with fine port for over eighty years; in fact, they owned the monopoly on brewing in the city. They had amassed a superb collection of Old Masters and furniture, which was presented to the nation when Finland regained its independence after the First World War. Maybe Rayner was dining off Sèvres porcelain every night or maybe he wasn't, but in any case he had flown so high that, sadly, his parents could no longer be expected to understand the social stratosphere he was living in. 'There has not really... been anything extraordinary to write about – a constant round of dinners, and suppers, and clubs, and private entertainments, and parties of all descriptions...'. He gave an account, which was not intended to dazzle but could not fail to, of the lives of those with whom he was now associating.

Mr and Mrs Uno Donner left Finland on February 20th for Italy. They spent a month at Milano and Florence, thence proceeding to the Riviera – Cannes, Nice, Mentone, Monte Carlo &c... [I] shall... sail for England by the boat which leaves Helsingfors on the 15th of next month. By that time the Donners will probably be in England – that is to say in London. If so I shall go straight to London, and then arrive in Birmingham on the 20th or 21st of May. The Donners would like me to stay at Birmingham for about a fortnight and then to spend a month in Switzerland with them – at Aix-les-Bains... From Switzerland we shall go to Mrs Sinebrychoff's [sic] country house for the summer, where there will be yachting, tennis, boating, swimming, riding horseback &c ad libitum. In the autumn the Donners will probably leave Finland for good, and settle down somewhere in England. For the autumn and winter they will hire a flat in London, and I shall begin studying Greek for Oxford. It will be impossible for me to join the University before January 1908.[6]

He was now part of a circle that included 'Consul Cooke', and
Count Sparre and his wife. Count Louis Sparre was a gifted and
famous Swedish artist who had trained as a painter in Paris. He
lived in Finland for nearly twenty years and married a Finn.
In the last decade he had been a pioneer of Finnish industrial
art and design; he had even founded a factory to produce Art
Nouveau furniture and other pieces.

> When Mr Donner returns to Finland in summer, he will prob-
> ably visit his father for some time, and I shall at the same time
> live at Count Sparre's country house near Borgå. He is an artist
> and will give me some drawing lessons there.

Oswald Rayner loved his family, but he would never again live
in a back-to-back terraced house with a draper's shop in the
front room. At Oxford he would study Modern Languages,
and entered the university in October 1907, graduating with
Honours in 1910. By that time Prince Felix Yusupov was already
at University College, where he occupied rooms on the ground
floor overlooking the street – rooms traditionally known, according to the Master, as 'the Club', no matter who lived there. It
was here in 1909, through a mutual friend, Eric Hamilton (later
Bishop of Salisbury and Dean of Windsor), that Oswald Rayner
met Felix Yusupov. The three scholars shared a mutual love of
languages and would remain close friends for the rest of their
lives. Indeed, Rayner would later name his only son 'John Felix
Hamilton Rayner' as a testament to his two closest friends.[7]

After university, Rayner applied for a post with the *Times* newspaper and, in November 1910, was duly appointed Second
Assistant Correspondent in the Paris office at a salary of £150
per year.[8]

The following year he moved back to London and embarked
on a career in elevated government circles as Private Secretary
to Sir Herbert Samuel, Asquith's Postmaster General. Samuel
and Rayner sailed together through choppy waters when,

in 1912, Sir Herbert, along with Sir Rufus Isaacs and David Lloyd George, was accused by Belloc and Chesterton of insider trading in Marconi shares (an enquiry later exonerated all three, although there can be little doubt that they successfully conspired to frustrate the process and conceal truth from Parliament). It was during the course of this long and drawn-out episode that Rayner made the acquaintance of Lloyd George, then Chancellor of the Exchequer, with whom he stayed in close contact for at least a decade afterwards.

Throughout his employment with Sir Herbert, Rayner was reading for the Bar. He was admitted with Honours in the Bar finals of 1914, and when the war began he joined the Officer Training Corps of the Inns of Court in September 1914. The Corps had immediately been embodied as a territorial force on the outbreak of war and had initiated a crash training programme for those seeking commissions. Rayner was among twenty-one new recruits to a company under Lt Reggie Trench, who initially described them as 'an awful rabble'. They were immediately sent off to Richmond Park to begin the basic training that would ultimately lead most of them to service regiments on the Western Front. Rayner appears to have been an exception. In October 1914, a little over a month after he joined the Corps, he was commissioned as Second Lieutenant, Interpreter. He was fluent in French, German, Russian and Swedish. It is generally known that Col Francis Errington, the Corps CO, actively resisted attempts by junior officers to transfer out. However, within three months Rayner had been seconded to 'special duties' in the Intelligence Department of the War Office.

Quite how and why, in January of 1915, he was given this secondment can only be the subject of speculation. Whether certain linguists like Rayner were simply identified by the War Office and transferred accordingly, or whether he had a sponsor who guided him in the direction of intelligence work, is unclear. He certainly had a number of influential political contacts in Whitehall through his employment with Sir Herbert Samuel, and as we shall see later on, he would not have been the first person to lobby for such a post.

It was while working for the War Office in 1915 that Rayner made the brief acquaintance of another junior officer, one Lt George Hill, who had initially gone to Ypres on the Western Front in a Canadian infantry battalion attached to the Manchester Regiment. Following a serious injury while on a mission in No Man's Land, the multi-lingual Hill had then been seconded to the War Office's Intelligence Department. Both Hill and Rayner, like other new recruits to the department, had a four-week course on intelligence work which covered shadowing, methods of using invisible inks, code and cipher systems and lock-picking among other skills. While their time together in London was to be brief, their paths would cross again some three years later when they would be among the first agents recruited to the new Stockholm SIS station run by Major John Scale.

Towards the end of 1915 Hill was sent to Greece, where he was to work with agents behind enemy lines. Not long after his departure, Rayner was also given his first intelligence posting abroad. In November of 1915 he and Major Vere Benet were assigned to the British Intelligence Mission in Petrograd, where they were to take up responsibility for censorship. In a memo to Sir Samuel Hoare written shortly after Rasputin's murder, Vere Benet discusses the nature of their censorship responsibilities and describes what 'Rayner and I have done, are doing and still hope to do':

> Censorship does not mean reading private correspondence in the spirit of inquisitive curiosity, but is rather a branch of military intelligence, which if rightly used, is of great assistance to the Allies.
>
> …I have avoided all interference in purely Russian affairs (except trade), and passed onto them all such internal matters as espionage and politics. I have impressed on them that my object, besides helping them, is to obtain information regarding the activity of

the Scandinavian and neutral countries, whose agents act as inter-
mediaries for German trade… MI8 wrote to me recently, 'The
copies you send are most useful to the Shipping Department
of the Blockade and give us an entirely new and fresh lot of
Scandinavian names'. Extracts from intercepted correspondence
also show the enemy's appreciation of 'English Censorship'.[9]

Despite his claim to have 'avoided all interference in purely
Russian affairs', it very much depends on how one interprets the
words 'avoided' and 'interference'. Benet and Rayner's definition
seems to have meant intercepting Russian communications of
all kinds on a grand scale and, when they felt so inclined, sharing
some of them with their Russian counterparts without playing
any active role in what ensued. The report is also a very firm
confirmation of the fact that very little news or information
was changing hands between friends and foes alike in Petrograd
without Benet and Rayner being in the know. Benet himself
states elsewhere in the memo that he has 'read, censored and
made notes on some 28,000 telegrams since April 1916'.

In wartime the Russian Imperial General Staff gave over part
of their offices to the French and British Intelligence Missions.
They were housed with various Russian government and
police departments in a semi-circular sweep of offices, pierced
by an arch over a busy road, overlooking the square in front
of the Winter Palace. Almost all the British contingent spoke
Russian fluently. Some, like Rayner, were censors. Others were
engaged in identifying enemy units on the Russian front. This
did not involve camouflage and binoculars. It was a desk job,
usually accomplished by piecing together whatever snippets of
news reached them from other theatres of war and working out
which Germans the Russians must be fighting by a process of
elimination.

Samuel Hoare, who had a nice eye for detail, wrote a wry
account of what he found when he arrived at the Mission in the
spring of 1916.

True to Russian type, the façade was the best part of the building. At the back of the General Staff was a network of smelly yards and muddy passages that made entrance difficult and health precarious. Inside, the bureaucracy showed its unshaken power by maintaining a temperature that in those days of fuel shortage was far beyond the reach of any private house... Our caps and galoshes were left in the keeping of a Finnish gendarme in a stuffy waiting-room. The Finn's other duty was to bring us tea during the day.

Soon after my arrival, two tiresome events happened in the Mission. One of my galoshes was missed from the waiting-room, and the samovar simultaneously struck work.

Inevitably, the two crises were linked, the galosh having been left to stew in the samovar for several days. Office life, with its hourly glasses of sugar-laden tea, crawled by at a sluggish pace. There were time-wasting formalities when Russians visited the British office and vice versa; according to Russian military protocol, all personnel had to shake hands with everyone in the room on arrival and departure, and must wear swords at all times. The system was almost paralysed by this kind of thing, not to mention other imperatives to stop work.

Upon all public holidays the General Staff was closed, and our office with it... There were no less than fifteen public holidays in the month of May and five on end in the last week of August owing to a perfect covey of saint's days and national anniversaries... Upon the Church festivals that were not important enough to be honoured with a whole holiday, services of considerable length would be held in the General Staff chapel... Even when the department was working, the hours were uncertain, and it was never easy to make an appointment with a Russian colleague. I remember, for instance, that at the time of my arrival the Quartermaster General, the senior officer of the General Staff, made a common habit of arriving at his office at about eleven at night, and of working until seven or eight the next morning.

Unsurprisingly, co-operation, indeed contact, through work was not so easy to achieve. Those members of the British Mission who already had Russian friends in Petrograd turned to them as a relief from life at the office. Rayner, of course, knew the second richest man in Russia, and it was not long before he and Yusupov renewed their acquaintance.

Yusupov was immensely generous, as only a man could be whose ancestors had been accumulating palaces, furniture, paintings, jewels, serfs, animals, factories, steppes, coastlines and oil fields since the founding of the family by a nephew of Mahomet; and like his great friend Dmitri Pavlovich, he was a great and enthusiastic anglophile. After his first year at Oxford he had invited Eric Hamilton to visit Russia as his guest. Hamilton, a friend of Rayner's, was quite overwhelmed by the wealth of his host, and his kindness too. He would not have seen the more dissipated side of Yusupov. Oswald Rayner, who probably did, could hardly fail to be dazzled and amused, though it is unlikely that he went native and began to see himself as a Petrograd socialite rather than a British intelligence officer.

Rayner was not alone in the British Intelligence Mission in having friends in high places. Captain Stephen Alley, who shared a Petrograd apartment with Rayner and Vere Benet on the top floor of the Swedish Church Building, had been born forty years ago in the Krivo, one of the Yusupov Palaces in Moscow. His father, John Alley, was an engineer employed in Russian railway construction. Although he had begun life in conditions of privilege by comparison with Rayner, he had wider experience. Many years later he made notes about his early life.

> I ran wild on our estate, called Malakhovo, until I was sent to the German school in Moscow, Fiedler's. I used to travel up by train from Malakhovo with our neighbours the Obolenskis. My father used to take a house for the winter in Moscow and we lived in the Malakhovo house in summer.

Prince Serge Obolenski was a great friend of Felix Yusupov.

> This went on until my father's partner, Colonel John Davis, brought me to England. Apparently I was too old for one class of school, and too young for another.

Alley was fifteen when he arrived in England in the summer or autumn of 1891. It was decided that he would be placed as an apprentice with Dewrance & Co., a London firm, and that his academic education would continue by means of evening classes at King's College.

It would, of course, have been possible to get a fifteen-year-old into a private school or even a crammer. Either because of business misfortune or illness, things at home in Russia may have been on a financial downturn when Stephen arrived in Britain.

But in 1891 he registered at King's College to study maths, mechanics, Junior French and Junior German (most likely the lessons at Fiedler's had been conducted in Russian).[10] At the time he was lodging at 39 Paulet Road, Camberwell; but for most of the next three years he would stay with a Captain and Mrs Moody in Blackheath.

He was then sent to Scotland to further his apprenticeship in the works of his uncle (also called Stephen) at Polmadie, an industrial suburb of Glasgow which made more locomotives for export than anywhere else in the world. Alley and McLellan at Polmadie were marine engineers and enthusiastic exporters (during the First World War they would manufacture barges for neutral countries).[11] In 1894 he enrolled at the University of Glasgow to study analytical chemistry, mathematics and English literature. He was then living at 2 Park Terrace, Ayr and his father was still alive.[12] He remained for a year, attending evening classes, and did not graduate, but accepted a job in London representing Alley and McLellan in their offices at 28 Victoria Street. 'My uncle Stephen put me up for the St Stephen's Club.' This was on the corner of Bridge Street and the Embankment, between the Houses of Parliament and Scotland Yard, and the members tended to be civil engineers (from their professional institution a hundred yards away) or Conservative politicians; Disraeli had been a founding father. At home in Russia there seems to have been some family upheaval, for the 1901 census shows that Stephen's mother, a British subject who had, like him, been born in Russia, was widowed and had come to live with her son in Greenwich.

The firm in Glasgow was also undergoing great changes at the end of the century. In 1898 his uncle Stephen of Alley and McLellan died, and his son, Stephen's cousin Stephen Evans Alley (who was only twenty-six), took over his share of the business. McLellan retired in 1903 and Stephen Evans Alley absorbed a rival firm, starting to develop the Sentinel Steam Wagon in Glasgow: it would eventually be used in road vehicles as well as railway locomotives.

With the new regime came the inevitable family dispute.

I disagreed with my cousin as to commissions and started my own office in Westminster.

He also joined the Surrey Imperial Yeomanry, whose 'A' Squadron was conveniently close to Victoria Street in Pimlico. The following year, with the Russo-Japanese War in progress, he translated the Japanese sappers' secret manual (obtained in Russian) into English for the War Office.

But there were business problems.

Whilst I was on my own I represented Hodgkinson, Stokers' tyre lever which I had patented and started pushing, but… the business went wrong and I got into debt. For the time being, I had a partner who helped me and took over my affairs. I went abroad in order to repay my debts.[13]

In 1910 he went to Russia for three years to help build the first heavy oil pipeline to the Black Sea. This was the period of the Caspian oil boom; the Nobels and the Rothschilds were backing

the Russian endeavour to transport oil out of Baku, then part
of the Tsar's empire. Huge fields lay beneath the Caucasus, and
Russian oil transported by Shell already accounted for about a
third of the world's production.

On the outbreak of war in 1914, having the rare advantage
of being truly bilingual, Alley was recruited by the Military
Intelligence Department and sent to Petrograd. On a brief period
back in London on leave, he attended a Secret Service course in
Russell Square where he was 'taught the art of counter-espionage
and many other things' by former Scotland Yard Superintendent
William Melville, by then MI5's Chief Detective. Back in
Petrograd as part of the British Intelligence Mission, he:

> ...collected a lot of suitable officers in Russia, all who really
> could speak the language, and popped them about to keep me
> informed as to what was happening. Folks at home were appar-
> ently not satisfied with the information they were getting and
> they sent out Sam Hoare.

At the outbreak of war Sir Samuel Hoare was a Conservative
MP. He later recalled that in August 1914 he knew nothing of
military matters and had no interest in them:

> Army affairs I had particularly neglected. Never even a territo-
> rial... year by year I had sleepily heard the debates on Army
> Estimates.[14]

Although initially commissioned in the (territorial) Norfolk
Yeomanry, he had, at the end of 1914, been declared unfit for
active service and faced the prospect of being invalided out
of the army. During 1915 he was running a recruitment office
in Norwich Cattle Market, growing increasing restive and
depressed at his misfortune. He therefore sought to pull political strings and find himself a job on 'one of the remoter fronts
where an Englishman might still be required'. In February
1916 a friend at the War Office told him of a possible post in

Petrograd. After taking a course of Russian lessons in Norwich, Hoare arranged, through his friends and contacts in government circles, an interview with 'C', Captain Mansfield Cumming, the Chief of the Secret Intelligence Service:

> I had expected to be put through an examination in the Russian language, and a questionnaire as to what I knew about Russian politics and the Russian army... instead, there were a few conventional words... a searching look and a nod to say that while it was not much of a job, I could have it if I wanted it.[15]

The job firstly involved going out to Petrograd to review the working of the British Intelligence Mission there, which was then being run by Major C.J.M. Thornhill, and secondly to assess the effectiveness of the Russian blockade on trade with Germany. After undertaking the usual intelligence course, Hoare left London for Russia in March 1916 and eagerly set about his task. Although his verdict on Thornhill's stewardship of the Mission was hardly a flattering one, it seems clear that he was completely unprepared for the inevitable consequences that would follow C's receipt of his report. Not only did C decide to dismiss Thornhill as Head of the Mission, he chose Hoare to succeed him, granting him the rank of temporary lieutenant-colonel in recognition of his new posting.

Hoare's appointment clearly created friction within the Intelligence Mission. It would seem that many of the officers under his command not only resented the appointment of a man who was seen as being responsible for the removal of the universally popular Thornhill, but more to the point was perceived as a politician with neither the military nor the intelligence expertise for the job in hand.

Alley, Thornhill's second in command, was in many ways the obvious person to step into his shoes, but he was overlooked on this occasion, although he was to remain as deputy to Hoare. Perhaps he was considered rather a loose cannon. He had certainly offended the Ambassador, as a terse note dated 15 March

1915 indicates. It is an explanation, point by point, to a third party of an internal row. (It may well be, in view of the style, that the third party was C in England; it reads like a telegram.) He and a Captain Simpson had been hauled over the coals by Sir George Buchanan one Friday afternoon. 'We were both rather hurt unsympathetic attitude which however caused us show extra deference. Ambassador requested me bring copy my instructions certain hour Saturday afternoon.' He goes on:

d) Saturday I was several hours Russian War Office renewing acquaintance various officers expecting finish in time appointment; but Chief of General Staff suddenly fixed unexpected hour receive myself Major Ferguson clashing Embassy hour. Telephones temporarily out of order sent deferential letter fully explaining asking Ambassador if he would postpone appointment until later hour but leaving barely time ensure punctuality.

e) Interview Chief of General Staff closely followed by General Leontieff unavoidably kept us until few minutes past our appointment. This was less than 15 minutes appointment. Meanwhile greatest possible speed I fetched my instructions drove to Embassy.

f) Near Embassy caught sight Ambassador excitedly hailing from pavement. Sprang out and ran towards him. Without waiting to hear any expression of regret, loudly assailed me with great violence action and with imprecation. Starting apologise he cut me short exclaiming he did not care damn what I had to say. Asking what I should do with paper in my hand I obtained no comprehensible reply. Then with further strong language he upbraided me for chucking appointment with Ambassador for Chief of Staff. Then he turned his back on me and walked away.

If Alley was in any way put out by Hoare's appointment, he never showed it. In fact, in another sense, the newcomer's appointment was tantamount to giving him a free rein, because Hoare was not worldly enough to perceive the subtleties of which some of his staff were capable.

Major Stephen J. Alley MC, as he later became, gets just one mention in Hoare's account of his year in Petrograd. Sir Samuel and Lady Hoare had a female cook who went berserk in their flat and held up Sir Samuel's soldier-servant at knifepoint. Hoare was bedridden, at the time, with a fever. (Never a well man, he would live to be seventy-nine.) The Hoares gave the cook notice, but she refused to leave, as under wartime regulations she was entitled to do. They must get rid of her, but could only shudder and discuss legal action until Stephen Alley introduced a visitor: the local Police Commandant. The policeman, who in the nature of his work had grasped the principle of direct action, unceremoniously booted her out of the back door in return for a twenty-rouble note. Local understanding had its uses.

Alley was a military man, not a socialite, but he understood the Russian ruling class because he had known them since he was born. Bruce Lockhart would probably have said he was 'incapable of forming a reliable political judgement', but his upbringing and experience of work in Russia would have helped him to recognise the disaster that Russia's war effort was fast becoming. Even Hoare, whose local knowledge was so much more superficial, could see the problems of social injustice and failing morale that had been intensifying since the war began. And even Hoare heard the stories of dark forces around the imperial household, misguiding them in the direction of defeat.

The Tsar and Tsarina believed 'the people' were fired with personal loyalty to them – naturally, for were not the Romanovs rulers by divine right? The Tsar believed so, and this self-righteousness was at once his only strength and his greatest weakness. With Western Europe becoming increasingly secular, Russia – and the imperial couple in particular – clung to the medieval religious outlook of the Holy Synod of the Russian Orthodox Church. Its political expression was feudal. The Tsar, not by nature a tyrant, had been brought up to believe that the vast mass of his subjects were a resource, like his land and rivers and mines, to be used for the benefit of Russia. And as his wife said 'The Tsar *is* Russia'.[16] The peasants were out there like fish in the sea. If men were lost in war, there were always more men, and in the Tsar's mind they so loved the monarchy and all it stood for that they would feel honoured to serve.

He persisted as far as he could in ignoring change. Perhaps change was easy to ignore because it had been so very slow. The serfs had been liberated in the nineteenth century. There had been some land reform. Soldiers and sailors had mutinied after the Russo-Japanese War in 1905, and revolution had threatened to spread; in October of that year the Tsar had been forced to grant Russia a constitution in order to pre-empt it. A constitution meant an elected government, the bi-cameral Duma. That had been instituted over a decade ago. But there was no universal suffrage and ministers were appointed by the Tsar. To a great extent government still operated by petition and dispensation, like a tribal society in which petitioners must queue for days to ask favours of a potentate.

Rasputin understood the system. He was the arch-fixer, and when, from 1915 onwards, the Tsar was at the Stavka, far from the capital, it was Rasputin, in his stuffy apartment in Gorokhovaya Street, whom people would queue to see, and Rasputin who would listen, and scrawl a note to whoever could give them what they wanted.

That the Duma had been emasculated, and that the workers were discontented and always striking, that there was a new urban middle class they did not understand at all and that soldiers at the front were deserting in droves, did not shake the imperial couple in their belief that the Tsar knew best. The Tsar's reaction to constructive criticism was not to listen or even to confront but to *shut out* challengers; to send them out of the room as would a vexed schoolmaster. Right-wing aristocrats would have had him do a lot worse, but he was temperamentally inclined to avoid confrontation.

Still worse, he was impressionable. Orders were issued and countermanded, ministers arrived and departed, with disconcerting frequency, as new arguments won him over.

His most obvious defect was his inability to form his own judgement; it was this trait which made his Generals contemptuous
of him.[17]

Back in 1905 only Grand Duke Nikolai Nikolaivich, the most
famous of Tsar Nicholas's uncles, had been able to persuade
him to sign the October Manifesto and grant a constitution.
The Grand Duke was older, more belligerent, and a lot taller; he
was six feet six, and his physical presence alone carried authority. And the soldiers respected him, so the Tsar had made him
Supreme Commander of the Russian Armies at the start of hostilities in August 1914.

Russia had been bound by treaty to join France and Britain
and its old enemy Japan (the Allies) in fighting the expansion-
ist Germans, the Austro-Hungarian Empire and later, the Turks
(the Central Powers).[18] So the Tsar had *had* to go to war; a
Romanov could not break his word. Unfortunately, Russia
was unprepared for war in any respect other than manpower.
They began with a massive 102 regular land divisions (each of
between 12,000 and 20,000 men), where the British began with
six. At the very beginning Grand Duke Nikolai, with 1.6 million
men at his disposal, sent several divisions to East Prussia, thus
gallantly diverting German forces from France and Belgium.
The German army was better supplied and vastly better pre-
pared for war than the Russian rabble, and although Russia
probably saved the British and French from an ignominious
rout, the Russians were easily outmanoeuvred, and tens of
thousands killed. This was the battle of Tannenberg, and a great
deal of outmoded but useful matériel was gained from it by the
Germans.

Before the end of 1914 Turkey had joined the Central Powers.
So in 1915, besides trying to defend its western borders, Russia
had to prevent Turkey from grabbing the oil fields of Azerbaijan
or shoving Russia out of the way right across Central Asia and
sneaking into British India. (Persia remained nominally neutral,
but unfriendly.) At Grand Duke Nikolai's request, the British and

French deflected Turkish aggression by opening the Dardanelles campaign, which failed.

The Russians were beaten steadily backwards in the west. Morale sank as the German front advanced east along a line approaching Riga in the north, and south to Czernowitz on the border with Romania. Around 750,000 Russians were captured in the summer of 1915 alone. Lines of defence simply crumbled. In Petrograd, Stopford confided to his diary:

> It will indeed be a tragedy if the enemy comes here, with all the factories and powderies and cannonries. At Riga there is sixty million pounds' worth of timber, and more than double that value here.[19]

At Tsarskoye Selo, the Tsar wrung his hands and did nothing. He and his family were self-contained to the point of isolation. From the Tsarina, he received a constant chiding stream of advice, usually presented as the thoughts and insights of their spiritual advisor, Rasputin. Society, liberal and otherwise, was appalled. Rasputin helpfully offered to come to the Stavka to give Grand Duke Nikolai the benefit of his wisdom. He got a telegram by return.

> Do come! I shall hang you.

It was never a good idea to offend Rasputin. Already the Tsarina could not invite her beloved advisor to the Alexander Palace, because her husband knew that Uncle Nikolai would find out about it and kick up a row; but this was the final straw. On 28 August 1915, Albert Stopford, dining with the usual clutch of Grand Dukes, heard that Nikolai Nikolaivich was likely to be relieved of his command.[20] He informed Buchanan on 1 September.

On 5 September 1915 the news broke decisively: the Tsar in person was to take over as Supreme Commander. Grand Duchess Vladimir, rushing to her palace with this information, was late for dinner. ('No Romanov is *ever* late for dinner,' commented Stopford, appalled.) Forty minutes after her delayed arrival, suppressing his pique and 'eating my lukewarm *potage St-Germain*'[21] among an assortment of Romanovs, he found them dreadfully despondent. Unlike the Tsar, many of these nobles understood only too well the cost of military mistakes. They had seen the wrecked lives of the poor at first hand and they feared an uprising that might threaten the survival of the monarchy. They were aware of the hostile intelligentsia, whose criticisms they abhorred as inspired by alien ideas. Also, they could feel an icy blast from the German approach in the west, and they did not trust the soldiers, sailors or poorly fed people in the streets to cling to the Allied cause.

> We all expect the Germans here sooner or later. Till Riga falls no one will know whether their *objectif* is Petrograd or Moscow; if Petrograd, their fleet could co-operate with them. The major part of the artillery and munition factories are here.
>
> On the other hand… the winter begins in about 6 weeks' time… If they come here, will there be a revolution? The fear is the *people* might rise and make peace to stop the German advance, feeling that the Romanovs have had their chance and been found wanting.[22]

A separate peace, the British estimated, would release 350,000 German soldiers to fight on the Western Front: it would mean almost inevitable defeat. Refusing to submit to despair, Sir George Buchanan did his best to make the Tsarina reconsider the Tsar's position.

> I took advantage… of an audience which I had early in September [1915] with the Empress to tell Her Majesty that I shared the apprehensions with which the Emperor's decision was viewed by the Council of Ministers. Not only, I said, would His Majesty have to bear the whole responsibility for any fresh disaster that might befall his armies, but he would, by combining the duties of

Commander-in-Chief with those of an autocratic ruler of a great Empire, be undertaking a task beyond the strength of any single man. The Empress at once protested, saying that the Emperor ought to have assumed the command from the very first and that, now that his army had suffered so severely, his proper place was with his troops. 'I have no patience,' she continued, 'with Ministers who try to prevent him doing his duty. The situation requires firmness. The Emperor, unfortunately, is weak; but I am not, and I intend to be firm.[23]

Grand Duke Nikolai Nikolaivich was despatched to defend Russia from the Turks in the Caucasus. Tsar Nicholas gritted his teeth and left Tsarskoye Selo to run the war from the Stavka at Moghilev. This, while several hundred miles from any front line, was distant from Petrograd and people said that Rasputin had got the Tsar out of the way in order to better influence policy through the Tsarina. The Tsarina showed Rasputin the maps and plans that her weak little husband had showed *her*; it was tantamount to treason. In intimate suppers in palaces and restaurants all over the capital and beyond, Grand Dukes and Duchesses began to talk about direct action.

A plot was hatched by the Grand Dukes and several members of the aristocracy to remove the Tsarina from power and force her to retire to a convent. Rasputin was to be sent back to Siberia, the Tsar deposed and the Tsarevich placed on the throne. Everyone plotted, even the generals. As for the British Ambassador, Sir George Buchanan, his dealings with radical elements caused him to be accused by many Russians of secretly working for the Revolution.[24]

Nothing came of it, perhaps because at first things did not seem to be turning out too badly. In October of 1915 Grand Duchess Vladimir volunteered brighter news. Stopford wrote home that she told me she found the Emperor – who had been to see her – quite a changed man, and with quite a different face. He now, for the first time in his life, knows everything, and hears the truth direct. Nikolai Nikolaivich never wanted to know anything, and of what he did know he only told the Emperor so little that it was hardly worth his hearing.[25]

But information was not enough. Tsar Nicholas was incapable of taking focused, decisive action without getting the go-ahead from his wife. He did have some strategic and logistic understanding, because he and his family between them controlled most of the country's resources and knew how much this war was costing to run. He now knew that, for Russian commanders at the front, getting munitions was like pulling teeth.

In November of 1915 the Tsar met Buchanan, and

…made an earnest appeal to His Majesty's Government to supply the Russian army with rifles. If only they would do so he could, he said, place 800,000 men in his field at once, and strike a crushing blow at the Germans… I could hold out no hope of our being able to supply rifles on so large a scale… I also pointed out that, apart from the question of supply, there was also that of delivery, and that if Russia was ever to receive from abroad the war material in which she was so deficient, drastic steps would have to be taken to expedite the construction of the Murman railway. The Emperor agreed that the work of construction ought to be placed under the control of some energetic and competent official, but he did not approve of the candidate whom I had ventured to suggest for the post.[26]

David Lloyd George, the energetic Minister of Munitions, was ensuring that Britain's manufacture and supply of arms was at last cranking into top gear. He was all for supporting the Russians by sending guns and tanks but clearly recognised that this was going to be of minimal effect unless the political paralysis that was engulfing Russia was addressed. It is clear from Lloyd George's papers that he was coming to the view that unless Russia's internal crisis was resolved the outlook was bleak, not only for Russia herself but for Britain and France, who would be left to stand alone in the event of a Russian collapse. It is also clear that Lloyd George was not relying totally on official channels to keep him informed of news and developments in Russia. Days after Buchanan's audience with the Tsar, he received a personal letter from Sir Ian Malcolm, the Conservative MP for Croydon, who was at the time in Petrograd on an unofficial fact-finding mission. Staying at the Astoria Hotel, Malcolm made his views clear to Lloyd George in no uncertain terms:

> The Emperor and family and Court have not a single friend. It is said they have made every possible mistake… when the Revolution comes – that is what it is openly called – comes, I am told that at least half the army is so enraged at the massacre of their fellows, consequent on the lack of munitions, that they will side with the rebellion.[27]

Back in Russia, Buchanan was experiencing impatience with what was starting to look like high-level sabotage by the politicians who had paid Rasputin to get them their jobs. Sturmer, for instance, a placeman of Rasputin's and known German sympathiser, was in charge of the Russian Ministry of Ways and Communications, which included railways. The railway between Petrograd and Alexandrovsk (Murmansk, in winter the only ice-free port) was imperative for the distribution of munitions and supplies but was taking forever to complete. Time and again, the Tsarina and Rasputin would persuade the Tsar to put someone useless in charge of an important government department, only to have the Allies get frustrated by inadequate Russian performance and insist that this person be removed. The Tsar would profess agreement with everything but usually he did nothing. Both he and his wife had a financial interest in the cosy relationship with Rasputin.

It seems barely credible that such a fabulously wealthy Romanov should take money in return for favours, but this is what appears to have been going on. The Extraordinary Commission that examined the death of Rasputin during the spring and summer of 1917 took depositions from Vyrubova and scores of others, and wanted to know what had become of Rasputin's money. Had there been half a dozen wads of cash under the bed, they could have been stolen. But over recent years hundreds of thousands of roubles had been passed to him in exchange for favours. Had Vyrubova received money from him? She pleaded poverty, but how had she paid for a hospital and a church at Tsarskoye Selo? She said that she had used 20,000 roubles of her 100,000-rouble insurance payout from a railway accident. This was an unconvincingly small sum and she knew it. Gradually, another story emerged. The money from petitioners was apportioned, a small cut to Rasputin, some to Vyrubova and the Infirmary, and the rest to 'the Empress's institutions'. At one point the going rate was 1,000 roubles.

> November 3rd, 1915, 'Alex to Nicky':
> …One thing Our Friend said, that if people offer great sums (so as to get a *decoration*), now one must accept, as money is needed and one helps them doing good by giving in to their weaknesses, and 1000 profit by it – it's true, but again against all moral feelings. But in time of war all becomes different.[28]

Weighed down by so much responsibility and so little power, the Tsar sank into an intermittent mild depression. His apathy was often remarked upon. When he was not doing what his wife told him to, he was said to exist in a kind of torpor. People said he was drunk or drugged, probably by Badmaëv (see chapter 5) – but given the common reliance on opiates in those years, he was probably getting whatever he wanted from the family medical advisor Dr Botkin.

He had no trusted, supportive friends at all. He took the Tsarevich to Moghilev for company. He told the Tsarina that he didn't want the boy to be over protected and fearful of grown-up life, as he had been. The little boy, who was twelve, and delicate, and always got his own way, was allowed to wear a specially made Cossack uniform. They were happy there, away from the women and the dark forces that enveloped the court.

FIVE

DARK FORCES

Not a single important event at the front was decided without a preliminary conference with the *starets*. From Tsarskoye Selo instructions were given to General Headquarters [the Stavka] on the direct telephone line. The Empress insisted on being kept fully informed by the Emperor on the military and political situation. On receiving this information, sometimes secret and of the utmost importance, she would send for Rasputin, and confer with him.[1]

How on earth had he done it? The Tsarina taking advice from a *peasant*? To the aristocrats of imperial Russia, it was as if she was taking advice from a chimpanzee.

For several years before his death, any outright reference to 'Our Friend', as the Tsarina called Rasputin, in the public press was forbidden; the generally understood code in subversive articles was 'dark forces'. This only served to increase his mystique. When people happened to see him they stared, fascinated. Meriel Buchanan, the Ambassador's young daughter, spotted

Rasputin in April 1916 as she waited to cross a busy Petrograd street. Along bowled an *isvostchik* with bright green reins, drawn by a shaggy white horse, carrying Rasputin –

> a tall black-bearded man with a fur cap drawn down over long straggling hair, a bright blue blouse and long high-boots showing under his fur-trimmed overcoat.[2]

She was describing, perhaps unconsciously, the costume he died in. Like everyone else, she mentioned his unusually pale, deep-set, staring eyes. She was not a careless writer, but about Rasputin she used the words 'compelling' and 'repellent' on the same page, which is significant in itself. His sexual attractiveness increased the more demonised he became.

Sir Paul Dukes, then a music student in Petrograd, shared a flat with Gibbes, the Tsarevich's English tutor, who told him that, if he cared to, he could see Rasputin on the station platform bound for Tsarskoye on a certain day (Rasputin was usually guarded, but on this day apparently wasn't). Dukes went along out of curiosity, and was not impressed by the man's scruffy appearance and 'rat-like' eyes. A girlfriend of his had once shared a carriage with Rasputin, only to be lunged at mid-journey; she slapped his face and got out. The same thing had happened to her cousin.

Rasputin was born some 1,600 miles from what was then called St Petersburg, in the village of Pokrovskoe in western Siberia. The village was made up of several streets of spacious one- or two-storey wooden houses, with framed windows and carved, painted beams. It was very much an ordinary village, more prosperous perhaps and more lively than most since it was on both the road and the river. In 1915, the Petrograd newspaper *Novoe Vremya*, in an anti-Rasputin article, described Pokrovskoe as a poor village, a wretched foggy place, remote and wild, inhabited by Siberian *zhigani* or rogues.[3]

Grigori Rasputin was the second son of Anna Egorovna and Efim Aklovlevich Rasputin, a carter and farmer. Maria

Rasputina gave her father's date of birth as 23 January 1871.[4] By the pre-revolutionary Julian calendar, this date corresponds to 10 January. Rasputin's exact date of birth has been an unresolved issue for over a century. Rasputin biographers have given a variety of dates ranging from the late 1860s through to the 1870s.[5]

During Soviet times, encyclopedias and reference books gave Rasputin's date of birth as 1864/65. Contrary to the generally accepted view that no authoritative contemporary evidence of his birth exists, the answer is to be found in the Tyumen Archives.

According to a Pokrovskoe church register entry, Rasputin's parents (his father was aged twenty and his mother twenty-two) were married on 21 January 1862.[6] Birth registers indicate that between 1862 and 1867 six daughters were born, but all died in infancy.[7] Eventually, on 7 August 1867, a son, Andrei, was born.[8] The registers from 1869 have regrettably not survived. Before 1869 there is no mention of Grigori Rasputin's birth in any of the registers. It can therefore be concluded that he could not have been born before 1869. However, this does not imply that it is impossible to establish Rasputin's exact date of birth. A census of the population of the village of Pokrovskoe, also in the Tyumen Archive,[9] contains the name Grigori Rasputin. In the column opposite his name is his date of birth – 10 January 1869, which happens to be St Grigori's Day. This corresponds to the date given by Maria Rasputina, although she places the year as 1871 not 1869.[10]

Rasputin himself was also responsible for the variety of dates given as his date of birth. In a 1907 ecclesiastical file on an investigation into his religious activities,[11] Rasputin declares that he is forty-two years of age, therefore implying that he was born in 1865. In a 1914 file on the investigation into an attempt on his life by Khiona Gusyeva, he declares, 'My name is Grigori Efimovich Rasputin-Novy, fifty years old',[12] which implies 1864 as his year of birth. In the 1911 notebook belonging to Tsarina Alexandra,[13] she recorded Rasputin as saying, 'I have lived fifty years and am beginning my sixth decade.' This suggests he was born in 1861!

Reporters covering the murder of Rasputin at the time stated his age as being fifty. When, six months later, the new Provisional Government set up an Extraordinary Commission of Inquiry to examine Rasputin's activities, evidence from witnesses who had known him in Siberia and elsewhere was collected by its chief investigator, E.P. Stimson, a respected lawyer from Kharkov. Stimson concluded that Rasputin was born in either '1864 or 1865'.[14] Tsarina Alexandra referred to him as 'elder'. He was in fact younger than the Tsar, and it was, perhaps, for this reason that he sought to inflate his age.

According to contemporary accounts,[15] Rasputin's father Efim was comparatively well-off in terms of Pokrovskoe peasants, who in turn had a better standard of living than the peasants in European Russia, who lived in chimneyless log huts. Efim's single-storey cabin had four rooms – unlike many peasants, who used stretched animal bladders to cover their windows, Efim could afford glass. In later years, Rasputin proudly recalled that as a child he ate white bread rather than the brown bread suffered by peasants in European Russia – and fish and cabbage soup.[16]

Rasputin's mother related that the young Grigori often 'stared at the sky' and at first she feared for his sanity.[17] Stories abound about his developing powers as a youth – he seems to have had a way with animals and became a horse whisperer. Efim Rasputin had a favourite story[18] of how his son's gift first showed itself. Efim mentioned at a family meal that one of his horses had gone lame that day and could have pulled a hamstring. Grigori got up from the table and went out to the stable. Efim followed and saw Grigori place his hand on the animal's hamstring. Efim then led the horse out into the yard – its lameness had apparently gone. According to his daughter Maria, Rasputin became a kind of 'spiritual veterinarian',[19] talking to sick cattle and horses, curing them with a few whispered words and a comforting hand.

Stories also abound concerning Grigori's supposed ability to discover missing objects. On one occasion, a horse was stolen. A village meeting was called to discuss the theft. Grigori pointed at one of the richest peasants in the village and declared him the guilty man. Despite his protests, a posse of villagers followed the man back to his homestead and discovered the stolen horse there. As a result, the man was given a traditional Siberian beating.

Rasputin's daughter Maria later wrote that he could also predict the deaths of villagers and the coming of strangers to Pokrovskoe.[20] Much of what Maria was to record in her book and published interviews is, however, very much open to question. For example, the Provisional Government Inquiry of 1917 found Pokrovskoe witnesses who had a somewhat different perspective on her father. 'They note that Efim Rasputin drank vodka heavily,' the investigator wrote. 'As a boy Rasputin was always dirty and untidy so that boys of his age called him a "snotter."'[21]

Maria's claims concerning her father's early life are typical of the retrospective accounts that have come to be accepted without question by many subsequent writers and researchers. It suited Rasputin's retrospective image to establish that his gifts were evident during childhood. A number of Maria's claims are very much open to question and are at variance with testimonies given by Pokrovskoe villagers.

In August 1877, when Grigori was eight years old, his ten-year-old brother Mischa died. The two brothers were swimming in the River Toura when Mischa was caught by a current, dragging Grigori with him. Although the two boys were pulled out by a farmer, Mischa contracted pneumonia and died shortly after.

At the age of nineteen, Grigori attended a festival at Abalatski Monastery, where he met a girl two years older than himself, named Praskovia Fyodorovna Dubrovina, from the nearby village of Dubrovnoye. Following a six-month courtship, they married. The precise date of their marriage is unknown, although the 1917 investigation believes it was 1889.[22]

Marriage seems to have had little impact on Grigori or his lifestyle. He continued to spend his evenings at the tavern. According to E.I. Kartavtsev, a neighbour of the Rasputins in Pokrovskoe, who was sixty-seven years old at the time of the 1917 investigation, he had 'caught Grigori stealing my fence poles'.[23] Kartavtsev went on to explain that,

> he had cut them up and put them in his cart and was about to drive off when I caught him in the act. I demanded that Grigori take them to the Constable, and when he refused and made to strike me with an axe, I, in my turn, hit him with a perch so hard that blood ran out of his nose and his mouth in a stream and he fell to the ground unconscious. At first I thought I'd killed him. When he started to move I made him come to take him to the Constable. Rasputin did not feel like going, but I hit him several times with a fist in the face, after which he went to the Constable voluntarily.

Not long after this event, Kartavtsev recalled that a pair of his horses was stolen from his meadow. 'On the night of the theft I guarded the horses myself… I saw that Rasputin approached them with his pals, Konstantin and Trofim, but I didn't think much of it until a few hours later I discovered the horses were not there. Right after that I went home to check whether Rasputin was in. He was there the following day, but his pals had gone.'[24]

As a result of the thefts of the poles and the horses, the Pokrovskoe villagers convened to discuss what should be done about Rasputin and his errant ways. Konstantin and Trofim were expelled from the village for horse-stealing. Rasputin was not, but he faced charges of stealing the poles and a consignment of furs in the local court. He was also accused of stealing a consignment of furs that went missing from a cart he was driving to Tyumen. In his defence, he claimed that he had been attacked by robbers.

According to his daughter Maria, he denied being a thief, and maintained that since he was convinced that other people shared his second sight, and so could track down any stolen object, he could never bring himself to steal.[25] Whatever the reality, Rasputin left the village for Verkhoturye Monastery, some 250 miles north-west of Pokrovskoe, shortly afterwards.

Maria asserted that his departure from the village was the result of giving a ride to a young divinity student in his cart, who apparently encouraged Grigori to go to the monastery.[26] Many years later Rasputin told a similar story to the Tsar and Tsarina. According to the imperial tutor, Gilliard, Rasputin had been hired to drive a priest to the monastery. During the journey the priest implored Grigori to confess his sins and urged him to devote himself to God. 'These persuasions,' said Gilliard, 'impressed Grigori so much that he was filled with a wish to abandon his dark and desolate life.'[27]

The reality behind Rasputin's timely departure from Pokrovskoe seems to have had little to do with such fantasies. Numerous witnesses told the 1917 Inquiry that Rasputin's involvement in local criminality was now such that he thought it best to make an exit, preferring Verkhoturye Monastery to a criminal record and a custodial sentence.

Rasputin's three-month stay at the monastery, according to the 1917 investigation, ended 'the first, early, wild, loose period of his life'. As a result, 'Rasputin was to become a different person'.[28] It left anguish in his soul '…in the form of extreme nervousness, constant restless, jerky movements, incoherent speech, the permanent interchange of extreme nervous agitation and subsequent depression'.[29]

When Rasputin came home he continued to express his delight in the natural world, which had impressed him deeply. He had given up meat and sugar and alcohol. He seemed to be in a state of ecstatic mysticism a lot of the time, but the people of Pokrovskoe snorted at his praying and his visions. He was the same old lying Grisha, as far as they could see.

Rasputin ignored them. Around the age of thirty, wild-eyed and unwashed, shouting and waving as he travelled, and sleepless for nights on end every spring, he was an eccentric figure who vaguely represented the Old Beliefs, the ancient Christian culture of 'Holy Rus' whose sorcerers, healers and false messiahs attracted many followers. In particular he headed north and west to the large monastery at Verkhoturye in the Urals, where he worshipped at the shrine of St Simeon of Verkhoturye. This St Simeon had died of fasting and self-neglect early in the seventeenth century, but Rasputin looked upon his spirit as his guardian and mentor.

At some time in his wanderings and contacts with the adherents of 'Holy Rus', Rasputin had become involved with the Khlysti. These were the followers of Daniel Filippovich, who had been crucified and resurrected more than once (a story reminiscent of Yusupov's later account of Rasputin who, allegedly, was poisoned and shot at point-blank range and left for dead before leaping scarily to his feet half an hour later). There were several messiahs like Filippovich in the sect's history and most of them were said to have been raised from the dead.

The Khlysti were harmless enough, but to the Orthodox mind they were the Devil incarnate. Adherents to the sect believed that repentance was insignificant unless they had something to repent for. So 'sinning' – fornication, and plenty of it – was a necessary preamble to repentance. Thus encouraged to indulge themselves, the Khlysti exulted in ecstatic secret meetings, with priests in nightshirts whirling like dervishes into elevated states of consciousness and behaving 'sinfully' with their attendant womenfolk before prophesying, praying and repenting.[30] Rasputin's gift of prophecy seemed particularly significant to his followers; he had a 'sense of catastrophe hanging over the kingdom'.[31] But none of this must be divulged… Orthodox priests were appalled when in 1903 they enquired into Rasputin and were told that he held dubious services in a secret chapel under a stable in Pokrovskoe.

Driven underground, the Khlysti referred to each other as 'Ours' or 'Our own'. It was a sect 'of the people' that laid claim to a special kind of truth vouchsafed only to the poor. At least, it was 'of the people', until Rasputin conquered the ladies of St Petersburg.

His climb was extraordinary; he leapt from one social foothold to the next, up and up in a matter of months. In 1903 his prophecies, and in particular his frankly expressed insights into the character and aims of his listeners, impressed the archimandrite of Kazan. Thus he obtained letters of introduction to an important bishop in St Petersburg, who in turn introduced him to Bishop Feofan, confessor to the Tsarina. Invited to stay at Feofan's St Petersburg apartment, Rasputin was introduced to Militsa, the wife of Grand Duke Pyotr Nikolaivich, who was sickly. Militsa was one of the two Black Sisters, as they were called, not only because they were dark but because they were from Montenegro. The other sister was Anastasia, the mistress (and later the wife) of that very tall and martial Grand Duke, Nikolai Nikolaivich, who would so badly offend Rasputin during the war.

At this time of social upheaval and impending international crisis, Militsa and Anastasia were close to the Tsarina. People sneered at them as her self-appointed 'procurers of Holy Men'. Rasputin was the last and cleverest of a long line of these. The Tsarina was credulous about occult happenings and omens, so much so that she seemed silly even in Russia, where the existence of the supernatural was generally accepted.

From her earliest youth it had been clear that the future Tsarina Alexandra of Hesse lacked a sense of humour. In her teens she had received a proposal of marriage from Prince Albert Victor, or Eddy as he was more commonly known, the heir apparent to the English throne. Eddy, who was to die young, leaving the throne to his brother George, was a sweet-natured dandy and not nearly religious enough. Nicholas, the young heir to the throne of Russia, on the other hand, lived in a permanent state of anxiety and would one day be head of the Russian Orthodox Church. But she was a Lutheran...

Alexandra struggled with her religious conscience for more than three years before she consented to marry the Tsarevich

Nicholas. He was a repressed, insignificant young man, physically almost the double of his English cousin Prince George. She made a more imposing figure than he did, in her clumpy heels beneath long swishing skirts, and a fussy hat like a huge meringue.

They had not been married long when Nicholas's father, Alexander III, died in 1894. To celebrate the coronation of Nicholas and Alexandra, an outdoor festival was arranged for the poor, but hundreds of thousands turned up in search of a free meal and over a thousand of them were trampled to death in the crush. Grand Duke Sergei was Governor-General of Moscow at the time, and his mismanagement was blamed. Nicholas and Alexandra had arranged to attend a ball being held in their honour by the French that evening, and did not cancel. As they danced, crushed bodies were still being removed from the scene of the disaster by the cartload. Insensitivity of that kind was not easily forgotten.

St Petersburg society despised Alexandra anyway. Had some gaiety relieved the severity of her character she would have been forgiven almost anything, but she was haughty and distant and did not make friends easily. She was appalled by anything remotely improper, while St Petersburg society was quite relaxed and unshockable.[32] Georgina Buchanan, Sir George Buchanan's wife, who knew her when she was young, accused her of a 'naïve simplicity' allied with 'uncompromising and domineering self-assurance'. She 'strove from the very first to influence her husband to what she considered was the right way of thinking'.[33] Alexandra seized upon the notion that the essence of Russianness was expressed by 'the people', and they all, from Archangel to Vladivostok, were fervently loyal. It followed that criticism was alien. In her mystic belief about 'the people' she echoed Militsa, but also her grandmother, Queen Victoria. The old Queen's principles had influenced her when she was a girl, and Victoria was fond of the illusion that she was closer to the spirit of the English than the aristocracy were. Like Alexandra, the old lady could be self-righteous and was deeply wounded by bitchiness. They both wallowed in dramatic self-pity when the opportunity presented itself. But Victoria was sharp and lively-minded and Alexandra was entirely unburdened by reason.

By the turn of the century the court was led by the Grand Duchess Vladimir in St Petersburg, while the Tsar and Tsarina and their three daughters were rarely seen outside Tsarskoye Selo. The magnificent Romanov palaces were rarely, some never, visited and even the treasures of the comparatively modest Alexander Palace were put into storage. Instead, Alexandra had the walls painted mauve and ordered ugly suites of furniture from Maples in the Tottenham Court Road. Queen Victoria herself, with her tartan and watercolour aesthetic, her fiddly little tables and hulking great ornaments, was never as tasteless as this.

To explain her neglect of society, her ignorance of science and her increasing dependence on mystics and clairvoyants and healers, Alexandra flaunted her preoccupation with motherhood. The empire must descend through the male line. Alexandra's existence would have no meaning for her unless she could produce a son. She must be able to pass the Tsardom to her own flesh and blood. Magic would work; she knew it. Around the turn of the century, Monsieur Philippe, a magician from Lyons, was presented to the Tsarina by Militsa.

Philippe was an obvious charlatan. Only an under-occupied woman half-crazed by a single obsession, as by that time Alexandra was, could have taken him seriously. Her mother-in-law, the Dowager Empress Maria Fyodorovna, interceded with Nicholas, but to no avail. Proofs of the Frenchman's rascality emerged and were put before the Tsarina. But Alexandra had a fatal flaw: the gift of faith. She was like the White Queen who had trained herself always to believe ten impossible things before breakfast. Once she had made up her mind that something was true, it became so. Nothing would shake her belief.

So when, in 1901, she gave birth to her fourth child, which Philippe had told her would be a boy – the new Tsarevich – and it was a girl, she was bewildered. Monsieur Philippe regretted that his prediction had been confounded, but had she had more faith, it would certainly have come true. She saw the point of this, and made herself believe even more.

A condemnatory Secret Service report on Philippe arrived from Paris. The agent responsible, Pyotr Rachkovski, who had run the Okhrana in Western Europe for a decade, was forced out of his job, while Monsieur Philippe stayed. The rest of the Romanovs fumed in the background. The Tsarina (and her husband too, because Nicholas preferred to concur with his wife rather than face the hysterics that would result if he contradicted her) paid Philippe more rapt attention than ever. In 1902 she seemed to be expecting a child. The magician from Lyons diagnosed her condition and announced that this time it would be a boy. After doctors expressed doubts that the pregnancy was genuine, Alexandra would allow no one else to examine her. Somehow Philippe was provided with papers certifying that he was a Russian doctor of medicine. In August, however, the Tsarina was losing weight, and got a second opinion. Hers had been a phantom, that is, imaginary, pregnancy.

With the Black Sisters as their only friends, the imperial couple were pretty well isolated by their faith in Philippe. Grand Duke Nikolai, notwithstanding his love for Anastasia, was embarrassed by his own indirect association with the whole affair. Alexandra's elder sister, Elizaveta Fyodorovna, who was almost as religious as she was and married to Grand Duke Sergei, tried to persuade her that the mystic must go. The Russo-Japanese War was in the offing and Nikolai needed all the help he could get. Regretfully, the imperial couple sent Philippe home to France with an opulent motor car and a generous pay-off.

In the summer of 1904, Alexandra gave birth to a boy. She was delighted that her faith had at last been sincere enough. However, the baby was susceptible to mysterious bouts of illness. Little was known about haemophilia at the time, and it would be a year before the doctors diagnosed his condition. The Tsarina, who was not amenable to science or reason, was deeply ashamed. The elder girls and everyone else in the tiny royal circle were sworn to secrecy. The baby suffered intermittent agonies and the doctors were helpless. Alexandra had nowhere to turn, for by the time haemophilia was suspected, Monsieur Philippe was dead; he died in France in 1905. He had told her, however, that he would 'return in the form of another'.

Bishop Feofan was introduced to the Tsar and Tsarina and became the Tsarina's confessor. He was a straightforward, ascetic, Orthodox priest. This was not exactly what they wanted, and Father Ioann of Kronstadt joined the circle. He too came from the regular Orthodox hierarchy, with many followers and a reputation as a healer. But neither he nor Feofan could wholly engage this nervous, superstitious, desperate pair.

Beyond the gates of all the palaces, the clamour for change was growing to a roar. Grand Duke Sergei was blown up by a bomb. Sailors mutinied and peaceful protestors were mown down by Cossacks.

In October 1905, just three days after Nicholas had counter-manded his wife's advice and signed the papers that promised his subjects a constitution, Rasputin came to tea.

The impression he made on that first visit was good, but not earth-shattering. By this time he was in his mid-thirties, could pass for older, and was no longer the wild man from Siberia. He had become used to bathing, for one thing, and wearing clean clothes, still in the peasant style – for he was not a priest. He had visited many houses where there was indoor sanitation and carpets and a piano; even electric light, in one or two. He still ate with his fingers, but he restrained his appetite, and his hollow-cheeked visage with its intense, pale-eyed stare had lost none of its magnetism. He spoke of the sin of pride. To say that he was fluent is an understatement; his words tumbled over each other in a torrent, and to one like Alexandra, who always heard what she wanted to hear, they were magical. He urged the Tsar and Tsarina to 'spit on all their fears, and rule'.[34]

By Rasputin's own admission, the Tsar was not immediately captivated as his wife was. He had rather a lot on his mind.

Rasputin decided to get out of Feofan's orbit (he had been staying at his apartment) before he made his second sortie into

the imperial presence. He must find somewhere else to live. This
was not difficult, for since his first visit to St Petersburg he had
acquired quite a following. Certain ladies even made a habit of
collecting his finger-nail clippings and sewing them into their
underclothing. And now he met the devoted fanatic who would
welcome him into her beautiful home. Within weeks of his
meeting with Nicholas and Alexandra, Rasputin left Feofan's
apartment and moved in with Olga Lokhtina, the wife of a key
official at Tsarskoye Selo. She had been called a 'Petersburg lion-
ess and fashionable salon hostess'.[35] That was before she met
Rasputin.

She became besotted. According to her, when they met she
was sick with an 'intestinal neurasthenia which tied me to my
bed'.[36] With or without intestinal neurasthenia, whatever that
is, there was to be quite a lot of tying to the bed in future. For
like many of the others she began a sexual relationship with the
magnetic peasant. In the first weeks, they shared the innocent
pleasures of kissing and communal bathing at Pokrovskoe. Six
years later, if Rasputin's friend and publisher Filippov is to be
believed, they had evolved a relationship that worked satisfactorily for both of them.

> Arriving at Rasputin's early in the morning for tea as was my
> custom… I saw him behind the screen that separated his bed
> from the rest of the room. He was desperately beating Madame
> Lokhtina, who was clad in a fantastic get-up consisting of a white
> dress hung with little ribbons, and who was holding onto his
> member while shouting 'You are God!' I rushed over to him…
> 'What are you doing? You are beating a woman!' Rasputin
> answered 'She won't let me alone, the skunk, and demands sin!'
> And Lokhtina, hiding behind the screen, wailed 'I am your ewe,
> and *you are Christ!*'

By 1911 Lokhtina had been banished from her husband and small
daughter and all her worldly goods, and spent her life wandering
the highways and byways of Russia, barefoot and unwashed in

a white dress with the word 'Alleluyah' painted on a bandeau around her forehead. On cold days she wore a wolfskin cap.

But in 1906 she was a fashionable and beautiful woman still married to the uncomplaining senior official at Tsarskoye Selo. At her house in St Petersburg Rasputin was in a position to hear all the gossip of the dwindling royal circle, and he learned that the Tsarevich was sick. What the Tsarina most desired was someone who could offer a cure for her son. Rasputin obtained an icon of St Simeon of Verkhoturye, Olga Lokhtina wrote a suitably deferential compliment slip to be delivered with it under Rasputin's name, and the Tsar received it.

So it came about that one year after their first meeting, Nicholas granted another audience to the peasant healer from Pokrovskoe, and this time, 'he made a remarkably strong impression on Her Majesty and on me'.[37] He was invited to see their little boy, who was then aged two and undergoing a crisis, and Rasputin's prayers were followed by the child's recovery. He seemed able to work miracles.

He did more than pray; he formed a relationship with the child, over the years that ensued. He was always good with children and animals and their instincts are generally acute. He knew how to approach them and was sincerely kind to them.

Had that been all there was to it – had Rasputin been simply a gifted healer who confined his attention to the heir to the throne – he would never have attracted the opprobrium he did. But the combination of a weak Tsar and a strong Tsarina, and the louche, sharp-witted side to this peasant, who quickly understood the role he must play to keep the Tsarina's loyalty, was an excuse for ribaldry, disrespect and ridicule. It was fear that had kept the people subservient for so long, not love, and the fear had been replaced with mistrust long before. Once the imperial couple were in thrall to an incoherent, semi-literate peasant, even common respect began to diminish.

For the first few years, however, few were aware that the Tsar and Tsarina had found this new miracle-worker. At first even Militsa was not allowed to know, because Rasputin had

purposely taken the initiative and presented himself to the
royal couple. He did not want to be paraded like a talking
dog, and nor did he want to be beholden to Militsa. She had
other things on her mind in any case. Her sister Anastasia was
to obtain a divorce in order to marry Grand Duke Nikolai.
The Tsarina was scandalised and angry, but did not ostracise
the couple because they were her friends. Still smarting from
this disgrace, Militsa discovered that Rasputin, far from being
her own personal discovery, was already an admired protégé at
the Alexander Palace; and, what was more, she, Militsa, was no
longer the Tsarina's best friend. Her position had been usurped
by a younger woman, Anna Vyrubova.

Militsa was furious, and suspected Rasputin of turning the Tsarina against her. Rasputin made one of his
journeys home with several adoring St Petersburg ladies in
tow only to find, once he got to Pokrovskoe, that the entire
Church establishment of Tobolsk was out to get him. They
were asking questions (not for the first time), taking witness statements and generally building a case that he was a
Khlyst, guilty of fornication, adultery and sexual orgies with
various women. Olga Lokhtina, who had not yet deserted
her family in favour of the bare feet, white dress and ribbons,
deduced that there must be a malicious and powerful influence
behind this sudden investigation. She concluded that the secret
enemy was Militsa, and she returned to Tsarskoye Selo and
made sure that the Tsar would bury the incriminating evidence
forever as soon as it reached him.

From 1907 Militsa, Anastasia and Grand Duke Nikolai were
the 'out-crowd'. Rasputin and Anna Vyrubova were in.

Vyrubova had been an unmarried girl called Anna Taneev
when she became intimate with the Tsarina. Her father was a
court official and she had never been far from the inner circle
– Yusupov remembered loathing her at school. She and the
Tsarina were already inciting gossip about a lesbian affair when
she married in 1907. Her husband, a nonentity who owned a
large estate, proved significant only as provider of a name and

a marital status; after a few years they divorced. She accused him of impotence and sadism, and it was true that the marriage had never been consummated. He married again quite soon, was perfectly happy with his new wife and lived quietly on his country estate. Vyrubova and the Tsarina, however, caused talk by sharing a bed.[38]

One of the most complicated issues in Rasputin's story is the relationship of the Tsar and the Tsarina. It appeared to be cloyingly affectionate, yet one partner constantly dominated. This is usually a dysfunctional arrangement for both parties. Their religious beliefs would have made it difficult for either of them to admit to marital problems, even to one another, and it seems that they found, over the years, a *modus vivendi.*

The trouble was, nobody quite believed in it. In 1909 the royal family's appointed religious advisor, Father Ioann, died. Rasputin, although unqualified as a priest, effectively took his place. By 1910 he was often mentioned in society, and not in flattering terms.

People assumed he was an adventurer, lining his own nest. He complained that the Tsarina paid him hardly anything, yet expected him to be at her beck and call. He was living in modest circumstances in St Petersburg – in fact, in other people's apartments – and it seemed that all the Tsarina donated was a few roubles and some hand-embroidered silk shirts. But he had always scorned money, and gave generously what little he had; perhaps nice clothes and important friends mattered more.

However, money was being sent home, so other admirers must have given him some. In Pokrovskoe a comfortable two-storey house was being built, the better to accommodate his lady visitors from the capital. Now that he was nearly forty, and those three of his five children who had lived were growing up, Rasputin may have recognised that soothsaying and healing might as well provide a living.

He made new friends. Among them were Bishop Hermogen of Tobolsk and the notorious Orthodox preacher Iliodor. It was the latter who introduced Rasputin to crowds of new followers and, in gratitude, Rasputin invited Iliodor to Pokrovskoe. There he showed him letters he had received from the Tsarina and her daughters; and there, in 1910, Iliodor stole one or two.

Particularly shocking, after 1910 especially, were persistent stories that Rasputin took his St Petersburg ladies to public bath-houses. He freely admitted to this and explained that the Tsarina knew all about it. 'I don't go with one person... but with company', he told his publisher, Sazonov.[39] He insisted that it was good for these women to reduce their pride by accompanying a peasant to a bath-house; pride was a sin. He was notoriously promiscuous. Two years later, watchful Okhrana agents would note Rasputin and Mrs Sazonov visiting a bath-house together.

By the end of 1910 Rasputin's friends were having second thoughts. Bishop Feofan, Bishop Hermogen and, thanks to them, the entire Synod wanted to keep Rasputin in check. The sly Iliodor already supported them, though he remained friendly with Rasputin. There were articles about Rasputin in the newspapers, none of them flattering to him or the Tsar and Tsarina. The imperial couple had not the wit to understand that public opinion mattered. Stolypin, Prime Minister and Minister of the Interior, thought Rasputin was a scoundrel; but Rasputin was like a lightning conductor, deflecting anger from its true target.

In 1909 Rasputin and Stolypin had been briefly on the same side. In a kind of dress rehearsal for 1914, the Orthodox Serbs in the Balkans asked for Russia's protection from the Austro-Hungarians. The Orthodox Synod wanted the Tsar to send troops to defend the Serbs; so did Grand Duke Nikolai and the Montenegrin princesses; so did all the young officers who had been humiliated when Russia lost the war against Japan. Only Stolypin talked sense, and pointed out that Germany would attack if the Tsar tried to defend Serbia, and Russia was unprepared to resist. So Serbia was occupied, and Russia humiliated, but the threat of war was allowed to subside. Not because of Stolypin, or even the elder statesman Count Witte, but because Rasputin had advised the Tsar to keep out of it.

The Tsarina

> …was grateful to Rasputin, and happy, for it had turned out that her own wishes were remarkably consistent with the commands of Father Grigori and heaven.[40]

This was the key to his influence. Pierre Gilliard, the Tsarevich's tutor who saw Rasputin often and was part of the imperial household from 1904 onwards, wrote in his memoir:

> Cunning and astute as he was, Rasputin never advised in political matters except with the most extreme caution. He always took the greatest care to be very well informed as to what was going on at court and as to the private feelings of the Tsar and his wife. As a rule, therefore, his prophecies only confirmed the secret wishes of the Tsarina. In fact, it was almost impossible to doubt that it was she who inspired the 'inspired', but as her desires were interpreted by Rasputin, they seemed in her eyes to have the sanction and authority of a revelation.[41]

Stolypin, like everyone else, blamed Rasputin rather than the Tsarina for a whole series of decisions, especially the one that placed a Rasputin loyalist called Sabler at the head of the Synod. He also loathed him for his association with the right-wing Iliodor. And now it came to his notice that Rasputin and Witte were getting quietly friendly, and that Count Witte wanted Stolypin's job as Prime Minister while he, Stolypin, was losing the Tsar's support for his reformist policies.

He began making his resentment public. He refused to censor articles appearing in the press condemning Rasputin. In his joint capacity as Minister of the Interior, he had already ordered Okhrana surveillance in order to gather evidence of Rasputin's behaviour, which he knew to be inappropriate for a person employed as imperial advisor. Rasputin must have been wary of snoopers, because Alexandra found out about the Okhrana operation almost at once and got her husband to put a stop to it. Stolypin was nonetheless able to report to the Tsar about Rasputin's

> ...private life, a series of drunken and sometimes scandalous sexual liaisons and recently, dealings with dubious entrepreneurs and backers trying to turn his influence to advantage.

This is an anonymous description of Stolypin's report from a book about Nicholas II, published in 1917. Its significance is that it places his drunkenness, and alleged venality, as early as 1910 or 1911, while other writers – relying on the testimony of Rasputin's friends to the Extraordinary Commission of 1917 – say that his corruption and drunkenness developed later. Jaundiced observers were more impatient. One such was Vladimir Nikolaivich Kokovtsov.

> I served eleven years in the Central Prison Administration... and saw all the convict prisons, and... among the Siberian vagrants of unknown ancestry, as many Rasputins as you like. Men who, while making the sign of the cross, could take you by the throat and strangle you with the same smile on their faces.[42]

Not long after Stolypin's allegations, Rasputin was advised to make himself scarce for a while, and decided to go on a pilgrimage to Jerusalem.

He stayed away for four months, returning in the summer of 1911 and publishing a short memoir of his travels. This was dictated to, and written down by, Lokhtina. Rasputin had learned to read and write by now, but not very well. Lokhtina made his ramblings readable, and captured what was inspiring in them.

In the autumn he went to Kiev, where the Tsar and Tsarina were to attend the opening of a new regional Duma. Stolypin would be there too, because it was thanks to his reforming zeal that regional government had at last arrived.

It is apparent from the evidence of an extreme right-wing politician called Khvostov (a fierce opponent of the progressive

Stolypin) that Rasputin had something to do with Stolypin's assassination at Kiev. Ten days before the Kiev ceremonies, Rasputin travelled to Nizhni Novgorod to pay Khvostov an unexpected visit. Khvostov had never met him before, and when Rasputin offered him Stolypin's job as Minister of the Interior he thought the man was mad. He pointed out that the position was already occupied. Ah, said Rasputin, but all the same, Stolypin would be leaving. Khvostov made some facetious remark and saw him off the premises.

> ...he departed angry. I didn't invite him to dine and refused to introduce him to my family, even though he asked me to do so.[43]

Ten days later, Stolypin was shot at the Kiev Opera. The assassin had warned the local Okhrana of the time and place of the shooting the night before, but they still let him into the Opera House, complete with revolver.

From the first, Rasputin was named in connection with the assassination. It was all too much for Bishop Hermogen and even Iliodor. On 16 December 1911 (a date that would prove fatal five years later) they tricked Rasputin into visiting the Yaroslav Monastery. There, in front of a kind of clerical kangaroo court, he was tried, found guilty and badly beaten up by the assembled holy men before being threatened at sabre-point, bashed over the head with a crucifix and sent packing.

Hermogen did not stop there, but publicly insisted to the Synod that Rasputin was a Khlyst and privately accused him of adultery with the Tsarina. This could not be allowed to go on, and both Hermogen and Iliodor were sent into exile. Defiantly, they refused to disappear, but holed up in St Petersburg, releasing snippets of scandal to the papers. Even now, Iliodor hung onto his secret weapon: the stolen letters. Meanwhile, the Minister of the Interior who replaced Stolypin was Makarov – and in January 1912 he ordered another Okhrana surveillance. He intended to bide his time and say nothing about what he discovered unless it should ever prove useful to do so. The Tsar agreed to Rasputin's being watched for purposes of protection; and later events would show that he did indeed need protecting.

Now, in 1912, the Okhrana agents watched Rasputin's comings and goings, his daily visits to the bath-house with prostitutes and followers, and his visits to the Golovinas' house on the Moika (Mounya Golovina had been among the faithful since 1908). In her own drawing room Mounya had introduced Yusupov to Rasputin in 1909, before the young playboy left for Oxford. The current Rasputinists gathered there: Zinaida Manshtedt – a lover of his, if the sworn statement of the Tsar's children's nurse can be believed – and Lili Dehn, a well-known actress and close friend of the Tsarina. On most days he also saw Akilina Laptinskaya, a nurse he had been close to for years; she had worked at the Verkhoturye Monastery around 1903.

Rasputin would spend all day with one or several of these women, running around the city by cab or carriage, and when left alone, would find a prostitute and take her to a bath-house or, very occasionally, to a room somewhere. These episodes, if challenged, were explained away by his assertion that he must tempt himself, and resist, in order to score points towards his own redemption. If he had intercourse with them, and several women later testified that (with or without consent) he did, no resulting pregnancy was ever revealed.

Sometimes he saw Badmaëv. Badmaëv was a well-connected Asiatic from the Far Eastern steppe who manufactured and peddled herbal remedies to the great and good. He had been a protégé of Alexander III, the Tsar's father. Mostly, his herbal remedies were prescribed as aids to potency, but he also sold happy pills: concoctions, maybe opiate-based, that made people calm, dreamy and dull-witted. Badmaëv was a friend of Rasputin's, but was also close to Hermogen and other clerics. He cultivated Rasputin in the vain hope of one day being appointed Supplier of Herbal Cures to the Tsarevich. The connection never worked.

Hermogen and Iliodor were still wanted men, but Makarov knew the stolen letters existed and were Iliodor's weapon for blackmailing the Tsar. He ordered an Okhrana search and they were found. They appeared to be (and were later confirmed by Alexandra as) perfectly genuine:

> My much-loved, never to be forgotten teacher, saviour and instructor. I am so wretched without you. My soul is only rested and at ease when you, my teacher, are near me. I kiss your hands and lay my head upon your blessed shoulders. I feel so joyful then. Then all I want is to sleep, sleep for ever on your shoulder, in your embrace. It is such happiness to feel your presence close to me. Where are you, where have you run off to?... Come back soon. I await you and yearn for you. I ask you for your holy blessing and kiss your blessed hands. Your eternally loving Mama.[44]

Like others before him, Makarov thought the Tsar would be appalled when he read this and would order Rasputin away from the court. Not a bit of it. Rasputin did leave St Petersburg for a while, but only because his presence was embarrassing; the Tsar was not at all angry (except with the unfortunate Makarov). A contemporary confided to her diary in despair:

> The tsar has lost all respect and the tsarina declares that it is only thanks to Rasputin's prayers that the tsar and their son are alive and well; and this is the twentieth century![45]

Nicholas was suspicious of the Duma. He had been gracious enough to permit its existence, but now it stood between him and 'the people'. It loomed in the tall, fat form of the Speaker of the Duma, Rodzyanko. Behind him lurked all sorts of liberals. Guchkev was particularly odious, for he despised Rasputin. Nicholas told Rodzyanko and the Duma to mind their own business. His family's relationship with Rasputin was a purely private affair. He was deeply offended; these people appeared to be challenging autocracy itself.

Within twelve months Rasputin was back in St Petersburg with his position consolidated, because he had effected an apparently miraculous cure.

Over the years, the Tsar and Tsarina had come to rely on him to relieve their son's illness. He had always managed to do it. He talked to the boy, and prayed with him, sat with him and was generally so comforting that it has been suggested his tranquil presence could have encouraged the release of agents into the child's body that constricted the blood vessels and staunched internal bleeding. In 1912, also, a cure took place that cannot be conclusively explained by science, since Rasputin was 1,000 miles from his patient when it happened. The royal family had spent most of the summer in the Crimea and now, as autumn began, were at their hunting lodge in Poland when the Tsarevich had a minor accident. Any other child would have had a nasty bruise. Surgeons rushed in from St Petersburg but had to give up; a great tumour had formed in his groin, threatening blood poisoning, but they dared not operate, for he would almost certainly bleed to death.

Rasputin had been in Pokrovskoe all summer. Djhunkovski, Head of the Okhrana, had been quietly keeping an eye on him. Rasputin got a telegram. He prayed. He prayed so intensely that his face was 'grey and streaked with sweat'.[46] He sent a telegram back: the doctors must not be allowed to tire the boy, who would recover.

Indeed he did. Nobody could explain it, but he did. After this, the Tsarina would never allow Rasputin to stay away so long. Soon he was back in St Petersburg, and more secure than before. He brought his two elder daughters to the city to be educated. There was not much money left over, because the Tsarina seemed unaware that he and his family needed money to live, but he rented his own apartment not far from the smart English Quay. He drank a little wine, only rarely too much. He still restrained himself in the matter of food, eating only vegetables and fish and avoiding sugar. Akilina Laptinskaya and young Katya Petyorkina kept house for him.

The old round of visits to Tsarskoye Selo recommenced. This was his heyday; his position had never been more assured. Yet instead of growing fat and complacent he behaved like a man with hounds at his heels. Never exactly well organised, in a matter of months he adopted what we now call a 'chaotic life-style'. He stayed up all night and slept late, and spent the waking hours receiving petitioners and followers, visiting friends and gossiping. Increasingly, there were meetings about deals and favours and money, the whole merry round accompanied by glass after glass of Madeira. Rasputin visited bath-houses daily, usually managed to pick up a prostitute somewhere, and was rarely sober. He liked sweet wine and gypsy music, and would dance himself into a frenzy every night if he got the chance. Night life in the capital was sophisticated and entertaining for those who could afford the Villa Rhode or the restaurant at the Astoria, where the 'marble stairs and plate glass windows, thick red carpets and graceful palms, gave it a glow of comfort unknown in any other hotel in Petrograd [sic]'.[47] Rasputin was frequently seen there; and years later, the head waiter at the Villa Rhode would recall his disgusting table manners.[48] After an evening at a night club or a restaurant, he often took his entourage across the Neva towards the Islands, the wilderness, the gypsies – and champagne.

The gypsies were famous; people were in awe of their singing. Bruce Lockhart was stationed in Moscow, and, during his first few days there in 1912, his host at a spectacular ball got up a small party that would go on to Streilna, a night club far from the city centre, to hear the gypsies.

This gypsy music, in fact, is more intoxicating, more dangerous, than opium, or women, or drink, and although champagne is a necessary adjunct to the enjoyment, there is a plaintiveness in its appeal which to the Slav and Celtic races is almost irresistible. It breaks down all reserves of restraint. It will drive a man to the moneylenders or even to crime... It is very costly. It has been responsible for the bulk of my debts. Yet tomorrow, if I had thousands and the desire to squander them, there is no entertainment in New York, Paris, Berlin or London or indeed, anywhere in the world, which I should choose in preference to a gypsy evening...[49]

The British diplomat is unconsciously describing a shared passion, for Rasputin, whom he despised, was as much addicted to gypsy music as he was.

As for the deals and favours, Rasputin was in a position to provide plenty of those. Yusupov, who is not to be trusted in these matters, wrote about seeing a chest full of little parcels wrapped in newspaper in the flat on Gorokhovaya Street in 1916.

'Surely that isn't all money?' I asked.

'Of course it is – nothing but bank-notes; I got 'em today,' he answered without hesitation.

'Who gave them to you?'

'Various kind people. I just fixed up a little affair, and out of gratitude they made a donation to the Church.'[50]

It is plausible enough. For as long as Rasputin dominated the Tsar and Tsarina, placemen appeared at the head of the Synod, and later in key positions in government, and money certainly changed hands. Bruce Lockhart saw the result:

From time to time... I saw the mark of the beast at Chelnokov's house, where the Mayor would show me a short typewritten note requesting him to fix up the bearer in a safe and comfortable job in the Cities Union. The note was signed in an illiterate scrawl 'GR' – Grigorii Rasputin. The requests were invariably turned down by the sturdy Chelnokov.[51]

Rasputin was not necessarily directly in contact with the supplicants. He was not interested in money, just in having enough of it to do what he wanted and to help others when he wanted to. From early in 1914 his long-time mistress, Akilina Laptinskaya,

who had once been a nurse at Verkhoturye Monastery, acted
as his 'secretary' and passed on to him the cash inducements
provided by those who wanted favours. His friend Filippov, a
banker and publisher, testified to the Extraordinary Commission
in 1917:

> Laptinskaya, being a person of exceptional intelligence and per-
> severance, was guided exclusively by mercenary considerations;
> various people made presents to her of specific sums on the
> occasion of Rasputin's arrival or for Rasputin. And Rasputin
> threw her out a couple of times… on suspicion of stealing sums
> in the thousands.[52]

There must be a go-between. Rasputin himself had to be careful because there were people watching him; Rodzyanko and
most of the Okhrana were out to get some dirt on him and
Djhunkovski, Head of Police at the Ministry of the Interior, was
quietly employing Okhrana surveillance teams. With a rather
different agenda, the Tsar still expected the Okhrana to guard
Rasputin round the clock because of numerous threats to his
life. One of these almost succeeded.

In 1913, Iliodor, now excommunicated from the Orthodox
Church and living under his original name of Sergei Trufanov,
concocted a plot. A number of prostitutes were to seduce
Rasputin and castrate him. This came to nothing, because
Rasputin got wise to it before it happened, but Trufanov did not
give up.[53] He knew that Rasputin was in Yalta, in the Crimea,
advising 'the tsars' in the spring of 1914. Everybody knew
– people were selling photos of him outside his hotel. Vyrubova
visited him constantly (she was staying at the royal household's
summer palace at Livadia) and he boasted to the hotel staff about
his hold over the imperial couple. In the end, Rasputin became
such a tourist attraction that Nicholas had to send him away. He
collected his wife and daughter, who were visiting St Petersburg,
and travelled home with them to Pokrovskoe; and Iliodor knew
about this, too. One of the women who had been involved in the

castration plot was Khiona Gusyeva, 'a once good-looking ex-prostitute now seriously disfigured by syphilis'.[54] She followed Rasputin to Pokrovskoe.

On 28 June 1914, the Archduke Ferdinand and his wife were shot in Sarajevo, and Rasputin came face to face with Gusyeva, in Pokrovskoe, disguised as a beggar-woman

> ...who asked him for money. As he put a hand in his pocket she pulled out a knife and stabbed him in the stomach, driving the blade up to the rib cage and wounding him badly. Yet as she pulled the knife back for a second blow Rasputin had strength enough left to hold her off with his stick until an angry crowd grabbed her and allowed the *starets* to collapse.[55]

The nearest doctor was a six-hour ride away, but he came as fast as he could, and got Rasputin back over the agonising six-hour journey on bumpy roads to the hospital in Tyumen. Thanks to his sturdy constitution he survived, although he was in hospital until late August 1914. Russia by then had declared war. It is quite likely that the Tsar would have vacillated, or even kept his country out of the war, had Rasputin been around to advise him. As it was Rasputin sent telegrams – indeed, prophecies of doom: he said that if Russia entered the war the autocracy would be finished; there would be untold misery and loss of life. He was right on both counts, but his was an emotional appeal innocent of the counter-arguments: the defence of resources, and the honour of Russia, which would be forfeited if the Tsar broke promises. Grand Duke Nikolai understood these points rather better, and was there in person to present them forcefully. Popular sentiment supported war in any case. At first there was an upsurge of support for the fight and the monarchy. It did not survive Tannenberg.

Back in St Petersburg – renamed Petrograd at the start of hostilities in August 1914 – Rasputin rented a new apartment. Akilina Laptinskaya found the one in Gorokhovaya Street, which was comfortable enough to live in with his daughters and Katya, the maid, and to use for entertaining.

Rasputin drank more after the stabbing. He had sipped Madeira or champagne before. Now he turned to vodka and was visibly drunk during the day, not just after an evening's carousing. Probably vodka helped dull the pain and the fear of another assassination attempt. He was soon a notorious drunkard. This was particularly scandalous because prohibition was in force, as a wartime measure. For those who could afford it, illicit alcohol simply cost more. Night clubs resorted to serving vodka out of teapots.

Alcohol was an expensive habit, and the Tsarina was still mean with money. Rasputin had long ago become reconciled to Akilina's acceptance of bribes. Soon he had a friend, Rubinstein the banker, who managed his financial affairs and another friend, Aron Siman-ovich, who acted as secretary, agent and gatekeeper.

All observers agree that Rasputin was able to sober up remarkably quickly if he had to. The years of fasting and self-denial had taught him a rare self-mastery, and now, if he was called unexpectedly to Tsarskoye Selo when in his cups, he was able somehow to control himself and appear steady and coherent.

Although the Tsarina was as dependent on the *starets* as ever, there was a coolness in Nicholas. Despite all Rasputin's predictions, cheering crowds had greeted the Emperor when war was declared in 1914, and he loved adulation. Also, he was probably fed up with the endless intriguing of Vyrubova, Alexandra and Rasputin. As tends to happen in these small cliques, there had been an internal cataclysm: Vyrubova and Alexandra had gone off each other, while Rasputin was still friendly with both. Vyrubova was reinstated to best friend status, however, after injuries sustained in a railway accident made Nicholas and Alexandra fly to her side. She was given the last rites, but recovered when Rasputin revived her on her deathbed in the royal presence. This made even Nicholas soften towards him – which was fortunate, because Rasputin was soon to disgrace himself more outrageously than ever before.

The incident took place in Moscow. Bruce Lockhart came across Rasputin on the fateful evening in the first half of 1915:

One summer evening I was at Yar, the most luxurious night-haunt of Moscow, with some English visitors. As we watched the music-hall performance in the main hall, there was a violent fracas in one of the neighbouring *kabinet*s. Wild shrieks of women, a man's curses, broken glass and the banging of doors raised a discordant pandemonium. Head-waiters rushed upstairs. The manager sent for the policeman who was always on duty at such establishments. But the row and the roaring continued. There was more coming and going of waiters and policemen, and scratching of heads and holding of councils. The cause of the disturbance was Rasputin – drunk and lecherous, and neither police nor management dared evict him. The policeman telephoned his divisional inspector, the inspector telephoned to the Prefect. The Prefect telephoned to Djhunkovski, who was Assistant Minister of the Interior and head of all the police. Djhunkovski, who was a former general and a man of high character, gave orders that Rasputin, who after all was only an ordinary citizen and not even a priest, should be arrested forthwith. Having disturbed everyone's enjoyment for two hours, he was led away, snarling vengeance, to the nearest police station. He was released early next morning on instructions from the highest quarters. He left the same day for St Petersburg, and within twenty-four hours Djhunkovski was relieved of his post.[56]

It was said that Rasputin had hit a woman and exposed himself. The Tsar would not listen to such stories. Not long afterwards, Samarin, a loyal and honest man in charge of Church affairs, was sacked at Rasputin's behest; murmurs of protest grew louder.

Rasputin was accepted by nearly everyone in Moscow as a complete proof of the Tsar's incompetence. 'Down with the autocracy!' cried the Liberals. But even among the reactionaries there were those who said: 'If the autocracy is to flourish, give us a *good* autocrat.'[57]

In other words, everyone wanted change, but not the changes they were getting. Urged on by his wife and Rasputin, the Tsar took over from Grand Duke Nikolai as Supreme Commander of the Russian Armies, and with Nikolai's departure, despair grew deeper. More plots seethed around the *starets,* and anti-Semitism too, because Simanovich (who had, as it happened, been baptised) and Rubinstein were his friends.

From here on in, the Tsarina kept up an endless stream of wifely notes to her husband, which frequently cited 'Our Friend' and his opinions. To many others, Rasputin was seen as the evil genius in a triumvirate, the other pillars of which were Vyrubova and the Tsarina. By the time Romania entered the war in August 1916, Rasputin was widely supposed to be running the country.

SIX

ON THE BRINK

With the approach of midsummer in 1916, Sir George Buchanan's struggle to keep Russia in the war was getting harder. Russia's infrastructure was as hopelessly underdeveloped as ever and the haemorrhage of men, weaponry and equipment was disastrous. By mid-1916 Russia was calling up her thirteenth million.[1] Help had to come from the Allies if Russia were to keep fighting.

Traditionally, finance for Russia's big projects had been raised in the City of London, but British financiers were in no position to help and money must be got from America, where the British had useful contacts. So, in the first week of June 1916, a few months after his first personal audience with the Tsar ('I was summoned by an attendant in the livery of an 18th-century courier, wearing a flat hat with a huge bunch of red and yellow ostrich feathers on the left side'), Albert Stopford was cutting a deal. He noted in his diary:

Monday June 5th

To the Embassy, to speak to His Excellency about an American loan offered to Russia by the National City Bank, which had got hung up and seemed more than likely to fall through. Without hesitation he said he would do all he could for it. The Bank representatives who had come from New York wanted him to say a word to Sazonov. The matter was in the hands of Bark, Minister of Finance.

Returned to the hotel to tell the financiers, who asked if I thought the Ambassador would receive them before speaking to Sazonov. I immediately wrote to him and took the letter myself.

Tuesday June 6th

Met the Ambassador on the quay. He stopped me and said he had seen the financiers and agreed with all they said, and had laid the position before Sazonov, who was going that night to Stavka. At the hotel dined on the roof with the Americans, and afterwards went to their apartments to play bridge.[2]

Sazonov, the Foreign Minister, was tremendously useful to the British, for the Tsar was rarely willing to listen to Allied advice direct; he thought the British were much too pushy. Sir George 'ventured to suggest' change in a way that he resented and was forever nagging him to let the Duma make more decisions about which Ministers should be in charge. The French Ambassador was just as bad. Both despaired of the inadequacies of Russia as an ally, and privately recognised that these arose inevitably from a creaking political system which placed so much responsibility on the shoulders of one person – who might, as in this case, prove inadequate to bear it, and who was too stubborn to take their advice, preferring to listen to his wife.

As the war on the Eastern Front went from bad to worse, the British government's concern about a possible Russian collapse heightened. Such a collapse would be fatal for the Western Front, as the Germans would then be able to direct their full military might in the west instead of fighting a war on two fronts. Britain's Secretary of State for War, Lord Kitchener, was only too painfully aware of this impending danger, and sought Prime Minister Asquith's approval for an urgent initiative in the form of a special mission to Russia. Asquith gave his consent and agreed that Kitchener himself was the best man to lead it, for he believed that he was possibly the only British figure the Tsar might listen to. Kitchener, more than most, had always taken a particular interest in Russian affairs, and as a consequence had long foreseen the upshot of a Russian collapse. He was convinced that the fate of Russia was of overriding importance to Britain's interests, and had spoken in Cabinet on several occasions during the spring of 1916 warning of the forces within Russia trying to bring about an armistice with Germany and consequently a separate peace treaty. Furthermore, Kitchener's stock in Russian military circles was high and his opinions and reputation carried much weight with the Tsar personally.

As a result of secret diplomatic overtures, the Tsar indicated that he would welcome a delegation led by Kitchener. A secret invitation formally inviting Kitchener to visit Russia and meet with Nicholas was therefore sent in early May 1916. While the supply of munitions was high on Kitchener's agenda, he particularly wished to impress on the Tsar the destructive effect Rasputin's influence was having on Anglo-Russian relations and to urge the appointment of a genuinely national government that would draw together Russia's most able and effective politicians. In light of the fact that the supply of munitions would be one of the mission's major priorities, Asquith envisaged Lloyd George accompanying Kitchener. However, after the restoration of order in Dublin following the Easter Rising the previous month, the Prime Minister

> went over to Dublin to examine the situation on the spot. Martial law was still in force, and the three principal officers of the crown – the Lord Lieutenant, Lord Wimbourne, the Chief Secretary for

Ireland, Mr Birrell, and his Under-Secretary, Sir Matthew Nathan – had all resigned their posts.[3]

Lloyd George recalled that on his return

> Mr Asquith approached me with the suggestion that I should take up the task of trying to negotiate a settlement with the Irish revolutionary leaders. The request came at an awkward moment... Lord Kitchener was to proceed to Russia via Archangel to consult with the military authorities there about closer co-operation in the field, and it had been arranged that I should go with him to find out for myself the truth about the appalling shortage of equipment of which we had heard, and see in what way the Ministry of Munitions could best help remedy it. These were the matters in which I was for the moment far more closely interested than I was in the pitiable and rather squalid tragedy which had overtaken our lack of policy in Ireland. But my plans were upset by Mr Asquith's proposal.[4]

In fact, Asquith wrote a personal, handwritten letter to Lloyd George on 10 Downing Street notepaper on 22 May:

> SECRET
> My dear Lloyd George,
> I hope you may see your way clear to take up Ireland; at any rate for a short time. It is a unique opportunity and there is no one else who could do so much to bring a permanent solution.
> Yours very sincerely
> H.H. Asquith[5]

Although Lloyd George felt he could not refuse the Prime Minister's request, he obeyed him with some reluctance. In fact, this decision saved his life, for on 5 June HMS *Hampshire*, which was taking Kitchener and his mission to Russia, was sunk by a German mine off the Orkney Islands. Kitchener and most of the crew drowned (only twelve of some 200 crew survived). A month later, on 6 July, after some deliberation, Asquith appointed

Lloyd George Secretary of State for War, a post that in wartime
was second only to that of Prime Minister.

While Lloyd George and Kitchener certainly had very different
views about the virtues of the Russian imperial system, they were
at one on the issue of Rasputin. When Lloyd George took over
the War Office, he urged on the Prime Minister the formation of
another British mission to Russia, but for months nothing happened. Without a solid Allied-approved agenda for his conduct of
the war, the Tsar would not be able to get finance from America or
Britain, and would ultimately have to seek peace with Germany.

The Tsar was left prey to Rasputin, Vyrubova and the Tsarina.
He was weak, but they supported whatever self-belief he had:
his mystical view of his own divine right to be the Tsar, but also
and most importantly his terror of relinquishing power. Nothing
must weaken the monarchy. He never forgot that his grandfather, Alexander II, had been preparing to make concessions to
the liberals when he was assassinated, while his father Alexander
III, a fierce exponent of nationalism, orthodoxy and autocracy,
had died in his bed.

Nicholas welcomed the Tsarina's constant reminders to be
firm, because she said it was Rasputin's advice. Nicholas was well
aware of Rasputin's faults but had faith in him, as weak people
have faith that they are protected by brass Hands of Fatima and
St Christopher medals and rabbits' feet. When others warned
him, as they did, that Rasputin's proximity to the Tsarina was
undermining public respect for the imperial family, he found
refuge in a sense of martyrdom. He saw himself and the Tsarina
elevated from the ignorant world, bearing the banner of holy
truth regardless of jeers and brickbats. Psychologically at least,
he was the perfect model of a *mari complaisant*.

Rasputin's influence over the Tsar rose as the Allied star fell.
The Tsarina was already passing on to him Rasputin's com-
plaints about the pointlessness of so much loss of life. Paléologue,
the French Ambassador, pooh-poohed the idea that she was
working against the Allies; to him the Tsarina seemed English in
every respect. Sir George Buchanan was not so sure.

All the same, the Tsarina kept in touch with her brother, Prince Ernest of Hesse, intermittently throughout the war, and in 1915 came close to treason when Prince Ernest prevailed upon a Russian expatriate in Germany to convey a letter to her.[6]

> April 17th, 1915, 'Alex to Nicky':
> I had a long, dear letter from Erni... He longs for a way out of this dilemma that someone ought to begin to make a bridge for discussion. So he had an idea of quite privately sending a man of confidence to Stockholm, who should meet a gentleman sent by you... So he sent a gentleman to be there on the 28th... So I at once wrote an answer... and sent it the gentleman... he better not wait – and that tho' one longs for peace, the time has not yet come. – I wanted to get all done before your return, as I know it would be unpleasant for you.

Nicholas did not want to go crawling to Germany – to Alexandra's bullying Uncle Willy. He honourably passed this letter to the Ministry of Foreign Affairs. But instead of confirming that the Tsar and Tsarina were entirely behind the Allies, it confirmed doubts about the Tsarina's loyalty to them. After Kitchener's death in June, there were at least two formal contacts with German emissaries.

In July 1916, Protopopov, then Deputy Speaker of the Duma, visited Stockholm as head of a Duma delegation to Sweden. While there he met an official from the German embassy by the name of Fritz Warburg.[7] The German outlined to Protopopov the Kaiser's desire for a separate peace with Russia and touched on the terms that Berlin was minded to offer. While we have only a fragmentary idea of the terms Warburg put to Protopopov, his claim that they represented an 'honourable and advantageous' settlement was probably not an inaccurate one. Indeed, by comparison with the terms the Germans offered the Bolsheviks some two years later, this was as good an offer as the Russians were ever likely to get.

When Protopopov returned to Petrograd he sought an audience with the Tsar at which he reported on the meeting with

Warburg and suggested that Russia might open peace talks with the Germans. The Tsar rejected this overture on the basis that he had given his personal word to the Allies that Russia would not seek a separate peace. With that, Nicholas dismissed the suggestion. Channels between the Germans and Protopopov, however, remained open.

While British Intelligence soon picked up word of Protopopov's encounter in Stockholm from their agents there and monitored developments on his return, the public at large were blissfully unaware of it. Neither did they or his Duma colleagues know that Protopopov had, for some time, been in close and secret contact with Rasputin. The two had met in 1915 through their mutual friend Pyotr Badmaëv, the Siberian doctor and peddler of Tibetan medicine. Known for many years for his participation in the most outlandish of orgies, Protopopov's neglected venereal disease had finally caught up with him to the extent that he now sought the questionable remedies offered by Badmaëv. He is also reputed to have had incipient 'general paralysis of the insane', as it was then known: the symptoms of tertiary syphilis.[8]

Later that year, Buchanan, no doubt drawing on an intelligence report, asked the Tsar (whose loyalty to the Allies he claims never to have doubted)

> …whether it was true that, in the interview that Protopopov had had with a German agent at Stockholm, the latter had stated that, if Russia would make peace, Germany would evacuate Poland and raise no objection to Russia's acquisition of Constantinople…

These were among the political aspects of the conversation Proto-popov had with Fritz Warburg, but there were also financial ones, for Warburg was an economic adviser at the Stockholm embassy and younger brother of Max Warburg, the Hamburg banker.[9] That generation of seven siblings also included the brothers Paul Warburg of Kuhn, Loeb & Co. in New York, reformer of the Federal Reserve Bank; Felix Warburg, a powerful New York banker whose father-in-law was the legendary

New York financier Jacob Schiff; and Aby, the eldest, a scholar.[10] Fritz's account, as related to the family, may be somewhat disingenuous:

> In July 1916 Fritz stumbled into the history books quite by accident. A Russian delegation was passing through Stockholm on its way home from financial talks in London, when a Count Olusfiev asked to meet a German from the economic sphere. Having sounded out the mood in France and England, he said offhand, he wanted to do the same for Germany. The casual request concealed a serious agenda. During talks at the Foreign Office in Berlin, Fritz had received instructions to follow up on such overtures, and von Lucius encouraged him to meet with the Russians... Perhaps to give the German government some self-protective distance from the talks, Fritz claimed that he attended the Grand Hotel meeting with little official coaching and that he was astonished when the door opened and Alexander Protopopov, vice-president of the Russian Duma, strolled into the room. Suddenly Fritz was engaged in high-level, if discreetly unofficial talks, looking toward a separate peace between Germany and Russia... Felix was careful to stress that he was voicing his own views and not those of his government... [and that Germany's] real grievance lay with France and England, not Russia. He proposed a swap in which Germany would get Baltic territory and Russia parts of German-occupied Poland, followed by stepped-up trade between Russia and Germany.[11]

The Warburgs were on shaky ground. Having established the family in Germany some time between the fourteenth and seventeenth centuries, they were now impelled to demonstrate their loyalty to the country. This should not have been necessary, for they were patriotic Germans; Aby loathed Anglo-Saxon culture and Max had won an Iron Cross. Max had been livid when the Chancellor discriminated against Jews in the German army and his disgust at this had been made public only weeks before. The Hamburg bank had financed the construction of Germany's navy and its merchant fleet before the war. Only last year, Max had sent Carl Melchior, his own closest advisor, to Romania to do deals over grain supplies that were tempting enough to keep Romania neutral.

But Felix now could only offer territorial advantage, and the Tsar did not need any more land, resources or coastline. At this point the Tsar needed generous capital incentives to make peace. He had been here before, in 1905; he would need money to rebuild the country and repress the rebellious element.

Russian Jews, in general, were pro-German, and in view of the cruel pogroms and daily insults, as Sir Bernard Pares wrote in a despatch to the Foreign Office, 'it is difficult to blame them'. German propaganda suggested (with dubious sincerity) that peace with Germany would mean liberation. But Max Warburg could not offer to reconstruct Russia for the Tsar. Germany was suffering from the Allied blockade and so was his bank. By this stage in the war the German Warburgs, and German and Russian financiers in general, could *only* have got money for Russia from America – and they knew Wall Street would refuse to lend it to them. Felix Warburg's father-in-law, Jacob Schiff, so detested the Tsarist regime that he strenuously prevented Russia from getting Wall Street money. Partly out of his hatred for the Tsar's victimisation of Jews, Schiff had organised finance for the Japanese victory in 1904–5.[12] From an old Frankfurt banking family, he could not see why the Germans and Allies were fighting; as his biographer points out,

> Schiff banked on a neutral Wilson to engineer a status quo peace.
> Objecting to the craze for military preparedness in America, he
> opposed the export of munitions and funds to the belligerents.[13]

With the Warburgs and the Rothschilds, he was Jewish royalty. Together the distinguished old man Schiff, and Felix and Paul Warburg, would decide who got American money and who didn't. They could make business difficult for banks that propped up the Tsar.

On the other hand, if Felix Warburg was in a position to offer Protopopov nothing the Tsar would want, this calls into question the provenance of the New York money that Buchanan was able to promise the Tsar in the summer of 1916. It may possibly have come from J.P. Morgan Jnr, a noted anglophile whose *Britannica Online* entry includes the lines

> …during the first three years of World War I, he became the sole purchasing agent in the United States for the British and French governments, buying about $3,000,000,000 worth of military and other supplies from American firms on behalf of those countries. To finance the Franco–British requirements for credits in the United States, he organized more than 2,000 banks to underwrite a total of more than $1,500,000,000 in Allied bonds. After the end of the war his firm floated loans totaling more than $10,000,000,000 for European reconstruction work.[14]

The Americans were in a position to impose conditions. They could well have been persuaded by Buchanan's argument, often stated, that *providing Rasputin were out of the picture*, the Tsar would concede power to a pro-Ally, progressive Duma.

In addition to the feelers put out to Protopopov, and Nicholas's subsequent reaction, there is evidence to believe that Berlin was also considering other options in terms of brokering a peace with Russia. A decade after the events of 1916, Alexei Raivid, a Soviet consul in Berlin, was having one of his occasional meetings with Baron von Hochen Esten, when the subject of Rasputin cropped up. The Baron, a German specialist in Russian affairs employed by the Hungarian embassy, told Raivid that, in the summer of 1916, he and a number of others were sent to Petrograd. The purpose of their mission was to establish contacts with certain elements of the Russian court who sought a separate peace with Germany. Raivid recorded in his diary an account of what von Hochen Esten told him that day:

In his own words, the ties between the two courts never broke during the war and were maintained unofficially and through illegal means by different elements close to the courts. The main purpose of the mission was to take advantage of the difficult domestic situation in Russia and to warn the influential elements of the Russian Court that the only way to save Russia from the forthcoming revolution would be Russia's withdrawal from the war with Germany and some domestic reforms. He was charged, if necessary, to cooperate with other persons in preparation of a coup to remove Nicholas II from the throne. On his arrival he got in touch with the following three persons who together with Tsarina Alexandra worked on the development of the separate peace treaty: Sturmer; Beletsky, Director of the Department of Police; and one of the synod leaders, Vasily Mikhailovich Skvortsov. The group, in cooperation with other German agents, sought to persuade Rasputin that he and the Tsarina should lead a movement for peace with Germany. Because Nicholas opposed the idea of signing a separate peace treaty with Germany (he explained his position by the fact that as a nobleman he could not break the promise that he had made to the Allies) he was to be persuaded to abdicate the throne on 6th December (his Saint's Day) in favour of his heir Alexei. This would then allow Alexandra, as Regent, to conclude a separate peace treaty, as neither she nor the Tsarevich had given such a promise to the Allies. According to a further plan, the Regent would publish a manifesto stating that the difficult domestic circumstances in Russia required the conclusion of a peace treaty and carry forward a programme of reforms in the country. The manifesto allegedly promised to 'give land to the people'. Von Hochen Esten claims that Rasputin was among those who wrote a draft of the manifesto and that he favoured the idea of a separate peace and totally approved of the slogan promising land for the people.[15]

While Raivid's diary represents only one small fragment of documentary evidence to support the notion of such a plot, it was anecdotally well supported in the summer of 1916. It was taken equally seriously by David Lloyd George, on whose desk intelligence reports warning of future catastrophe were beginning to pile up.

SEVEN

WAR GAMES

In August 1916 there was good news and bad. The good news was that Romania had at last declared war against Germany. The bad news was that Romania was so ill-prepared that the country would inevitably be overrun, south of the Carpathians at least, and Russian and Allied military assistance must be given. This expert intervention would destroy the resources that would otherwise allow the Germans to pour across Romania to the Black Sea and stay there. The British Intelligence officer whose team would follow the retreat, burning grain stores and destroying factories, oil fields and oil refineries, was Captain John Dymoke Scale.

Scale was six feet four, a thirty-four-year-old Indian Army officer with a wife and young children in England. He was from a genuine British background, the son of a Merthyr solicitor,[1] educated at Repton and trained as an army officer at Sandhurst. He had learned Russian before the war, during a previous posting in Russia. He fought on the Western Front in 1914, sustaining a serious shrapnel wound to the leg. He was posted to France in the summer of 1916 and, also that summer, was assigned to accompany a party of Russian parliamentarians visiting England, which included Protopopov, the spokesman of the delegation, Milyukov and Shingarev, who were opposition leaders, and many others representing different shades of opinion.

With the entry of Romania into the war in August 1916, Scale was attached to the Petrograd SIS station. He was already well connected in Petrograd society, not only through his parliamentary contacts but because of his acquaintance with Robert Wilton, the *Times*'s Petrograd correspondent, who had accompanied a party of Russian journalists in England a few weeks before his own trip with the Duma members. Among Wilton's party had been Vladimir D. Nabokov, the Kadet leader. Scale knew his brother, the diplomat Konstantin D. Nabokov, who had from 1912 been Russian Consul-General in Calcutta; he was now at the imperial Russian embassy in England.[2] Konstantin Nabokov corresponded with Scale and undoubtedly primed him with current opinion, such as 'rumours… of Rasputin's evil orgies and of the loss of prestige which the monarchy was suffering owing to the disastrous influence of this hysterical and vicious scoundrel blindly believed to be a saint and a miracle-maker'.[3]

Scale arrived in Russia on 31 August, via Finland, and headed directly for the Astoria Hotel in Petrograd, where most of the British Intelligence Mission was billeted.

The Astoria was a fine five-storied building, built round a large dining hall, down onto the coloured glass roof of which the windows of the inner rooms looked… German-owned… it had been taken over by the Government… and was now the 'official' hotel, open only to diplomats, officers and officials… Many people lived there indefinitely, in spite of a regulation that no one save the diplomats and officials of allied powers could stay there longer than a certain number of days. From lunch time till late at night its salons were kaleidoscopes of movement and colour. Cossacks, Guardsmen, naval officers, in fact men in every Russian

uniform imaginable (most civilians in Russia wear uniform) sat
at tables or stood in groups chatting to their womenfolk. Often
very beautiful women they were too, in wonderful clothes and
jewellery. Here and there among the throng, officers in the uniform of one or other of the Allied powers were conspicuous. A
Romanian military mission had just arrived, and was the centre
of new interest. No taciturnity or absence of smiles was notice-
able here. In fact one could hardly recognise the airs played by
the military band so loud was the buzz of talk and laughter. A
cheery, careless place was the Astoria (a happy hunting ground
for enemy agents too!).[4]

He set to work for the British Intelligence Mission. His immediate duties were to exchange news of German troop movements
between Russian and British staff officers. Cypher telegrams
would arrive from London, explaining which German units
were operational in France; they would have to be deciphered
and compared with Russian intelligence about the Russian and
Romanian fronts. There were endless misunderstandings, que-
ries and frustrations ('…thus the 21st Reserve Regiment has
now been established as belonging to the new 216th Division
but it is always down as of 36th Reserve Division…'[5]) caused
by a combination of German cunning, Russian carelessness,
and sometimes, in Scale's view, London's willingness to believe
French intelligence from Moscow rather than British.

   It is pretty certain that Scale placed himself firmly on Alley's
side of the 'show' rather than Hoare's. Hoare, bright and per-
sonable as he was, was essentially a desk wallah. Alley and Scale
already knew each other from the time in 1913 when Scale
qualified, in Russia, as an interpreter, first class. He would have
heard all the Rasputin-related gossip relayed by Alley, Rayner
and Felix Yusupov,[6] who he had also made the acquaintance of,
through Alley, on his previous Russian posting. Quite what this
Indian Army man and veteran of the trenches made of Yusupov
and his louche social connections can only be imagined. Perhaps
by this time nothing surprised him. Yusupov and Pavlovich were

fabulously exotic; the Yusupovs were descended from the Tartar hordes who once overran southern Russia, and were said to be the second richest family in Russia. Yusupov wrote of his childhood:

> We seldom went abroad, but my parents sometimes took my brother and myself on a tour of their various estates which were scattered all over Russia; some were so far away that we never went there at all. One of our estates in the Caucasus stretched for one hundred and twenty-five miles along the Caspian Sea; crude petroleum was so abundant that the soil seemed soaked with it, and the peasants used it to grease their cart wheels.
>
> For these long trips, our private coach was attached to the train… [it] was entered by a vestibule which in summer was turned into a sort of verandah containing an aviary; the songs of the birds drowned the train's monotonous rumble. The dining-drawing room… was panelled in mahogany, the chairs were upholstered in green leather and the windows curtained in yellow silk. Next came my parents' bedroom, then my brother's and mine, both very cheerful with chintzes and light wood panelling, and then the bathroom. Several compartments reserved for friends followed our private apartments. Our staff of servants, always very numerous, occupied compartments next the kitchen at the far end of the coach. Another coach fitted up in much the same way was stationed at the Russo-German border for our journeys abroad, but we never used it.
>
> On all our journeys we were accompanied by a host of people without whom my father could not exist…[7]

Felix Yusupov would in due course inherit palaces and estates in seventeen Russian provinces. There were several in St Petersburg, several more in Moscow and its environs, a few in the Crimea. His account of his family's many mansions is littered with throwaway lines such as (about the palace at 94 Moika) 'the house was a present from Catherine the Great to my great-great-grandmother, Princess Tatiana'. All the palaces were resplendent with the work of the most accomplished sculptors and painters and furniture makers of Russia and Europe, collected over hundreds of years. Several, like the Yusupov Palace, had more than one ballroom, a picture gallery, and a series of opulent reception rooms; there were billiard rooms and libraries, nurseries and boudoirs, bathing pools and hot-houses, music rooms and secret rooms. At least two of the palaces contained full-size private theatres; the one in the Yusupov Palace was exquisite. Chaliapin, Chopin and Liszt had given concerts there and Alexander Blok had given poetry readings. At the country mansions were acres of conservatories, marble fountains, rivers, lakes. 'At Moscow, as at St Petersburg, my parents kept open house.' As a decorative touch, Yusupov's mother, the exquisite Princess Zenaïde, littered her state room with bowls of precious stones. Her husband, his imagination exhausted, had once presented her, as a birthday gift, with a mountain.

Felix was an obnoxious child, wild and by his own admission dreadfully spoiled. He hated to be bored, but when his parents were not giving receptions and balls the state apartments of the palatial town houses would be closed, and the children confined to the duller utilitarian rooms. Tedium was at last alleviated when Nicholas, Felix's elder brother, introduced Yusupov the schoolboy to the Bohemian circles of St Petersburg and his then mistress, Polya. Felix had a passion for furniture, interior design and clothes – women's clothes, particularly, when he got the opportunity to wear them, and as a boy of about thirteen, he did. He and Nicholas and Polya would visit, in secret and in disguise, the night haunts of St Petersburg, with Felix dressed as a pretty girl. After all, as he disingenuously protested, he would hardly be admitted as a schoolboy.

The 'pretty girl' was quite a success, and much emboldened one particular night they went to the theatre. Yusupov was aware he was attracting interest from an old gentleman and when the lights went up, he recognised King Edward VII. An English equerry stopped Nicholas in the foyer during the interval and asked the name of 'the lovely young woman he was escorting'.

I began to lead a double life: by day I was a school-boy and by
night an elegant woman. Polia [*sic*] dressed very well and all her
clothes suited me to perfection… I haunted *café-concerts* and knew
most of the popular tunes of the time and could sing them in a
soprano voice. Nicholas conceived the idea of turning this talent
to account by getting an engagement for me at 'The Aquarium',
at that time the smartest *café-concert* in St Petersburg.[8]

He auditioned in 'a grey tailored suit, fox fur and a large hat'
as a young French woman singing the latest songs from Paris,
and was engaged on the spot. New frocks and headdresses
were ordered. He appeared, took three encores on the first
night and was, of course, the toast of the town. For a week. And
then,

> …on the seventh evening I saw some friends of my mother
> staring at me through opera glasses. They recognised me from
> my likeness to my mother, and also knew the jewels I was wear-
> ing.[9]

There was of course a huge row, but this sort of scrape was just
the beginning. Scandal followed Felix and his brother wherever they went. They had nothing in particular to do, no role
at all – Nicholas at least would inherit the estates, but for Felix,
there was no particular future; he certainly did not want to go
into the army. They travelled a lot, most often to Paris, where
Nicholas fell in love with a famous courtesan and he and his
brother learned to smoke opium and escape from police raids.
The merry-go-round of pleasure rolled on for several years, but
ended in tears. In 1908 Nicholas fell desperately in love with a
girl who was about to be married. Married she became; and
he and she continued their affair. The husband found out, and
challenged Nicholas to a duel. Felix's beloved elder brother was
shot dead.

   The family was devastated. Princess Zenaïde never recovered. Prince Yusupov turned in his own fashion to religion and

practical philanthropy. With typical *savoir-vivre* he began as one of a party disguised as beggars who spent a night in the stews of St Petersburg where the homeless and the alcoholic, the desperate and the diseased, sought shelter. He was a kindly young man, and this came as a sad revelation to him. After this he volunteered regularly to help down-and-outs. Also, he was inspired by Elizaveta Fyodorovna, who, since the assassination of Grand Duke Sergei, had turned to good works and the Orthodox Church.

Prince Felix Yusupov, too, began to have spiritual thoughts. In support of this new interest, Mounya Golovina introduced him to Rasputin in 1909, but he was not impressed.

> The longer I examined him, the more I was struck by his eyes; they were amazingly repulsive. Not only was there no trace of spiritual refinement in the face, but it called to mind that of a cunning and lascivious satyr... His smile, too, was arresting: it was sickly yet cruel, cunning and sensual. Indeed, the whole of his being was redolent of something unspeakably revolting, hidden under the mask of hypocrisy and cant.[10]

Felix's spirituality and generosity to the poor having failed to keep him entirely on the straight and narrow, his parents were still concerned for him. After his brother's death, the fate of the Yusupov fortune lay in his hands, and he now proposed that when he inherited he would give most of it away. His parents could see that there was not much hope that a good wife might cure him of this exaggerated tendency to *largesse,* and were probably quite relieved when, despite their protests, he took himself off to Oxford for three years of pleasure, followed by many months of dissipation in London. One photograph from 1910 shows Felix in a braid-encrusted costume and hat as a dashing sixteenth-century *boyard*, his diffident smile enhanced by lipstick and kohl.

Григорій Распутинъ

Above: 1 Rasputin and his family *c.*1900.

Right: 2 Rasputin *c.*1906.

3 Rasputin with Bishops Hermogen and Iliodor, *c.*1906.

Above: 4 Rasputin and his admirers, 1914.

Right: 5 Rasputin and his children, 1910.

6 Rasputin surrounded by his admirers, 1915.

Above left: 7 Rasputin, 1916.

Above right: 8 Cartoons mocking the influence Rasputin had over the Tsarina were widely, if covertly, published.

9 Cartoonists saw the Tsar as being in the palm of Rasputin's hand.

Above left: 10 This cartoon is
the most overt suggestion that
Rasputin and the Tsarina were
having a sexual relationship.

Above right: 11 The belief that the
Tsar and Tsarina were Rasputin's
child-like pawns is again advocated
in this cartoon.

Left: 12 Mother Russia is
portrayed here as the victim of
Rasputin's influence and control
over the Tsar.

Above left: 13 British Ambassador Sir George Buchanan.

Above right: 14 Lord Kitchener boards HMS *Hampshire.* Within half an hour of this photograph being taken, Kitchener was dead.

Right: 15 The Tsarina and Rasputin on the front cover of the withdrawn December 1916 edition of the *Metropolitan* magazine.

Above: 16 Capt. Stephen Alley was born in the Yusupov Palace and remained close to the Yusupov family.

Left: 17 Lt-Col. Sir Samuel Hoare in the Russian coat worn by British officers in Petrograd during the winter of 1916.

Below: 18 Capt. John Scale, a lynchpin in the plot to kill Rasputin, was also close to the Yusupov family.

Right: 19 Oswald Rayner, *c.*1916; he had known Felix Yusupov since their days at Oxford University.

Below: 20 The Tsar and his family, 1913.

Above left: 21 Prince Felix Yusupov at Oxford University.

Above right: 22 Prince Felix Yusupov and Princess Irina at their marriage, 1913.

Above left: 23 Grand Duke Dmitri Pavlovich was regarded as the most pro-British of the Russian Grand Dukes.

Above right: 24 Vladimir Purishkevich, a late recruit to the conspiracy, whose unstable personality blew the plot wide open.

25 The Yusupov Palace.

26 Police Scene of Crime Photograph – the Yusupov Palace Courtyard; the pool of blood left by the fatal third shot is to the left of the open gates.

27 Police Scene of Crime Photograph – the door to the study and cellar is to the right; a temporary repair has been made to the bottom right-hand window.

Above: 28 Police Scene of Crime Photograph – two individual pictures joined together; the police have marked the trail of blood with red ink dots.

Left: 29 The door to the courtyard from the inside staircase in 2004.

30 The cellar of 92 Moika in 2004 – Rasputin's waxwork sits at the dining table.

31 Police Scene of Crime Photograph – Rasputin's frozen corpse is removed from the river; a close-up of his chest, head and shoulders.

Left: 32 Police Scene of Crime Photograph – Rasputin's body is put on a sledge; wooden planks lead from the hole in the ice to the river bank.

Below: 33 Police Scene of Crime Photograph – a close-up of the frozen body; while in the water the rope detached and the arms rose before the corpse froze.

Top: 34 Police Scene of Crime Photograph – a close-up of the hole in the ice; Petrovski Bridge, from where Rasputin was thrown, can be seen in the background.

Middle: 35 Police Scene of Crime Photograph – Petrovski Bridge; the car tyre tracks are still visible in the snow.

Bottom: 36 Police Scene of Crime Photograph – traces of blood are in evidence on the girders.

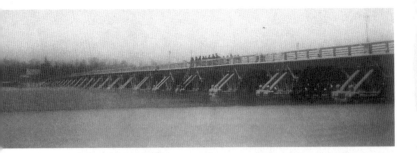

Above: 37 Police Scene of Crime Photograph – investigators can be seen examining the spot on Petrovski Bridge from where the body was thrown into the water.

Right: 38 Petrovski Bridge in 2004, now a pedestrian bridge.

Below: 39 Autopsy Photograph – Rasputin's still-clothed corpse before the autopsy commenced.

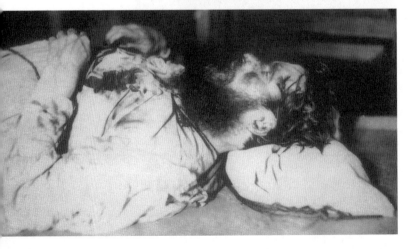

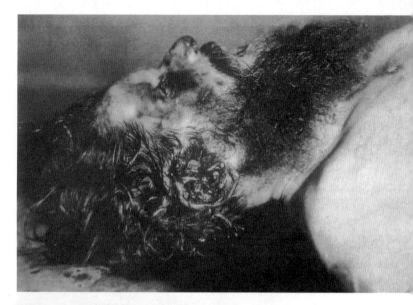

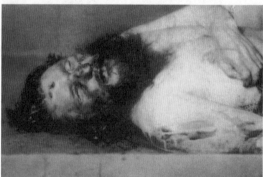

Above: 40 Autopsy Photograph – right-hand side of Rasputin's head; damage to the ear, eye and nose are particularly evident.

Left: 41 Autopsy Photograph – the fatal third shot to the forehead.

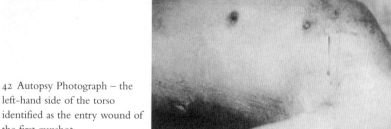

42 Autopsy Photograph – the left-hand side of the torso identified as the entry wound of the first gunshot.

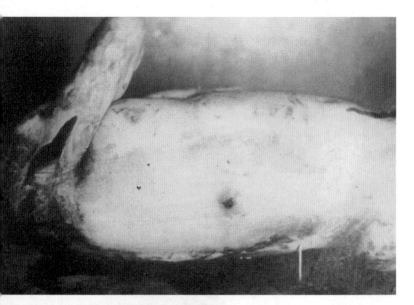

Above: 43 Autopsy Photograph – the right-hand side of the torso identified as the exit wound of the first gunshot.

Left: 44 Autopsy Photograph – indicating the entry wound from the second gunshot and the 'gaping wound' to the left lower back caused by a knife or sword.

45 A Webley revolver and unjacketed .455-inch lead bullet as carried by Oswald Rayner.

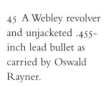

46 A Savage pistol and jacketed 7.65mm bullet as used by Vladimir Purishkevich.

47 A Browning pistol and jacketed 6.35mm bullet as used by Yusupov and Dmitri Pavlovich.

DEATH OF A BRILLIANT SCHOLAR 10.361

WAS IN PALACE WHEN RASPUTIN WAS KILLED

ON March 6, Major Oswald Rayner, M.A., Oxon., M.B.E., died peacefully at his home in Oxford. Major Rayner was a cousin of Mrs. D. S. Jones, of Old Meadow, Bulkington Lane, Nuneaton.

He was a brilliant scholar, a barrister-at-law, and spoke five languages fluently, including Russian. During the First World War he became a King's Messenger and it was his duty to carry messages between Buckingham Palace and St. Petersburg.

He was a personal friend of Prince Youssupoff who organised the plot against Rasputin, and was actually in the Palace when Rasputin was killed. Later when the Prince wrote a book about Rasputin it was Major Ray-

ner who translated it into English.

It was his sad duty to announce to King George V the tragic death of the Russian royal family in 1918.

Major Rayner had his roots in Nuneaton, for his grandfather, the late Thomas Rayner, was manager of Nuneaton Gas Works for many years.

48 On Rayner's death in March 1961 the *Nuneaton Observer* revealed that he was present at the scene of the murder.

The real trouble began when he got back, and Felix Yusupov and Dmitri Pavlovich got together. They had known each other since they were small children. Dmitri's mother had died when he was small and his father, Grand Duke Paul Alexandrovich, had married again, to a Madame Pistolkors, who already had two children. Morganatic marriages such as this must be discouraged, and Dmitri's father was banished to live in exile. Dmitri Pavlovich and his sister remained in Russia to be brought up by their uncle and aunt, the Grand Duke Sergei Alexandrovich and his wife Elizaveta Fyodorovna, the Tsarina's elder sister. Grand Duke Sergei was homosexual and they had no children; in 1905 he was shot dead by an assassin.

Dmitri grew up against this turbulent background, and in due course went into the army.

In 1913, after three years in England, Prince Felix Yusupov was in his twenties, sophisticated, cosmopolitan and still not really the marrying kind. And on his return,

> ...I saw a great deal of the Grand Duke Dmitri Pavlovich, who had just joined the Horse Guards. The Emperor and Empress both loved him and looked upon him as a son; he lived at the Alexander Palace and went everywhere with the Tsar. He spent all his free time with me; I saw him almost every day and we took long walks and rides together.
>
> Dmitri was extremely attractive; tall, elegant, well-bred, with deep thoughtful eyes, he recalled the portraits of his ancestors... Almost every night we took a car and drove to St Petersburg to have a gay time at restaurants and night clubs and with the gypsies. We would invite artists and musicians to supper with us in a private room; the well-known ballerina Anna Pavlova was often our guest. These wonderful evenings slipped by like dreams and we never went home until dawn.[11]

The Tsar and Tsarina were outraged that Dmitri was falling under Felix's spell, for they were 'aware of the scandalous rumours about my mode of living'. Dmitri was confined to Tsarskoye

Selo, and Felix tailed by Okhrana agents. Finally, Dmitri escaped the Alexander Palace, and, as young people will, moved into a palace of his own – the Sergei Palace on the Neva. His surrogate mother, Elizaveta Fyodorovna, now in a convent, had made him a present of it. 'He asked me to help with the re-decoration of his new home', explained Felix artlessly in his book. This kept the heir to the Yusupov fortunes delightfully occupied, but Princess Zenaïde could see that her son's aimless mode of life could not be allowed to go on. She found him a wife. She knew Felix well, and perceived that only a beautiful, slender, elegant young girl, who looked very like him, would do: and she found one. Early in 1914, to the dismay of the Tsar and Tsarina, Felix Yusupov married their niece Princess Irina, the daughter of Grand Duke Alexander Mikhailovich and Grand Duchess Xenia. In 1915 their first and only child, a daughter, was born. The couple adored each other, but Irina was under no illusions about her husband's sexuality.

Late in 1915 he entered the *Corps des Pages,* the Junior Guards, for a year's training. This was not so much because, despite his anti-militarism, he was unable any longer to resist expectation that he do the right thing; by his own admission it was because he had no social life, since everyone he knew was in uniform.

By the autumn of 1916 he was preparing for his final exami-nations. His military training was not arduous, and he got plenty of leave – as did Dmitri Pavlovich, stationed at the Stavka with the Tsar. Irina and the baby remained in the warmer climate of the Crimea while Yusupov spent every spare moment supervis-ing the preparation of their new private suite of apartments at the Yusupov Palace. A few rooms within it were to be set aside for him personally, as a kind of bachelor *pied-à-terre* for use whenever the rest of the family was out of town.

Four thousand miles away in New York City, Rasputin's former intimate, Bishop Iliodor, had resurfaced to find himself at the centre of a storm that would have far-reaching reper-cussions. The chain of events began within a day or two of his arrival on 18 June, when he met with H.J. Wigham, the president of *Metropolitan* magazine, at his Manhattan office. As a result, a deal was agreed whereby Iliodor would be interviewed by a Russian-speaking journalist named Tobenkin (Iliodor himself spoke no English), who worked for *Metropolitan* magazine. The interview would centre on a number of new revelations principally concerning Rasputin, the Tsarina and moves to conclude a peace treaty between Russia and Germany. The source of the story, according to Iliodor, was letters, documents and information that he had brought with him from Russia. The contents of the interview would then be used for a series of five articles appearing under Iliodor's name. It was agreed that he would receive a full and final payment of $5,000 by 1 August 1916.

The interview duly took place in early September and resulted in an initial article entitled 'Rasputin: The Holy Devil of Russia'. Trailed in the September edition as being scheduled to appear in November, it was billed as 'The Biggest Magazine Story of the Year!' Several days afterwards, Iliodor received two unexpected visitors at his home in the Bronx – Archbishop Evdokin and one Mikhail Ustinov, the Russian Consul-General. They told him that they had read in the *Metropolitan* magazine that he was to write a number of articles about Rasputin and the Tsarina. They urged him not to go ahead with the publication deal and offered him $25,000 if he withdrew them and further agreed not to publish them elsewhere either. Should he not agree, he was told in no uncertain terms that the Russian Consulate would use its influence to prevent publication.

Back in Petrograd, there was a flurry of activity behind the scenes, as the Tsarina began urging her husband, at Rasputin's behest, to appoint Protopopov to the all-powerful post of Minister for the Interior. On 7 September she wrote:

My own sweetheart... Grigori begs you earnestly to name Protopopov [as Interior Minister]. I believe in Our Friend's wisdom and guidance... His love for you and Russia is so intense and God has sent Him to be to yr. help and guide and prays so hard for you.

From his reply two days later, it is clear that even the Tsar was somewhat doubtful about the wisdom of appointing such an erratic and questionable character as Protopopov, saying that he 'must think about that question… one should be careful, especially where high positions are concerned'.[12]

Whatever his doubts, Nicholas does not seem to have held out long, for on 18 September, to the absolute astonishment of virtually everyone, Protopopov's appointment as Interior Minister was announced. David Lloyd George made clear to Prime Minister Asquith, in a 'confidential' memo, that:

> Germanophile influences have been considerably strengthened by recent changes. Our friends have disappeared one by one and there is no man now of any influence in the Russian Bureaucracy who can be said to be favourable towards this country.[13]

In Petrograd, the Tsarina and Rasputin congratulated themselves over Protopopov's appointment. On the same day as the announcement was made, Alexandra sent the first in a series of telegrams to the Tsar, begging him to halt the latest offensive, which he initially appears to have done. However, acting completely in character, he quickly changed his mind, having come under pressure from military aides at the Stavka. With equal predictability, Alexandra rushed off another missive on 24 September, telling her errant husband that, 'Our Friend is much put out… says that you were inspired from above to give that order and God would bless it – Now he says again useless losses'. Nicholas countered that changed circumstances had prompted him to reverse the order, to which Alexandra obliviously retorted, 'Oh, give your order again to Brussilov – stop this useless slaughter… Our generals don't count the lives – they are hardened to losses and that is a sin… spare those lives'.[14]

On the other side of the Atlantic, the proprietors of *Metropolitan* magazine formally announced the cancellation of Iliodor's articles on 3 October. This was obviously a decision the publishers did not take lightly, as the November edition had already gone to press. The printers had to be instructed to physically remove the article. From a practical point of view, there was nothing that could be done about the front cover, which featured a colour illustration of a sinister Rasputin looming over a helpless Tsarina. Readers were left to puzzle about the contents of the article, which had obviously hit a raw nerve so far as the Russian authorities were concerned.

The veil was finally lifted when officers of the magazine were summoned to appear before the New York Supreme Court on 2 November as defendants in an action brought by an enraged Iliodor. He told the court that he had formerly 'been a confidential friend and advisor of Rasputin' and that his account of Rasputin's influence over the Tsarina had been suppressed by the Russian government. He alleged that Rasputin

is strongly pro-German and has such influence over the Tsarina as to obtain her influence against the Allies… he is now engaged in a conspiracy to bring about a separate peace, with the Russian Government to apply for a loan of three million roubles from the English government, with the threat that in case the money is not forthcoming a separate peace will be signed this winter.[15]

Before the case could reach the point of judgement, the magazine settled out of court. Whether Iliodor's motives were guided by his fear and hatred of Rasputin or the sizeable sum of money being offered for his story is very much open to conjecture. The essential threads of his story were certainly taken seriously by the SIS station in New York, headed by Sir William Wiseman. We know too that one of Wiseman's officers, Captain Norman Thwaites, made several reports to C in London, and to the British Intelligence Mission in Petrograd, concerning Iliodor's claims. There is also good reason to believe that these reports were not simply second-hand reworkings of information Thwaites had gained from his network of sources. After the case had been settled, Iliodor told the *New York Times* that:

> Prior to the suppression of my articles I was called upon by an
> agent of the British Government and to him I told some of the
> facts in my possession concerning Rasputin.[16]

More compelling evidence still comes from the papers of Station
Chief Sir William Wiseman, which indicate that not only had New
York SIS had direct contact with Iliodor, but they later actively con-
sidered sending him back to Russia on a propaganda mission.[17]

Matters had now, undoubtedly, come to a critical head so far
as Britain was concerned. To Lloyd George, the prospect of a
peace deal between Russia and Germany, and the horrendous
consequences it would bring for Britain and France on the
Western Front, was looming large with each passing day.

> Such news as came through to us during the autumn of 1916
> from Russia showed what a fatal blunder the abandonment of
> the mission was proving. All the omens were pointing to a break-
> down of the Russian military effort and to a separate peace with
> Germany. The King of Sweden (who was pro-German in sym-
> pathy) had remarked to the British Ambassador at Stockholm,
> on hearing this news, that there would be peace between Russia
> and Germany within two months! Sir George Buchanan… men-
> tioned in a private letter to Lord Charles Beresford on 17th
> October the prevalence of rumours of a separate peace, which
> Stürmer had officially denied, and reported the growth of a pro-
> German sentiment in official circles.[18]

In his letter, Sir George identified Stürmer (now at the Foreign
Office), Protopopov and Rasputin as the leading Germanophiles.
To further compound Lloyd George's suspicions, yet another
intelligence report landed on his desk.

SECRET
NOTES FROM A RELIABLE SOURCE
There is talk in various circles in Switzerland about supposed pri-
vate conversations between Germany and Russia. It is impossible

to get proof of this, but it is said that these conversations are taking place between the Crown Princess Cecilia and the Empress of Russia with Rataieff [sic], Chief of the Russian Secret Police, in Switzerland as an intermediary. The last speech of Bethmann Hollweg seems to corroborate this. Its tone is courteous towards Russia and the assurance that Germany does not want to interfere with Russian internal politics, as well as the complete absence a statement concerning Poland looks as if Germany wanted to leave this question open in order to eventually settle it with Russia. Bethmann's vehemence against England and her presumed use of her Allies to serve her own ends leads to the belief that if these conversations really exist they must be on a strong anti-English basis. Bethmann's words 'we will not interfere' seems to contrast to the fears always expressed by the reactionary parties in Russia that the Allies will want to interfere.[19]

Lloyd George was not the only one with an impending sense of doom. Many in Russia tried to get Nicholas to send Rasputin into exile. The Tsar's mother, the Dowager Empress Maria Fyodorovna, had long ago been alienated by the Tsarina and had moved away from Petrograd to live in Kiev. She hardly saw the couple, or her grandchildren. 'In the twelve years I was with [the Tsarina] Alexandra Fyodorovna, I saw Maria Fyodorovna maybe three times', Vyrubova later testified.[20] But in October 1916 the Dowager Empress made a special journey to warn her son, in pretty much the same terms that Sir George Buchanan had, that the pernicious influence of 'advisors' on his wife was endangering the monarchy. He changed nothing.

EIGHT

CARDS ON THE TABLE

There was a lot of talk about murdering Rasputin, and that is what most of it was: just talk. The *muzhik* was seemingly so well guarded that practical possibilities could apparently not be found. Aristocratic officers were the most likely to assassinate him because they despised all he stood for, and would have had no compunction about killing such an upstart.

Some time in the autumn of 1916 a carefully thought-out plot to murder Rasputin began to take shape in somebody's mind.

The murderer must be someone whose proximity would not cause Rasputin, or his minders, any concern.

This person should have a perfect alibi.

Rasputin should simply disappear. People would guess that he could have died in a drunken brawl on the Islands he was so fond of visiting. Were the body found, this would be confirmed.

Had the person who considered these principles been British, he would not pass the first hurdle; he would never get close to Rasputin.

Prince Felix Yusupov, on the other hand, had met Rasputin and knew Mounya Golovina, one of his intimate disciples, very well. He was married to a Romanov, which meant that he would probably be safe from prosecution. Also, he had personal reasons for taking revenge on Rasputin. According to Yusupov, his father had lost his job as Governor-General of Moscow because he denounced to the Tsar, with anger, the pro-German schemers who hampered his work.[1]

As for whether Yusupov could kill Rasputin in cold blood... the Prince had a lot to prove. As a member of the *Corps des Pages,* he was part of a militaristic band of brothers to which his reputation hardly qualified him for admittance. People suspected that he would fail his exams on purpose to avoid active service. On the other hand, participation in Rasputin's murder would make him a hero in the eyes of his peers.

Grand Duke Dmitri Pavlovich had something better than an alibi. No Romanov could face a firing squad.

The identity of those involved in the planning of Rasputin's murder is reasonably clear. What remains unclear is whether British intelligence officers proactively approached Yusupov and Dmitri Pavlovich with the idea of carrying out a murder by proxy or whether they heard about their desire to kill Rasputin at a very early stage and sought to exploit this opportunity for their own ends. Either way, the longstanding personal rapport between Yusupov, Stephen Alley, John Scale and Oswald Rayner was absolutely key to the collaboration.

John Scale's two daughters, Betty and Muriel, have clear memories of hearing their father's account of his involvement. According to Betty, he told them that he was 'involved in the planning but was not at the murder'.[2] Muriel also confirmed that

He was involved in the planning of it; they were all together... You see they had to do something, but in fact he wasn't there

when they actually killed him, he was somewhere else, so he
didn't actually take part in that, but he was involved in all the
planning and how they were going to get rid of him… He
knew the Yusupovs very well. He used to stay at their palace…
palaces.[3]

We also have corroboration of British involvement in the planning from another source. William Compton was a chauffeur
who worked for the Anglo-Russian Hospital from his engagement in June 1916 until its closure in February 1918 and the
evacuation of its staff to England. He left a diary, from which it
is clear that some of the chauffeurs used to moonlight as driv-
ers for other members of the British community in Petrograd.
Compton in particular drove Oswald Rayner and John Scale.
Most significantly, his diary (in this respect, an account-book)
confirms that on six occasions between late October and mid-
November of 1916, he took Rayner and Scale to and from the
Yusupov Palace. Two further visits are recorded after Scale's
departure for Romania on 11 November, the last of which was
the night before the murder.

Whether the idea to murder Rasputin was initially Yusupov
and Dmitri Pavlovich's or the intelligence officers', it is clear
that the pair were to be the means of physically carrying out the
deed. The Achilles heel of involving the two playboys was that
everyone knew their business.

The first rumours of approaching murder reached Simanovich
at the Fire Club, a gambling club he ran in Countess Ignateva's
house on the Champ de Mars… Ivan came to him to say that
there were mysterious meetings at the National [a rival club]
where a lot was said about Rasputin. Alexis sometimes worked
in the room where the meetings were held. Simanovich gave
him 500 roubles and told him to ask Alexis to find out as much
as he could. Alexis reported back that the meetings were chaired
by Purishkevich and were attended by Grand Duke Dmitri
Pavlovich, Prince Felix Yusupov, and some young officers. 'They

spoke a lot about Rasputin in these meetings,' Simanovich said; the name of the English Ambassador, Buchanan, and those of the Tsar and Tsarina were also mentioned.[4]

Yusupov's famously gothic account of the murder, translated by, and essentially co-written with, Oswald Rayner in 1927, naturally makes no mention of British involvement. Despite a degree of cynicism about Yusupov's account on the part of historians, the book more or less became the authorised account of the murder for the best part of nine decades. Rayner himself certainly felt that it was very much a shared endeavour and ensured that his name appeared in big bold letters, only slightly smaller than Yusupov's, on the title page of the British edition. In fact, it seems that it was he, rather than Yusupov, who initially approached London publishers Jonathan Cape with a proposal for the book. According to Yusupov, the conspiracy was all his own idea. He talked to Princess Irina first, and she agreed with him that something must be done. He began (no date is given) by making sure he was doing the right thing.

> I decided to attach no particular importance to all the disturbing rumours which were rife, but first of all to obtain irrefutable evidence of Rasputin's treason.[5]

He put the case against Rasputin to Mounya Golovina, and she happily admitted that the Tsar and Tsarina discussed affairs of state with the man he called an 'unenlightened and uneducated *muzhik*.' 'There are obviously people behind him who are secretly directing him,' he told her sternly.

She wouldn't listen; he didn't understand the essential holiness of Rasputin, she said. That was enough.

> I realised that no more time must be wasted in talk; it was necessary to take action, deliberately and with energy, while all was not yet lost.[6]

He decided 'to consult certain influential people' and to tell them all he knew of Rasputin's doings. These were all people who in the past had bemoaned the man's influence, but now that he approached them with a view to taking action, backed off. They had 'an addiction to a quiet life, and an eager desire for their own welfare'. One who saw the point of what he was saying, but was not in a position to do anything, was Rodzyanko, a relation of Yusupov's, a huge fellow who was Speaker of the Duma at the time. He agreed that it was all quite dreadful, but what could one do when 'the entire Government, and those who are in close contact with the Emperor, are without exception Rasputin's nominees?' The only way out, said Rodzyanko, was 'to kill the blackguard'.[7]

This was more like it. Yusupov was full of trepidation, but an inner voice strengthened his resolve:

> Every murder is a crime and a sin, but in the name of your country you must take this sin on your conscience. You must take it without faltering. At the front, millions of innocent men have been killed…[8]

His decision was made, and he wondered 'to whom I could entrust my secret'. This is typical of Yusupov, as it begs the question of why he didn't just get on and figure out how to do it alone, or pay for it to be done, in a way that would remain undiscovered. But his first impulse was to unburden himself – of what by now was barely secret.

He decided on Dmitri Pavlovich and Lt Sukh-otin. Sergei Sukh-otin, from the smart Preobrazhenski Regiment, was twenty-nine, like Yusupov, and currently convalescing in the Anglo-Russian Hospital from wounds received in action. Yusupov visited him practically every day.

Both agreed at once to participate in the plot. Yusupov dismissed a qualm of trepidation about 'the most distressing possibilities' that might arise from all this, as

I was buoyed up by the hope that the destruction of Rasputin would save the Tsar's family, and that the Emperor, roused from the spell which had been cast on him, would lead the country to a decisive victory at the head of his united people.

Somehow, all three of them convinced themselves that inside that weak little man was a valiant warrior, all ready to burst forth in shining armour brandishing the sword of freedom. Yusupov's inner hero was not much in evidence at the moment; Dmitri Pavlovich, who had to go back to the Stavka soon, was sure he was being drugged.

They arranged that when Dmitri next returned from the Stavka, between Saturday 10 December and Thursday 15 December, they would 'work out a detailed plan for Rasputin's destruction, and prepare everything for its fulfilment'.[9]

When Dmitri left Petrograd, the convalescent Sukhotin (who had been upstairs from Dmitri's in the Anglo-Russian Hospital all the time) paid Yusupov a visit 'at home' – possibly at the palace of his father-in-law, Grand Duke Alexander, where he was staying while the Yusupov Palace apartments were being finished; or, more likely, privately at the Yusupov Palace. They decided that Yusupov should get to know Rasputin better, and try to persuade or bribe him to go away from Tsarskoye Selo. But,

…we had to decide on the method to use in case this failed and we were obliged to resort to violence. I proposed that we cast lots to decide which of us would shoot the *starets*.[10]

Two meetings took place between Yusupov and Rasputin; the first on the pretext that Yusupov required healing, and the second because Rasputin wanted to hear gypsy music (which the Prince was still good at, despite no longer being a soprano). Then he had to work for an exam, and did not see Rasputin for a while, until Mounya Golovina insisted he go with her to Rasputin's flat.

When their car was quite close, she told the driver to stop around the corner, and explained to Felix that Okhrana men watched Rasputin round the clock and kept a record of visitors. Yusupov explained later that she 'knew how intensely my family disliked the *starets,* and spared no effort to keep my relations with him secret'.[11]

After the meeting at Gorokhovaya Street, Yusupov was sure that Rasputin was too comfortably set up to leave Petrograd of his own volition, and not at all in need of money; he could have as much as he wanted from people seeking positions of power. He went back to Rasputin's again, this time for a hands-on healing session. 'After this hypnotic séance I repeatedly went to him, sometimes with Mounya, sometimes alone.' He recounts Rasputin's boasting in detail and claims that Rasputin, drunk, told him,

> When it's all settled, we'll hail Alexandra as Regent for her young son and we'll send 'him' [the Tsar] to Livadia for a rest... There! Won't that be a treat for him? To be a market gardener! He's worn out... he must have a rest.[12]

At one point in this account mysterious strangers enter and Yusupov peeps from behind a door.

> Four of them were typically and unmistakeably Jewish in appear-ance. The remaining three were singularly alike; they were fair-haired, with red faces and small eyes.[13]

German spies, the lot of them! That settled it. Yusupov was now convinced that Rasputin 'was at the root of all the evil, and the primary cause of all the misfortunes which had befallen Russia'.

However he also perceived that, were Rasputin to be shot in his own flat, the Tsar would interpret his death as a 'demon-stration against the Tsar and his family'. The consequences that might arise from this are not stated. Yusupov, therefore, thought it would be best for Rasputin to disappear in such a way that assassination, rather than accidental murder, was not provable and no perpetrators could be discovered.

If he really wanted this, he had certainly failed to grasp that the more people knew about the murder, the more likely it was that he would be found out. And as if being overheard in the Fire Club was not bad enough, he proceeded to enlist more conspirators.

There had recently been two outbursts against Rasputin in the Duma: one from Maklakov, and one from Purishkevich (on 19 November). This was significant in that it was the first time that Rasputin had been openly denounced by name, as opposed to coded references such as 'Dark Forces'. Maklakov was a distinguished lawyer. Purishkevich was the same monarchist anti-Semite who before the war had so despised the Duma that he once attended a session wearing a flower in his fly-button. Since the Tsar had fallen under Rasputin's spell, Purishkevich had changed. He now saw the point of the Duma, and was an active member. With his loudly expressed disdain for 'titled riff-raff', as he called them, he had even attracted a popular following.

Yusupov resolved to go and see both of them. Maklakov was intrigued, but claimed a prior engagement. He did, however, encourage him with the gift of a truncheon.

Purishkevich was keen, although he pointed out at once that Rasputin was well guarded and it would be hard to get close to him. Yusupov explained that that aspect of the affair had already been sorted out. Purishkevich then suggested they also enlist the help of Dr Lazovert – the medical doctor of his military detachment, who would be a useful driver. Now they were five: Dmitri, Yusupov and Sukhotin the original conspirators, and Purishkevich and Lazovert the second rank.

Certain decisions were taken. The problem of gunshot noise and wounds was addressed. Rasputin would be poisoned by cyanide of potassium because 'poison was the surest means of killing him without leaving any trace of murder'. He would be lured to the basement dining room in Prince Yusupov's private apartment, which 'lent itself admirably to the accomplishment of our scheme'. It was at a distance from the rest of the palace, nobody could approach without being heard, the walls were thick and the windows high and small. And there was no way out.

The date of 16 December was chosen, as this was the date by which Princess Irina was expected back from the Crimea. Rasputin had always wanted to meet her. (It was also the day before Yusupov expected to *go* to the Crimea – he told different stories at different times – and the day before Purishkevich was to receive the entire Duma on his hospital train, but apparently neither would require cocoa and an early night).

Irina's real position in all this – she rather fades out of it in her husband's account – was that she didn't like it one bit, but if it was going to take place she had better be there. (Indeed, as a Romanov, she would be further back-up against police intrusion.) Her letter to Yusupov on 25 November makes her feelings clear:

> …Thanks for your insane letter. I didn't understand half of it. I see that you're planning to do something wild. Please be careful and don't stick your nose into all that dirty business. The dirtiest thing is that you have decided to do it all without me. I don't see how I can take part in it now, since it's all arranged. Who is 'M.Gol.'? I just realised what that means and who they are while writing this! In a word, be careful. I see from your letter that you're in a state of wild enthusiasm and ready to climb a wall… I'll be in Petrograd on the 12th or 13th, so don't dare to do anything without me, or else I won't come at all. Love and kisses. May the Lord protect you.[14]

Yusupov would invite Rasputin to the Moika on the promise of meeting Irina. 'You will serve as the lure',[15] he wrote back to her on 27 November. And Rasputin would cheerfully deceive his minders that night, as he did not want to make things awkward for his new friend Yusupov. He would know that if the Tsarina heard, from the Okhrana, that Yusupov was visiting Rasputin, then Yusupov's parents would sooner or later find out and be angry.

All went according to plan, but for one thing: Princess Irina, overwhelmed by trepidation or horror at the last moment, stayed in the Crimea. Yusupov kept this from Rasputin. He had agreed to come, and did not suspect anything was amiss. He told Yusupov to collect him from Gorokhovaya Street after midnight, when the minders had been dismissed, and to come in by the back door.

Purishkevich's account of Yusupov's approach to him, and of the night of the murder, is presented as a diary. He recounts his triumphant denunciation of 'Dark Forces' in the Duma on 19 November and the many congratulations he received then and on the following day. One of them, from Prince Yusupov, whom he did not know, he found particularly intriguing, and when the Prince visited him the next day in uniform ('evidently he is fulfilling his military obligation as an officer') Purishkevich

> was very much taken with both his external appearance, which radiated inexpressible elegance and breeding, and particularly with his inner self-possession. This is obviously a man of great will and character – rare qualities among Russians, especially those in aristocratic circles.[16]

He goes on to describe a meeting between himself, Sukhotin ('slow-moving but forceful') and Dmitri ('a tall, stately and handsome man'). In this company, Purishkevich, with his gleaming bald pate, thick black beard and black-rimmed pebble glasses, must have felt conspicuously out of his element.

According to him, Yusupov said Irina was in the Crimea and had no intention of returning, but Rasputin was being enticed to Yusupov's palace on the promise of her presence. They must now decide how to kill him, how to avoid suspicion, and how to get rid of the body. They all decided on poisoning: 'Yusupov's palace, which stands on the Moika Canal directly across from the police station, ruled out the use of a revolver.' Getting rid of the body was more difficult. They needed a driver and didn't want to use the servants. Hence 'Dr S Lazovert, an old [*sic*] doctor who had served with me for two years in my military unit' was to be roped in. Purishkevich made the first mention of time constraints. 'I intended to leave for Iasi on the Romanian front in the middle of December, once I had procured all the necessary supplies for my work in our army zone there.'

On the evening of 24 November, he and Lazovert, Yusupov, Dmitri Pavlovich and Sukhotin met at precisely ten o'clock in the library coach of his hospital train, which was parked in the freight section of the Warsaw Station.

> At this point Prince Yusupov showed us some potassium cyanide which he had obtained from V. Maklakov. Some of this was in the form of crystals and some in a solution contained in a small phial which he continued to shake during the whole time he was in the coach.
>
> Our conversation lasted almost two hours and together we worked out the following plan: on the appointed day, or rather night, we would all meet at Yusupov's at precisely midnight. At 12.30, having completed all the necessary preparations in Yusupov's dining room in the lower storey of the palace, we would go up to his study. At approximately one o'clock Yusupov would leave in my car to pick up Rasputin at Gorokhovaya. Dr Lazovert would be his chauffeur.

From then on, the plan was neither economical nor elegant. In the hands of men as undisciplined, intemperate and unpunctual as these, it bristled with opportunities for error and misunderstanding.

Lazovert was to drive Purishkevich's car into the courtyard of number 92 Moika and park close to the side door, so that Yusupov could take Rasputin straight into his wing of the palace and show him directly downstairs to his private dining room.

Lazovert would then take off the chauffeur's uniform he would be wearing and climb the staircase to Yusupov's study, where Dmitri Pavlovich, Purishkevich and Sukhotin awaited, ready to rush downstairs if things went wrong.

Within ten or fifteen minutes of arriving, Rasputin would have drunk poisoned Madeira and died. Prince Yusupov would report to the others, who would follow him downstairs and bundle up his clothes. Sukhotin, wearing Rasputin's overcoat, and Dmitri Pavlovich, with a bundle of other clothes, would then leave in the car. The car would be driven, as before, by Lazovert dressed as a chauffeur. He would take them to the hospital train where Mrs Lazovert and Mrs Purishkevich (who had not so far as we know been consulted on this point) would burn the clothes. Presumably this was intended to delay identification, were the body to be found. However, it never quite makes sense. Rasputin wore a selection of smocks hand-embroidered by the Tsarina, but it later transpires that only his outer clothing was ever meant to be burned.

Purishkevich's car would be loaded onto the train. Lazovert, Sukhotin and Dmitri Pavlovich would go 'by taxi or by foot' to the Sergei Palace on Nevski Prospekt (which is quite a distance from the Warsaw Station). There they would pick up Dmitri's car, again drive it into the courtyard and park it close to the wall, and go up to the study to collect Yusupov and Purishkevich.

Together they would descend to the basement dining room, truss Rasputin up like a mummy in 'some suitable material', heave him upstairs and drive with the body in Dmitri's car to a spot yet to be arranged, where they would drop it in the water. It would be bound with chains and 'two-pood weights'[17] to prevent it from resurfacing through a hole in the ice – although by now, the winter was so far advanced that finding some un-iced water in the first place was going to be the hard part.

They parted, Purishkevich having agreed to buy chains and weights at the Alexandrov market. On 28 November, Yusupov invited him to view the room where the dark deed was to be carried out. Purishkevich entered through the main entrance of 94 Moika, a baroque foyer designed on an appropriately palatial scale and illuminated by a blazing chandelier, the better to display a rich carpet laid on a pale marble floor which led up a wide marble staircase which divided and soared up out of sight under an exquisite moulded ceiling. It was the foyer through which glittering throngs of princes with medals and princesses afire with jewels customarily passed before making a grand entrance to the *enfilade* of reception rooms and galleries on the first floor.

But Purishkevich noticed none of it. Instead, he was horrified by the number of servants, and especially by the faithful Tesphé, an Ethiopian manservant Felix and Irina had picked up in Jerusalem.

> 'Listen, Prince,' I said, 'Surely this whole gang sitting in your hallway, headed by that liveried blackamoor, won't be around on the night of our reception for Rasputin?'

He was reassured that there would be only two men on duty, and they would be in the main palace, not in Felix's wing. The rest of the servants would have the night off 'including the blackamoor'. As for the basement dining room, currently a chaos of builders' gubbins and workmen installing electricity, he could see its thick walls and scant windows would make it perfect for their purposes because 'even if shots had to be fired from there, the sound of their report would not be heard in the street'.

He asked Maklakov to participate. Maklakov said he would be in Moscow on and around the projected date but he would act in their defence if required. He asked Purishkevich to send a telegram when the assassination had been carried out successfully; the message would be 'When are you arriving?'

On 29 November, Purishkevich took his wife with him to Alexandrov market to help carry the weights and the chains back. They carried them carefully onto the train so that the crew would not get curious. (It is hard to imagine a well-born, well-dressed St Petersburg lady lifting so much as a Fabergé egg, far less staggering, red-faced, across the goods yard with a 16-kilo weight – but she was a nurse. And she had put up with Purishkevich for many years, indicative in itself of considerable grit.) They hid their booty in the pharmacy and behind books in the library coach. Purishkevich spent the afternoon being driven around by Lazovert 'examining every ice-hole in the Neva and in the little streams and bogs around Petrograd'. They found just two that were suitable. One was on a canal that ran from the Fontanka to the Tsarskoye Selo station; it was badly lit at night. The other was outside the city limits, on 'the old Neva' by the bridge across to the Islands.

The following day,

> I saw the costume Dr Lazovert acquired today on my orders for 600 roubles: a chauffeur's fur coat, a sort of Astrakhan cap with ear flaps, and chauffeur's gloves. Lazovert modelled all of these for me, looking like a typical chauffeur – foppish and impudent. For the time being he took all these purchases to the Astoria Hotel, where he stays during our visits to Petrograd.

The next decision was serious. They had to fit the murder into their busy schedules. Yusupov and Dmitri Pavlovich wanted to have it over with by 12 December, but Dmitri's diary was full until Friday 16 December. In passing, Yusupov told them (as his own account confirms) that Rasputin had offered to get him a job in government.

> 'And what did you say to that?' the Grand Duke asked, throwing him a meaningful look while taking a drag on his cigarette.
>
> 'I?' replied Yusupov, who lowered his gaze and, fluttering his eyelashes, assumed an ironically languid look, 'I modestly informed him that I consider myself too young, inexperienced and unprepared for service in the administrative field, but that I was gratified beyond belief that one so well known for his perspicacity as Grigori Efimovich should have such a flattering opinion of me.'
>
> We all burst out laughing.

They were concerned that Rasputin might tell his Okhrana minders where he was going. To deflect suspicion, they decided that after the clothes had been taken for burning to the hospital train, Sukhotin would telephone the Villa Rhode from a phone booth in the Warsaw Station. He would ask whether Rasputin was there, and on being told that he wasn't, would be overheard saying 'He's not there yet. That means he'll be arriving any minute.' So that if they were later asked whether Rasputin had been at the Yusupov Palace they would say yes, he came and later left for the Villa Rhode.

They were swept along on a tide of bravado. Plan A could go wrong at any juncture; but there was no Plan B.

On Tuesday 13 December they met for the last time. 'Vanya has arrived', the telephone signal, summoned them to the Yusupov Palace. Friday 16 December was to be the night. Another refinement was bolted onto the plan: a gramophone was to be put in the lobby outside the study, on the floor above the basement dining room. It would drown the voices of the men and make Rasputin understand that he must wait for the Princess Irina who, he would be told, was entertaining some ladies upstairs. And Yusupov showed them the sort of Indian club, or 'two-pound rubber dumb-bell like those used for indoor gymnastics' he had got from Maklakov and was keeping 'just in case'.

On the day before the murder, a Thursday, with Purishkevich and his family no longer living in their town apartment but having moved into the hospital train,

> Dr Lazovert having bought a brush, khaki paint, and dressed in a leather apron, spent all day today on the car which will serve us tomorrow night to fetch our exalted guest. All the cars in my detachment have inscribed on them, in large red letters, SEMPER IDEM, my motto. This inscription... could be that clue that could immediately lead the authorities to the Yusupov Palace and to my train.

Quite. Temperatures well below freezing are not generally the best for allowing paint to dry; but no matter. And Dr Lazovert, busily daubing icy coachwork in the freight area of the Warsaw Station, did look a little conspicuous. 'The train crew crowded round him', asking questions. He told them he was off on a spree to the Islands tomorrow night, and didn't want the car to be spotted – the motto could be painted on again later, en route for Romania.

Purishkevich gave his staff Friday night off, to get them out of the way. He was perfectly satisfied there was no circumstantial evidence to link him with Rasputin's murder.

Purishkevich's *Diary* was published in Russia in 1918 and in Paris in 1923, when, its author having died, Maklakov was asked for his comments before publication.

Maklakov was now living in Paris. He had served as Ambassador to France under the Provisional Government in 1917. His letter makes certain points which are worth bearing in mind. One thing he very much doubted was the dates. As for the bits he was certain of, because he was there, they are all wrong in essential aspects.

> Purishkevich's diary is not a diary at all. It is merely the literary form he chose for his memoirs... This story of Purishkevich's is a nonsensical mixture of various conversations which took place at different times and even with different people, about which Purishkevich could only have learned at second hand...
>
> I remember his first approach to me and even my surprise at it – a surprise related exclusively to the fact that *Purishkevich* was in the plot... Purishkevich told me the names of the participants, the *day* of the murder and that was all... I would never have talked to Purishkevich about it, since I did not consider him to be serious enough nor especially discreet enough for such an undertaking.

It seems that Yusupov approached Maklakov first, and got a dusty answer; then he asked Purishkevich, who agreed to participate; and then went to see Maklakov again and was given a truncheon (according to Yusupov). This Maklakov did not deny, but as to the potassium cyanide,

> It was not I who gave Yusupov potassium cyanide, or more pre-
> cisely, what to Yusupov passed for potassium cyanide – had it
> been genuine no amount of hardiness on Rasputin's part would
> have saved him.[18]

At the very least, Yusupov had told Irina, Purishkevich, Maklakov
and Rodzyanko; Pavlovich had told Stopford and Purishkevich
had told Hoare in November. Purishkevich had also enlisted
Lazovert, who had told the train crew he was going to the Islands.
Purishkevich was a blabbermouth, as were Dmitri Pavlovich and
Yusupov. If this murder were to take place, it would be a miracle
if all eyes did not turn in their direction. Yusupov was a tad worried about his legal position if he got caught, and Maklakov was
a distinguished lawyer.

> Just before the murder the participant, with whom I happened to
> talk, began to beg me urgently not to leave Petersburg on the day
> of the murder but to be there in case my advice might be needed.
> I will emphasise that… I did not suggest at any time to any of
> the participants that I would be their *defender at a trial*.[19]

Maklakov made it clear, he later wrote, that while he thought it
impossible that the perpetrators would be tried, as it would be
'too upsetting for Russia', on the other hand 'to allow obvious
murderers to go unpunished would also be impossible'.

> Therefore it was their duty to act in such a way that they would
> not be discovered. In essence this would not be difficult since
> the authorities, understanding the significance of the affair, would
> hardly try to find the murderers. They need only *make it possi-
> ble* that they not be discovered. Therefore the conspirators must
> refrain from any vainglorious urge to reveal themselves, must brag
> to no one, and on no account should they confess.[20]

Maklakov was close to putting off his prior appointment, which
was a speaking engagement at the Law Society in Moscow,

but found at the last moment that he couldn't; he must catch a train out of town. He happened to meet Purishkevich at the Duma late in the afternoon of Friday 16 December, and told him to pass on that message to Yusupov. It was now, he said, that Purishkevich agreed to send him a telegram 'if the affair ended successfully'.

NINE

A ROOM IN THE BASEMENT

The Yusupov Palace at 94 Moika had a long, high façade with twenty-six windows on each floor and a six-column Tuscan portico extending up to the second storey; high above this was a central attic carrying the Yusupov coat of arms. The façade ran along the pavement of the narrow road alongside the canal. At the back, projecting wings enclosed a colonnaded courtyard on two sides with a carriage entrance onto a street at the rear.

Adjoining the palace at the eastern side was a much more subdued building, number 92, also owned by the Yusupovs. It stood back about twelve metres from the façade of number 94. In front of it was a cobbled courtyard with handsome street railings made out of solid timber in the Russian style, having three sets of double gates along their course. Two of the sets of gates had high ornamental gateposts.

Prince Yusupov and Princess Irina had been having their private apartment in the eastern side of the palace remodelled since they married two years before; the work was still incomplete. Felix was at this time refurbishing his own set of private rooms within this partment, near the road alongside the Moika Canal. He would use them whenever he came to St Petersburg without his wife and baby. The ground-floor rooms were slightly above ground level. They were accessible from within the main palace, or from a small private door set centrally in the wall of the east wing overlooking the courtyard of number 92. This door opened onto the dog-leg landing of a narrow stairway. Six stairs led up to a large study with windows overlooking both the courtyard of number 92 and the canal, and more stairs led down to a roomy, vaulted basement, the street end of which had been converted into a dining room. Here, almost below ground, the front windows were small, set high in the walls, and gave onto the road at pavement level. The back windows were similarly small and high and gave onto the courtyard.

The small door, the basement dining room, the upper-ground-floor study, the windows and the courtyard figure crucially in the events of the night of the murder.

The Ministry of the Interior and its adjoining police station stood no more than fifty metres from the façade of number 94, across the frozen Moika Canal. On the east side of number 92, at right angles to the Moika, is Prachesni Lane. The temperature on the night of 16 December was well below freezing; snow was falling at least some of the time, certainly between the time of any activity in the courtyard and the time when the three police scene of crime photographs were taken at around midday on Saturday 17 December.

What happened in the basement room of number 92 Moika in the early hours of 17 December 1916, and who was ultimately responsible for the death of Grigori Rasputin, has been the subject of many theories over the years. With the wealth of original investigation documents and testimonies, the 1916 autopsy evidence, the subsequent forensic reviews and the new evidence, which has only recently come to light, we can now begin to eliminate some of the more fanciful and intangible accounts that have muddied the waters over the past nine decades.

The Police Department Report, written on 17 December, was compiled from police interviews the morning after the affair. It states[1] that at half-past two on the Saturday morning, the policeman on guard at the Interior Ministry across the canal from the Yusupov Palace heard 'a detonation' from the palace. The terms of his duty did not allow him to leave his post, so he went into the Ministry and phoned the Duty Sergeant at the police station next door. The police station notified the District Office, and the Chief Police Officer, Colonel Rogov, went to the palace with a detachment of men. They made enquiries of the janitor at the palace and were told that 'the shot' had been fired from the Prince's wing. Rogov's assistant, Krylov, entered the building (presumably the main palace) and was told by the butler that there was a party going on, and one of the guests had aimed at a target but hit a window. He was shown 'the broken window on the ground floor overlooking the forecourt of the adjoining house'. Rogov reported back to his senior officer, Grigoriev, and to an official on duty at the Prefecture.

> Scarcely had the police officers left the palace when a motor-car drove up along the Moika Canal quay and stopped near a small foot-bridge almost facing the palace. Four men were seen to alight from the car. The moment they had left it the chauffeur extinguished the lights, and putting on full speed, made off along the canal. This scene was witnessed by a detective belonging to the Okhrana, named Tihomirov, who had been detailed by the Police Department to look after Rasputin.

The men did not go into the palace through its main entrance. They entered through Yusupov's private door from the courtyard of number 92.

Tikhomirov thought they were robbers, ran across the canal to the police station, and telephoned the Chief of the Okhrana. Colonel Rogov, having put in his report and gone home, got there only to be alerted to the 'attack' on the palace by the Okhrana (Rogov, as a senior officer, would no doubt

have had a telephone at home). He sent some police officers there, and the butler came out and told them that 'some
very highly placed guests had just arrived from the environs
of Petrograd'. The policemen went back and put in a report
to the Governor of Petrograd, General Balk. Shortly after
six o'clock in the morning, when the policemen going off duty
were, as was their routine, answering questions about the events
of the night, 'the sound of several police whistles was heard from
the street'. They all rushed to the police station windows and
saw that from the main entrance to the palace 'two women were
being helped out, and that they were offering resistance to their
ejection and refusing to enter a motor-car, and doing their best
to force a way back into the palace'.

The police had blown their whistles in response to the protestations of the women, but by the time the police rushed out
to assist, 'the motor-car was already whirling off along the quay'.
Rushing out in pursuit of his men, their senior officer Colonel
Borozhdin 'hailed the motor-car belonging to the secret police,
which was permanently on duty at the Home Office building, and started off in pursuit'. His men ran to the palace. They
were told that the two women had been *demi-mondaines* who
were 'misconducting themselves' and had been asked to leave.
Borozhdin's car was not fast enough to catch the other one,
'which carried neither number nor lights'. He returned, and he
and Rogov (who must by now have needed some sleep) put in
a joint report 'in the morning' to General Balk, about the events
of the night.

The whole affair seemed to be at an end when suddenly from
the forecourt alongside the palace four shots were heard in rapid
succession. Once more the alarm was sounded in both police stations, and again detachments of police appeared at the palace. This
time an official wearing colonel's uniform came out to them and
announced categorically that within the Prince's palace there was
present a Grand Duke, and that HIH would make in person to the
proper quarters any explanations that might be necessary.

Thus dismissed, the police retreated to base, leaving a patrol on the palace side of the canal. An hour later, a car drove up from the direction of the Blue Bridge.

> The servants, assisted by the chauffeur, in the presence of an officer wearing a long fur cloak, carried out what looked like a human body and placed it in the car. The chauffeur jumped in, and putting on full speed, made off along the canal side and promptly disappeared. Almost at the same time General Grigoriev was informed from the Prefecture that Rasputin had been killed in the Yusupov Palace.

Meanwhile, another party of policemen arrived at the palace. Soon afterwards, the palace was visited by 'the Director of the Police Department, the Chief of the Okhrana, and all the Generals of Gendarmerie'. In the course of the day, all the police patrols were questioned. At five o'clock on Saturday afternoon, a secret telegram went to every police station in the city asking about the cars that had been seen overnight; the idea was to find out where they had come from and gone to. Patrols were sent to the Islands 'and to the suburban districts'.

While the Police Report is clearly of the view that a murder had taken place at the Yusupov Palace during the course of the previous night, and that Rasputin was the likely victim, it points no fingers in terms of culpability. The only names mentioned in the report, in the sense of circumstantial involvement, are Yusupov and an unnamed Grand Duke.

The following day, however, a privately circulated memorandum, thought to have been written by Albert Stopford,[2] gained widespread circulation among the British community. Unlike the Police Report, this story was not short on names.

According to this account, Rasputin was shot in a room in the basement of the Yusupov Palace shortly after seven o'clock on the Saturday morning. Grand Duke Dmitri Pavlovich, Prince Fyodor and Prince Nikita, who were Princess Irina's brothers, and Felix Yusupov were all present. They and others, including the sons of the late Grand Duke Konstantin, had made the general decision some time earlier to remove Rasputin because his behaviour was bringing the empire and the Romanovs into disrepute. There were many rumours, as far back as the previous Monday, that one of the sons of Grand Duke Konstantin had been chosen by lot to carry out the murder, but he had 'hesitated' and it had been postponed.

Rasputin often met Yusupov and his brothers-in-law and other young Romanovs at the Yusupov Palace; at these meetings, when drunk, he would talk about goings-on in the imperial circle and ministerial changes. Only with the sudden prorogation of the Duma on 16 December was the decision finally made; the others thought Rasputin was partly responsible. So that he would not be suspicious, they invited 'some of Rasputin's lady friends' that night.

From the Police Report of 17 December and from other information gained by reporters on the staff of *Novoe Vremya*, it appeared that at half-past two in the morning Rasputin was told he must die, and was given the option of shooting himself or being shot. A revolver was given to him and he fired it in the general direction of Dmitri Pavlovich. It smashed a pane of glass and the police heard it. Rasputin was then killed and his body removed to a place unknown, presumably Tsarskoye Selo.

This account seems to have drawn together the numerous rumours and tales, from a wide variety of sources, that were circulating around Petrograd during the twenty-four hours following the incident at the Yusupov Palace. By the very nature of its immediacy, the memorandum contains a number of statements that had had no opportunity for verification on the part of the writer. Furthermore, it is claimed that Rasputin often met Yusupov and Princes Fyodor and Nikita Romanov at the Yusupov Palace. However, detailed Okhrana observation reports of Rasputin's movements show conclusively that his fatal visit on the night of the murder was the first and last he made to the palace.

While we shall consider Yusupov's detailed 1927 account of the murder in the next chapter, we should perhaps remind ourselves that this was, in fact, the third version of events he had offered up by way of explanation, the two previous versions being the interviews he gave to the authorities on 17 and 18 December 1916 and the account he gave to Albert Stopford at Yalta on 6 June 1917, which Stopford wrote down and entitled 'The True and Authentic Story of the Murder of Grigori Rasputin'.[3]

In the version he related to Stopford, Rasputin was only with great difficulty persuaded to come to the palace. Yusupov had scheduled the murder for 16 December, as he was going to the Crimea the following evening. There was no supper party upstairs at 92 Moika, just Dmitri Pavlovich and Purishkevich. (Stopford could not get Yusupov to admit that a couple of women were also present, though, having seen the Police Report, he believed they were). Neither the Grand Duke Dmitri Pavlovich nor Purishkevich saw Rasputin while he was within the palace. In the basement dining room, Rasputin, during the course of conversation, 'positively asserted' that the Tsarina intended to make herself Regent on 10 January.

Rasputin apparently drank the poisoned Madeira, although Yusupov, as 'a total abstainer' drank nothing. The poison had been bought three weeks earlier and had lost its strength, resulting in Rasputin merely experiencing drowsiness. Yusupov then went upstairs to borrow Purishkevich's revolver. Downstairs, he shot Rasputin through the left side below the ribs, and left him on the bearskin rug. Stopford points out that the Police Report 'makes it evident that this was the moment when the ladies who had been entertained in the *salon* on the ground floor were persuaded to leave the palace'. Yusupov then went downstairs to check that Rasputin was dead, only to find that his eyes were not only wide open, but gleaming 'with tiger-like fury'. Rasputin then leapt up 'with amazing vitality', seized Yusupov by the throat and tried to strangle him. He succeeded only in pulling off Yusupov's epaulettes before making off upstairs and through the unlocked door to the courtyard, where he fell exhausted in the snow. Yusupov rushed up to call Purishkevich, who came out and fired four shots at Rasputin.

Two missed, one went into the back of the head and one into the forehead.

The body was then carried back into the house to await the return of the car (presumably after removing the women). It was put into the car and driven out to Kristovski Island and thrown into a hole in the ice of the Little Neva. Yusupov went to the Sergei Palace with Dmitri Pavlovich and stayed there, while it was given out that he had left for the Crimea.

Stopford is careful not to examine the obvious anomalies in this account, such as the inquest's finding or common-sense ballistics, which make nonsense of Yusupov's claim that the two wounds caused by Purishkevich's shots were in the back of the head and in the forehead. The Autopsy Report and the autopsy photographs make it clear that there were three bullet wounds; one to the left-hand side of the chest, a second to the right-hand side of the back, and the third to the forehead.[4]

By contrast, Rasputin's family tell a very different version of events.[5] According to Rasputin's daughter Maria, Yusupov asked Rasputin to accompany him back to his palace as his wife Irina had a severe headache. When they arrive at the palace, Yusupov tells Rasputin that Irina 'is having a party… she somehow manages to get through even though her headaches are so painful'.[6] Yusupov suggests that they wait in the downstairs room, where he offers Rasputin the poisoned wine, cakes, bonbons and sweatmeats. Rasputin, who 'had never cared for sweets',[7] declines the food but accepts the Madeira. When Rasputin becomes impatient of waiting any longer for Irina, Yusupov says he will go upstairs and get her. Instead he returns, with a pistol given to him by Dmitri Pavlovich, followed by Dr Lazovert, Dmitri Pavlovich, 'two other men',[8] Sukhotin and Purishkevich. Rasputin is then attacked *en masse* by the seven men. As he struggles to get up off the floor, Yusupov fires a single shot into his head and Rasputin falls backwards onto a white bearskin fur rug. There follows an even more severe beating, after which they leave him for dead and return to the study above. While there, they hear noises on the stairs and rush out to find that Rasputin is not only still alive but has managed to crawl up the stairs and through the side door into the yard outside.

Purishkevich then runs out into the yard in pursuit and fires four shots, although the account does not say how many hit Rasputin or where. The body is then taken away by car to Petrovski Island and thrown into the river. Despite his serious wounds, Rasputin is apparently still alive when he hits the water and dies from drowning. Of all the rival accounts, this one is most at odds with the forensic facts. The Autopsy Report not only concludes that the shot to the forehead was the third shot, not the first, but affirms that, although there was a small amount of water in the lungs, he did not die from drowning.[9] One of the two 'other men' is named as Paul Stepanov, although no one by this name was known to be an associate of Yusupov or indeed anyone else even vaguely connected with the story. The claim that Rasputin did not eat the food is, however, supported by the Autopsy Report, and was one of the issues taken up by Russian historian and playwright Edvard Radzinski eighty-four years after the murder in his biography *Rasputin – The Last Word*.[10] While Radzinski's account is very much in line with the facts of the case, he offers a very different ending to the traditionally accepted story.

According to Radzinski, Yusupov shot Rasputin in the chest with Dmitri Pavlovich's Browning pistol. Having left him for dead in the basement dining room, the conspirators returned to the study upstairs to celebrate with the two women whose presence was referred to in the initial Police Report. It was then decided that the two ladies should be taken home, and they were taken down the staircase to the small doorway and out to the car by Dmitri Pavlovich. While all this was going on, Yusupov had gone down to the basement and discovered Rasputin was not dead. Rushing back up the stairs he shouted, 'Shoot! He's getting away!' By this time, Rasputin had regained consciousness, crawled up the staircase and made a last-ditch attempt to flee across the courtyard. Purishkevich ran out behind him and fired two shots, both of which missed. Fortunately, Dmitri

Pavlovich was already in the courtyard and fired two shots with the Browning pistol that had been returned to him by Yusupov – 'the first shot brought Rasputin to a halt; the second one, in the back of the head, laid him out on the wet snow'.[11]

According to Radzinski, it was Dmitri Pavlovich who had the most convincing personal motives for killing Rasputin – it was Rasputin who had ruined the prospects of him marrying the Grand Duchess Olga, the Tsar's daughter, by telling Nicholas of his homosexuality. It was also Rasputin who had caused a rift in the Romanov family in which he had grown up and also in his father's immediate family.[12] As impeccable as the motives sited by Radzinski are, the theory again falls flat when confronted by the forensic evidence.

If Dmitri Pavlovich had indeed fired the second and third shots with the same Browning pistol that he had initially lent to Yusupov to fire the first shot, then one would expect all three bullet wounds to have been caused by bullets of the same calibre. However, the Autopsy Report, as we have already noted, states quite clearly that 'the bullets came from revolvers of various calibre'.[13] Furthermore, the Autopsy Report and accompanying photographs show that the bullet wound to the head 'hit the victim on the forehead',[14] and not 'in the back of the head'[15] as maintained by Radzinski. Most persuasive of all, in terms of eliminating this theory, are the conclusions of subsequent forensic reviews of the 1916 autopsy evidence, the most recent of which[16] indicates that the fatal forehead wound could not have been inflicted by the Browning pistol Dmitri Pavlovich had in his possession that night.

In the same year that Radzinski published his *Last Word* biography, another Russian playwright, Oleg Shishkin, also published a book,[17] setting out his views on Rasputin's murder. Shishkin began by examining the rumours abounding at the time of the murder that there had been British involvement. Drawing on Sir George Buchanan's account of his audience with the Tsar during which Nicholas's suspicions regarding the involvement of a British subject were aired, he began the search for the unnamed individual. He eventually concluded that Lt-Col. Sir Samuel Hoare, the Head of the British Intelligence Mission, was the mysterious college friend of Yusupov, and that he had fired the fatal shot into Rasputin's forehead. Shishkin correctly deduced that Purishkevich's account of firing the fatal shot from behind was not compatible with the autopsy evidence. Shishkin further hypothesised that, having been told by Purishkevich of the intention to 'liquidate' Rasputin, Hoare turned up at the Yusupov Palace on the night of the murder and entered by the side door of number 92.[18] Having been shown Rasputin's corpse by Yusupov, Hoare then supposedly left by the unlocked side door through which he had entered. This, in Shishkin's view, gave Rasputin a last-ditch opportunity for escape. When Hoare was almost at the gate, Rasputin came running out of the unlocked door into the courtyard, pursued at a distance by Purishkevich. His failed attempts to hit Rasputin from behind left Hoare with no alternative. In order to prevent Rasputin's escape, he fired at the figure looming towards him out of the shadows, fatally hitting him in the forehead.

In addition to the serious doubts that must be raised (and which will be further explored in chapter 11) as to whether Rasputin was ever physically able to leave the basement dining room, climb the stairs and run or stagger across the courtyard, the identity of Hoare as the mystery man must also be seriously questioned.

Hoare was indeed an Oxford University graduate like Yusupov, although an inspection of New College, Oxford records shows that Hoare matriculated in October 1899 and graduated in Classics in 1901 and Modern History in 1903. Yusupov, by comparison, matriculated in October 1909 and graduated in 1912. They were not, therefore, college friends or indeed contemporaries – in fact, there is no evidence that Hoare and Yusupov ever met at any time in their lives, let alone at university.

As we have already noted, while Hoare was indeed informed of the plot by Purishkevich, he did not take it seriously. On the night of the murder he was apparently at home with his wife and dinner guests.[19] Although invited by the police to see Rasputin's body following its discovery, Hoare did not, as Shishkin claims, actually accept the invitation, due to a bout of recurring illness.[20]

Having considered the versions of events proffered by those who were not present on the night of the murder, we must now turn directly to compare the accounts of three individuals who, by their own admission, were present and playing an active part in the events that took place – Yusupov, Purishkevich and Lazovert.

TEN

Once Upon a Time

In 1918, V.M. Purishkevich published his account of the murder of Rasputin in Russian, and after his death this was republished in Paris in 1923. Purishkevich's *Diary* sheds a far from flattering light on the events of the night, but it seems the word 'incompetent' was not in his lexicon. He begins his tale early in the evening of Friday 16 December. He has been in the hospital train, reading, all day, a statement which does not tally with Maklakov's assertion that he met Purishkevich in the Duma late that afternoon, but no matter.

He intended to leave the Warsaw Station at half-past eight that evening, and catch a tram to a meeting of the Town Duma. There he would stay, 'in order to kill time', until a quarter to midnight, when Dr Lazovert, in his chauffeur's uniform, would pick him up at the Duma watchtower for the drive to the Yusupov Palace. Just in case, at seven o'clock, he pocketed his Savage revolver and a brass knuckleduster.

He set off late; he left the station at half-past nine, and took the short ride by tram only to find the Town Duma building empty and the hall unlit. A quorum had failed to assemble, so the meeting had been abandoned. Making the best of things, he got the janitor to open up the Deputy Mayor's office so that he could write some letters and wait for Lazovert.

He spent an hour on his letters, but at a quarter to eleven had nothing left to do. He did not want to hang around in the street outside wearing military uniform.

> I decided to spend the rest of the time on the telephone and, calling a lady-friend of mine, the actress N., I chatted with her until after eleven.
>
> To stay any longer in the Duma, however, would have been awkward, so I put on my coat and went out to the sidewalk. As the clock in the Duma tower struck 11.15, I dropped my letters into a mailbox and began to stroll along the side streets near the Duma. The weather was mild. It was no more than two or three degrees below zero and a light, moist snow was falling.[1]

He dawdled. Minutes passed 'like an eternity to me', and at the appointed time there was no sign of Lazovert. When the car did turn up, more than five minutes late, he was cross, and shouted at the doctor, who said he'd had a puncture.

They drove to the Yusupov Palace. The courtyard of number 92 had an iron [*sic*] grille fence separating it from the street, and two pairs of iron gates... which nobody had remembered to open.

Thinking they must be too early, Purishkevich and Lazovert drove on, circled around Mariinski Theatre Square, and came back to the palace down Prachesni Lane. The gates were still shut.

Purishkevich, who was already on a short fuse, had had enough. They pulled up outside the towering central doors of the palace.

> I rang. A soldier opened the door to me and, without taking off my overcoat, but looking around to see who else was in the foyer

(there was one other man dressed in a soldier's uniform sitting on a bench, but no-one else), I turned to the door on the left and went into the apartment occupied by young Yusupov.[2]

He stomped in and found Yusupov, Sukhotin and Dmitri Pavlovich in the study. They accused Purishkevich of being late; this did not have a calming effect. Yusupov went away to have the gates opened, and shortly afterwards Lazovert appeared in his chauffeur's coat, having now been able to park the car, according to plan, close to the courtyard door. They all trooped downstairs to the dining room, where the tea table was 'abundantly spread with cakes and other delights'. The basement room was unrecognisable in its new, tastefully furnished state. They ate and drank slowly, aware that Yusupov must not leave until after half-past midnight to collect Rasputin. They disarrayed the table to make it look as if a party of ladies had been disturbed 'by the arrival of an unexpected guest' and had left hurriedly. Then they turned their attention to the poison. Dr Lazovert put on gloves 'which Yusupov had procured' and grated potassium cyanide 'pieces' onto a plate with a knife. There were two kinds of cake, sandwiched with either a pink or a chocolate mixture. Lifting the top halves of the pink ones, he concealed cyanide inside. Other pink cakes were cut and left as if half-eaten on the plates. Lazovert then burned the gloves. The chimney began to smoke. 'We had to spend at least another ten minutes clearing the air.'

Once they were upstairs in the drawing room,

> Yusupov took two phials of potassium cyanide in solution from his desk and gave one to Dmitri Pavlovich and one to me. Twenty minutes after Yusupov had left to pick up Rasputin we were to pour these into two of the four glasses sitting behind the bottles on the table in the dining room below.[3]

By twenty-five to one, Lazovert in his chauffeur's uniform and Yusupov in his coat with its upturned collar had left. Sukhotin went to see if the gramophone worked. Purishkevich put his heavy Savage pistol on the table. They were all quiet, and worried about whether they could smoke, for the smell of cigars or cigarettes would make Rasputin suspicious. Here Purishkevich points out for the first time that Rasputin had insisted that no other men be present on the night he came to the palace.

Purishkevich and Dmitri Pavlovich went downstairs to doctor the wine glasses. Upstairs again, they waited, and, when the car was heard, Sukhotin set the gramophone and started to play *Yankee Doodle* – 'a tune which haunts me even now'.

On the other hand, we have Yusupov's point of view.

The fateful day arrived. This was to be murder *de luxe*. Our hero, a set designer *manqué*, returned in the afternoon from his in-laws' palace down the road to spend a blissful afternoon supervising the arrangement of furniture in the vaulted basement.

> Arches divided it in two; the larger half was to be used as a dining-room. From the other half, the staircase… led to my rooms on the floor above…. The walls were of grey stone, the flooring of granite…
>
> When I arrived, I found workmen busy laying down carpets and putting up curtains. Three large red Chinese porcelain vases had already been placed in niches hollowed out of the walls. Various objects which I had selected were being carried in: carved wooden chairs of oak, small tables covered with ancient embroideries, ivory bowls, and a quantity of other curios… I have good reason to remember a certain cabinet of inlaid ebony which was a mass of little mirrors, tiny bronze columns and secret drawers. On it stood a crucifix of rock crystal and silver, a beautiful specimen of sixteenth-century Italian workmanship. On the red granite mantelpiece were placed golden bowls, antique majolica plates and a sculptured ivory group. A large Persian carpet covered the floor and, in a corner, in front of the ebony cabinet, lay a white bear-skin rug.

In the middle of the room stood the table at which Rasputin was to drink his last cup of tea.

My two servants… helped me to arrange the furniture. I asked them to prepare tea for six, to buy biscuits and cakes and to bring wine from the cellar. I told them that I was expecting some friends at eleven that evening, and that they could wait in the servants' hall until I rang for them.[4]

He spent much of the evening praying at the Cathedral of Our Lady of Kazan. When he came back, he was delighted by the effect his efforts had produced:

Comfortably furnished and well lighted, this underground room had lost its grim look. On the table the samovar smoked, surrounded by plates filled with the cakes and dainties that Rasputin liked so much. An array of bottles and glasses stood on a sideboard. Ancient lanterns of coloured glass lighted the room from the ceiling; the heavy red damask *portières* were lowered. On the granite hearth, a log fire crackled and scattered sparks on the flag-stones. One felt isolated from the rest of the world and it seemed as though, no matter what happened, the events of that night would remain forever buried in the silence of those thick walls.[5]

It must have been a comforting thought.

A bell rang; Dmitri Pavlovich and the others had arrived. Once they were in the basement dining room, Yusupov took 'a box containing poison' from a cupboard and the cakes from the table. Three were iced with chocolate and three with almond icing. Dr Lazovert put on rubber gloves and took out potassium cyanide crystals. He crushed the crystals and 'sprinkled' them under the chocolate icing.

They would put potassium cyanide crystals into the glasses later, in case the poison evaporated. Dr Lazovert 'assured us that the dose was many times stronger than would be required to cause death'. They disarranged the room. Lazovert and Yusupov left; the others would go upstairs later. Dr Lazovert changed into chauffeur's uniform and went to start the car, while Yusupov put on a fur coat and hat.

Arriving at Gorokhovaya Street, Yusupov had a brief exchange with the yard man and went up the back stairs in pitch darkness. Rasputin led him in, through the kitchen. Yusupov felt someone was watching him 'from the adjoining room'. After that night, Yusupov was the only living witness of what followed:

> We went into his bedroom, which was partly lit by a lamp in the corner, in front of the ikons. Rasputin applied a match to a candle. I noticed that the bed was disarranged – he had evidently just been resting. His fur coat and beaver hat were in readiness. On the floor were a pair of snow boots.
>
> He was dressed in a white silk blouse embroidered with corn-flowers and girded with a thick raspberry-coloured cord with large tassels, wide trousers of black velvet, and long boots, brand new. Even his hair and beard were carefully combed and smoothed. As he drew nearer to me I felt a strong smell of cheap soap. He had obviously paid special attention to his toilet that day; I had never before seen him so clean and tidy.[6]

Rasputin began to talk about going on to the gypsies. He was worried in case Yusupov's mother would be there; he knew she disliked him. And then he said

> And what d'you think? Protopopov drove round here this evening and made me promise that I'd stay at home during these next few days. 'They want to kill you,' he said. 'Evil-minded people are plotting against you.'

Dismissing this warning, he decided to go with Yusupov anyway. Before he left he opened a chest full of money in bundles wrapped in newspaper. He talked about his daughter's wedding. He blew out the candle and they left.

After a momentary qualm, Yusupov regained his courage as they headed for the Yusupov Palace.

They drew up at the side entrance and Yusupov took Rasputin through the little door. At once Rasputin heard an American song playing on the gramophone above and asked whether a party was going on. Yusupov told him that Irina was entertaining friends and would join them soon. He took him down to the dining room.

The visitor refused tea and coffee. They sat at the table discussing mutual friends – the Golovinas and Vyrubova. After a while, Yusupov gave him tea and biscuits. Later, the cakes. Rasputin didn't want any of those; they were too sweet, he said.

Finally, he ate the whole plateful. They had no effect at all.

Yusupov urged him to try some Crimean wine. At first he gave him wine from a clean glass, and only later, after he had switched to Madeira, did he trick him into drinking from a glass that had crystals in the bottom.

> …he drank slowly, taking small sips at a time, just as if he had been a connoisseur.
>
> His face did not change; but from time to time he put his hand to his throat as if he found slight difficulty in swallowing.

Three glasses of Madeira later, Rasputin was still waiting for Irina's party to finish and they sat facing each other in silence. Yusupov thought his victim just might have caught on.

> A mute and deadly conflict seemed to be taking place between us. I was aghast. Another moment and I should have gone under. I felt that confronted by those satanic eyes, I was beginning to lose my self-control. A strange feeling of numbness took possession of me. My head reeled… I saw nothing… I do not know how long this lasted…

Yusupov pulled himself together and offered Rasputin a cup of tea; Rasputin accepted, saying he was thirsty. Then he asked Yusupov to play his guitar and sing, which he did… and another song, and another. Soon 'the hands of the clock pointed to half past two'. And there was a lot of noise from upstairs. Yusupov went up to investigate.

Meanwhile, the others had been eavesdropping (we revert to Purishkevich's point of view). No sooner had Lazovert the 'chauffeur' crept upstairs to remove his uniform than the whole party, under cover of the gramophone music, crept out and down towards the dog-leg landing and listened for noises from the basement dining room. As Purishkevich described it,

> We stood bunched together: I was first on the staircase, the brass knuckles in my hand; behind me was the Grand Duke; behind him Lt Sukhotin; and last was Dr Lazovert.

They stood on the stairs for about half an hour, putting the needle back and furiously rewinding 'Yankee Doodle' so that it boomed faster through the great brass horn whenever it threatened to slow down. From below, they heard nothing but a quiet murmur of conversation. Then they heard the door below opening, and scampered back to the study like mice.

Yusupov came in and told them that Rasputin would not eat or drink. What should he do? Dmitri Pavlovich told him to go back downstairs at once, in case Rasputin came up after him, saw the assembled company, and got suspicious – 'and then we would either have to let him go in peace or finish him off noisily – this could be fraught with consequences'. Felix returned to the basement. The others returned to their previous positions on the stairs. Half an hour later they heard a cork popping and the tinkle of glasses. (Through the solid walls, the curtains and the door with its thick *portière*, that is.) Then silence. Dmitri thought they would not have long to wait. They returned to the study.

Fifteen minutes passed and Yusupov came upstairs, pale-faced. Rasputin had eaten all the cakes and drunk two glasses of poisoned wine and 'nothing has happened, absolutely nothing' – Rasputin was belching and dribbling, but that was about it.

And he was worried about why Irina didn't come. Yusupov had told him she would be down in ten minutes.

Again they told him to go downstairs and wait five more minutes for the poison to take effect. When he had gone, Purishkevich noticed that Lazovert, who had proved brave and imperturbable when in the battle zone and under fire, was having a *crise de nerfs*. He was 'beet-red from apoplexy', and went missing. After an unspecified time, he returned, 'pale and haggard', and said he had felt ill, had gone down to the car, and had fallen face forward into the snow. The cold had revived him.

Yusupov came back; it was hopeless. Dmitri Pavlovich said they must abandon the plan and let the man go. But Purishkevich was resolute.

> 'Never!' I exclaimed. 'Your Highness, don't you understand that if he gets away today, he will have slipped away forever? Do you think that he will come to Yusupov's tomorrow once he realises that he was tricked? Rasputin cannot,' I continued in a half-whisper, stressing each word, 'must not, and will not leave here alive... If poison doesn't work... then we must show our hand. Either we must all go downstairs together, or you can leave it to me alone. I will lay him out, either with my Savage or I'll smash his skull in with the brass knuckles. What do you say to that?'

They began to creep downstairs in single file behind Purishkevich with the knuckleduster. Lazovert had been given the truncheon, despite his protests that he was feeling too ill to use it. But Purishkevich had descended only a step or two when Dmitri Pavlovich told him to stop, and took Yusupov aside. The others returned to the study. When Dmitri Pavlovich and Yusupov came in, they had agreed that Yusupov would shoot Rasputin. 'It will be quicker and simpler', the Prince said, and took a Browning from his desk drawer and went downstairs.

Five minutes later they heard a shot, a cry, and a body hitting the floor. They rushed downstairs and plunged headlong through the basement door, and one of them got caught somehow on the light switch, plunging them into pitch darkness.

They groped for the switch and turned it on, only to find Rasputin dying on the bearskin rug and Yusupov standing over him, holding the revolver behind his back. There was no blood. 'Evidently it was an internal haemorrhage – the bullet had entered Rasputin's chest and had not come out.'

Dmitri Pavlovich foresaw a nasty stain, so they moved Rasputin onto the tiled part of the floor, 'with his feet towards the window facing the street and his head toward the staircase from which we had come'. There was no blood on the rug. They stood around the body, overawed by the oddity of the situation and of the influence of the man who lay before them in his cream embroidered shirt, velvet trousers and magnificent boots. Then they trooped out, 'turning out the light and leaving the door slightly ajar'.

Yusupov's account, published nine years later than Purishkevich's, is a little different. When he went upstairs for the first time, Dmitri Pavlovich, Sukhotin and Purishkevich rushed towards him with revolvers, asking what had happened. He told them that Rasputin was unharmed, and they decided to go downstairs together and strangle him. Once they had set off, Yusupov called them back to the study; he was not at all confident that Rasputin, who was no ordinary man, might not overcome them all. Instead, he persuaded them, with difficulty, that he personally should shoot him.

He took Dmitri's revolver and went downstairs.

Rasputin was sitting at the table, looking a little off-colour. Yusupov sat down beside him. Rasputin asked for more wine and suggested a visit to the gypsies. Yusupov poured him some more. He was hiding the revolver behind his back. He got up and went over to the crystal crucifix, and stood admiring it.

In due course Rasputin followed him. He said he preferred the labyrinth cupboard, and began opening its little doors and drawers.

'Grigori Efimovich, you had better look at the crucifix, and say a prayer before it.'

Rasputin looked at me in amazement, and with a trace of fear… He came right up to me, looking me full in the face, and he seemed to read in my glance something which he was not expecting. I realised the supreme moment was at hand. 'God give me strength to end it all,' I thought, and I slowly brought the revolver from behind my back. Rasputin was still standing motionless before me, his head turned to the right, and his eyes on the crucifix.

'Where shall I shoot?' I thought. 'Through the temple or through the heart?' A streak of lightning seemed to run through my body. I fired. There was a roar as from a wild beast, and Rasputin fell heavily backwards on the bearskin rug.

The others rushed downstairs, plunging everything into darkness. When the light was switched on again, there lay Rasputin, twitching, with his eyes shut. 'There was a small red spot on his silk blouse.' He became still. The bullet had gone through the heart; he was dead. Dmitri Pavlovich removed the body from the rug, they switched off the light, left the room and locked the door, and went upstairs.

They now had to dispose of the victim. Lazovert as chauffeur, Dmitri Pavlovich, and Sukhotin wearing Rasputin's coat, were to leave, as planned, in the general direction of Gorokhovaya Street to convince any pursuant Okhrana men that Rasputin had left for the night, but in fact to take some of Rasputin's clothes for burning to the Warsaw Station. They would leave Purishkevich's car there and proceed by cab to the Sergei Palace to pick up Dmitri Pavlovich's car. In this they would return to the Moika to pick up the corpse.

They left; Yusupov and Purishkevich remained behind and exchanged views about the future of Russia, 'now forever delivered from her evil genius'.

In the midst of our conversation I was suddenly seized by a vague feeling of alarm; I was overwhelmed by the desire to go downstairs to the dining-room. I went downstairs and unlocked the door.

Rasputin lay motionless, but on touching him I discovered that he was still warm. I felt his pulse. There was no beat.

From his wound drops of blood trickled, and fell on the granite floor.

On an impulse, Yusupov seized the corpse and shook it; it dropped back lifeless. He stood over it a little longer, and was about to leave when

my attention was arrested by a slight trembling of his left eyelid. I bent down over him, and attentively examined his face. It began to twitch convulsively. The movements became more and more pronounced. Suddenly the left eye half-opened. An instant later the right lid trembled and lifted. And both eyes – the eyes of Rasputin – fixed themselves on me with an expression of devilish hatred.

Yusupov was rooted to the spot. Rasputin leapt to his feet, roaring, and grabbed him 'like red-hot iron' by the shoulder and 'tried to grip me by the throat', all the time repeating the Prince's name in 'a hoarse whisper'. But 'with a supreme effort I tore myself free'.

Rasputin fell back to the ground. Yusupov dashed upstairs yelling for Purishkevich. He had given his own revolver to Dmitri Pavlovich, so he was unarmed, and as Purishkevich took his revolver from its holster they were alerted by a noise on the stairs. Yusupov dashed into the study, grabbed the truncheon, and returned to the staircase. Rasputin was clambering up to them on all fours, 'bellowing and snorting like a wounded animal'. With a superhuman effort, he rose to his feet and lunged towards the door into the courtyard.

Yusupov was sure the door was locked and Dmitri Pavlovich and the others had the key. He was mistaken. Rasputin vanished through it into the darkness outside. Purishkevich raced after him and fired twice.

Yusupov thought: *Rasputin will escape through the gate*. So:

> I rushed to the main entrance...

That is, he rushed through his study, out of his bachelor apartments, through the apartment that was being refurbished for himself and Irina and the baby; past Irina's silver boudoir, with its exquisite silver alcove with a marble Diana on a plinth and vaulted ceiling painted with birds of Paradise; past his own sunken marble bathing pool and private sitting room with silk-upholstered art nouveau chairs and canapé; past his drawing room with its ornate plaster door-cases, white marble fireplace and Carelian birch parquet floor; past the Winter Garden with its ferns and tall, green marble pilasters; past the small ballroom with its pillars and an inlaid design on the parquet, and into the main house. Breathlessly, he raced along hundreds of feet of mahogany beneath gilded ceilings above which ran the great *enfilade* of drawing rooms on the first floor – the Red, the Green, the Blue, the large Rotunda, the small Rotunda – towards the picture galleries with their Canovas shrouded in dust sheets and their Rubens and Rembrandts mutely staring; past the Moorish room with its fretwork lanterns and glowing lacquerwork; past the unseeing eyes of a hundred onyx nymphs and naiads, towards the banqueting hall, the ballroom, the antique room, the Roman room and the theatre; on and on he ran, and through the colossal baroque marble foyer, and out of the great oak doors, and

> ...ran along the Moika quayside, towards the courtyard, hoping, in case Purishkevich had missed him, to stop Rasputin at the gates.

He heard two more shots. Rasputin fell near a snow-heap. Purishkevich stood over him for a minute and then turned and went back into the house.

Yusupov, 'after looking around, and finding that the streets were empty, and that the shots had not attracted attention', crossed to the snow-heap and saw that Rasputin was dead. 'On his left temple gaped a large wound which, as I afterwards learned, was caused by Purishkevich's heel'.

But people were approaching from two sides.

Purishkevich tells a less flattering story. Having seen the corpse and gone upstairs with the others, leaving the door ajar, he noted that it was now after three o'clock in the morning and they must hurry. Sukhotin put on Rasputin's fur coat and galoshes, and carried his gloves. Lazovert once again dressed as the chauffeur. They left in Purishkevich's car, with Dmitri Pavlovich, bound for the Warsaw Station, as planned, to burn Rasputin's clothes in his train's passenger coach, 'where by then the stove should have been hot'.

Yusupov left Purishkevich in the study and went out of his own apartments, into the lobby, and into his parents' apartments, empty at the time because they were out of town. In his absence, Purishkevich smoked a cigar and paced about. Then, compelled by an 'inner force', he picked up his Savage and put it into his trouser pocket, and

> ...under pressure of that same mysterious force, I left the study, whose hall door had been closed, and found myself in the corridor for no particular purpose.
>
> I had hardly entered the hallway when I heard footsteps below near the staircase, then the sound of the door – which opened into the dining room where Rasputin lay – which the person entering evidently had not closed.

A moment later, he heard Yusupov's wild cry below – 'Purishkevich, shoot! Shoot! He's alive! He's escaping!' – and Yusupov 'rushed headlong, screaming' upstairs, white as a sheet with bulging eyes, past Purishkevich and through the door to the main lobby and through to his parents' apartments (where

Purishkevich had thought he was all along). Purishkevich, momentarily dumbfounded, now heard

> ...rapid, heavy footsteps making their way to the door leading to the courtyard... There was not a moment to lose so, without losing my head, I pulled my Savage from my pocket, set it at *feu,* and ran down the stairs.

Outside, he spotted Rasputin, running swiftly on snow alongside the fence. Rasputin yelled 'Felix, Felix, I will tell the Tsarina everything' and, sure now that 'he might, given his phenomenal vitality, get away... I rushed after him and fired'.

He missed. His second shot missed as well. Purishkevich was mad at himself, because he had allegedly done quite a lot of target practice at the Semionovski parade ground, 'but today I was not able to lay out a man at twenty paces'. Rasputin was by the gate now. It was all a matter of concentration. Purishkevich bit his left hand as hard as he could, to focus his mind, and his third shot hit Rasputin in the back. He stopped,

> ...and this time, taking careful aim from the same spot, I fired for the fourth time. I apparently hit him in the head, for he keeled over face first in the snow, his head twitching. I ran up to him and kicked him in the temple with all my might. He lay there, his arms stretched far out in front of him, clawing at the snow as if he were trying to crawl forward on his belly. But he could no longer move and only gnashed and gritted his teeth.[7]

Purishkevich went back into the house the way he had come. Between his shots, he had noticed two men walking along the pavement outside; 'the second of them' had run away when he heard the shot.

Now he wondered what to do. 'I am alone, Yusupov is out of his mind, and the servants don't know what is going on'. And a corpse was in the yard. A passer-by might see it. And in particular –

Perhaps the servants had not heard Yusupov's shots in this room, but it was impossible to imagine that two soldiers sitting in the main entrance hall could not have heard four loud shots from my Savage in the courtyard. I walked through the lobby to the main entrance.

'Boys,' I addressed them, 'I killed...' At these words they advanced on me in real earnest as if they wanted to seize me. 'I killed,' I repeated 'Grishka Rasputin, the enemy of Russia and the Tsar.' At these last words, one of the soldiers became greatly agitated and rushed up to kiss me. The other said 'Thank God, about time!'

He made them promise to say nothing. They said 'we are Russians... we won't betray you'.

Purishkevich found Yusupov throwing up in a bathroom of his parents' apartments. He took him back to the study, while Yusupov mumbled 'Felix, Felix' over and over again. However, within moments of entering the study, the Prince broke free of Purishkevich, dashed to his desk, got the rubber truncheon Maklakov had given him, raced downstairs, berserk, and began to beat the corpse about the head with it.

It took two servants to drag Yusupov away, and there was blood everywhere. They 'carried him upstairs in their arms' all covered in blood, and sat him in the sofa, where he continued to roll his eyes, twitch, and repeat his own first name. Purishkevich told the servants to 'find some cloth from somewhere' and wrap the corpse and 'bind the swaddled thing securely with the cord'. One of them went off to do this while the other one told him that the point-duty policeman had been enquiring about the shooting, and was insisting that he'd have to put in a report about it.

Ten minutes later, when Vlasuk came in, Purishkevich realised that he had made a mistake in calling him in because the police-man was 'a veteran of the old school'. Perhaps he had hoped to bribe him. Anyway, he recognised Purishkevich at once, and, having had the case for murdering Rasputin put to him by the silver-tongued Duma deputy, was only too pleased to find out that the death had occurred. He promised not to say anything unless they made him swear an oath, in which case he would have to tell the truth. Purishkevich let him go, because 'his district chief was Lt Grigoriev (who was, as far as I knew, a very decent fellow of good family)'. He decided 'to leave the future to fate'.

Downstairs, the servant had wrapped the corpse, head and all, in what looked like a blue curtain and tied it with cord. Purishkevich told the servants to tidy Yusupov up and do the best they could with him.

The others returned. He told them what had happened. Hurriedly they dragged the corpse into the car 'together with the chains and the 2-pood weights I had brought to Yusupov's apartment that night'. (Maybe Lazovert had loaded them into his car, and out of it at the Yusupov Palace later. Purishkevich didn't take them with him on the tram to the Duma, or hang around in the snow before midnight with them.) Purishkevich deputed one of the soldiers to look after Yusupov.

Dmitri Pavlovich drove (he had several cars and was a keen motorist). Sukhotin sat next to him. Dr Lazovert sat in the back on the right and Purishkevich on the left 'and squeezed in with the corpse was one of the soldiers, whom we had decided to take with us to help us throw the heavy body into the hole in the ice'.

They had already set off when Purishkevich saw Rasputin's galoshes and fur coat in the back of the car. The redoubtable Mrs Purishkevich had refused to cut it up for burning, and when Dmitri Pavlovich protested, she had not been one bit intimidated. They had burned his 'sleeveless coat' and his gloves, but the rest would have to be drowned with him. They had made their phone call to the Villa Rhode.

After this they continued the journey in silence, enjoying the icy air blowing through the open windows, with Purishkevich silently daydreaming about the time when Grand Duke Nikolai Mikhailovich had summoned him to hear about his, the Grand

Duke's, anxiety about Rasputin and how it had been expressed to the Tsar.

This unlikely digression over, Purishkevich found himself still in the car, the corpse soft 'at my feet', and outside the city on a bumpy road. At last, Dmitri Pavlovich drove onto the bridge and coasted to a halt. They saw a sentry-box on the far side before the headlamps were extinguished. (The photograph taken on Monday 19 December shows that there were gas-lights at intervals on either side of the Petrovski Bridge.) Purishkevich was first out of the car and the soldier and Dr Lazovert and Captain Sukhotin helped him swing the corpse and fling it into the ice-hole (a drop of about five metres, to judge from photographs). Dmitri Pavlovich stood guard by the car.

Then they remembered they'd forgotten the weights, and dropped them after it; and weighted the coat with chains and hoisted that over as well. Dr Lazovert found one of the galoshes and threw it off the bridge. Then they drove across the bridge, and saw the sentry asleep, and returned by a route that would take them past the St Peter and St Paul Fortress. It wasn't an easy journey; the car kept stopping, the engine misfiring, and 'each time… Dr Lazovert jumped out, fiddled with the spark plugs, cleaned them, and somehow or other got us going again'. Despite all this, on the way back Purishkevich found time belatedly to express his doubts about the method of disposal to Dmitri Pavlovich. He hoped the body would be found, he pointed out, because otherwise 'false Rasputins' would appear; they should have left it somewhere conspicuous.

The last repair stop was almost opposite the St Peter and St Paul Fortress itself. After this, they bowled along without mishap to the Sergei Palace. On alighting from the motor, they found the other galosh and some bloodstains on the car's carpet. Dmitri Pavlovich's servant, 'who had met us on the steps and who struck me as having been initiated into the whole affair', was ordered to burn the carpet and the galosh. Then Lazovert, Sukhotin and Purishkevich took their leave. They took two cabs to the Warsaw Station where their womenfolk awaited

– including Mrs Sukhotin, who had also spent the night on the hospital train. It was after five o'clock in the morning when they got back, and all aboard the train were asleep, except for Mrs Purishkevich.

We return to the story from Yusupov's point of view. We left him in the courtyard with Rasputin's body, aware that people were approaching. They were his two servants from the house, and a policeman. He stood to block the policeman's view of Rasputin as the officer asked what was going on. He explained that the noise had been mere drunken revelry, and led him to the gates. When he returned, his servants 'stood there. Purishkevich had told them to carry the body into the house'. Rasputin was lying differently in the snow and Yusupov was terrified; thinking the man was still alive, he went indoors, calling for Purishkevich, and then into his dressing-room for water. Purishkevich came in and saved him from swooning, and took him to the study.

While they were there, Yusupov's servant came in and said the policeman was back; shots had been heard at the district police station, and he was being asked to tell his superior officer what he knew on the phone.

It was up to Yusupov and Purishkevich to persuade the man to keep his mouth shut. They had him brought in. Out of the blue, Purishkevich excitedly declared that Rasputin had been murdered. 'I was horror-stricken at this conversation, but it was quite impossible to intervene and put an end to it.' Afterwards, feeling ill, Yusupov left the study with his truncheon and saw the body below on the landing, pouring with blood. Like Purishkevich, Yusupov was overtaken by an irresistible, inexplicable impulse: this time, to batter the corpse to smithereens.

> At that moment all laws of God and man were set at naught. Purishkevich subsequently told me that it was such a harrowing sight that he would never be able to forget it.

After this, he fainted, and the others went off with the body.

When he came to, he told his servant to take a dog to one of the outbuildings and shoot it. 'He then dragged its body over Rasputin's trail, so as to frustrate any subsequent blood analysis, and threw it on the snow-mound where not so long before the dead *starets* had lain.'

Yusupov gathered his servants together and swore them to silence, and set off at around five o'clock in the morning for Grand Duke Alexander Mikhailovich's, where Fyodor, his young brother-in-law, was waiting up for him. He said he would explain everything in the morning; and 'I went to bed and fell into a deep sleep'.

We therefore have two 'first-hand' accounts of the night in question; two accounts which contain a substantial number of major and important inconsistencies, to such a degree that it is impossible to reconcile the two accounts. For example:

Yusupov says that Dmitri Pavlovich and the other three conspirators arrived together at the palace,[8] while Purishkevich says that he and Lazovert arrived together – Dmitri Pavlovich was already there.[9]

Yusupov says that the chocolate cream cakes were poisoned,[10] while Purishkevich says the pink ones were.[11]

Yusupov says he played the guitar for Rasputin,[12] but Purishkevich makes no reference to this at all.

Yusupov says he left Rasputin only once in order to go upstairs to the study,[13] while Purishkevich says he came up to three times.[14]

After Rasputin had taken several glasses of wine and eaten some of the cakes, Yusupov says he had an 'irritated throat',[15] while Purishkevich says there was 'constant belching and hyper-salivation'.[16]

Purishkevich says that, while in the study, Lazovert began feeling unwell and went downstairs to go outside. When he returned to the study he looked very ill and told the others that although he had fainted outside, the cold snow had revived him.[17] Yusupov makes no mention of Lazovert coming down the stairs or returning afterwards.

Yusupov says that when he returned to his fellow conspirators in the study he was handed a gun by Dmitri Pavlovich,[18] while Purishkevich says that Yusupov returned to the room and took his own 'small Browning' from the desk drawer in the study.[19] It should also be recalled that, in his June 1917 version of the story, Yusupov states that he was given the gun by Purishkevich.

After Yusupov had shot Rasputin and the others had gone down to see the body, Yusupov says that he turned off the electric light and locked the dining room door.[20] Purishkevich says that they switched the light off but left the door open.[21]

Purishkevich says that after he shot Rasputin in the courtyard he stood by the body for several minutes – Yusupov was not there.[22] In Yusupov's account he is standing there with Purishkevich.[23]

Yusupov was to deviate further from his 1927 account when he gave evidence, under oath, in two libel cases he initiated in 1934 and 1965. In the 1934 trial at the High Court in London, he claimed that Rasputin was still alive when he beat him with the truncheon. In his 1927 book, this happened after Rasputin was dead. In 1965, in a similar case in New York State Supreme Court, Yusupov claimed that not only had he fired the first shot, but had also fired the second shot, which in the book he attributes to Purishkevich.[24]

In addition to the conflicting written accounts of Yusupov and Purishkevich, the 1923 account of Dr Stanislaus Lazovert, 'The Assassination of Rasputin', adds further seeds of doubt and incongruence:

When Yusupov and Lazovert went to Rasputin's apartment to collect him in the car, Lazovert says that 'he (Rasputin) admitted me in person' and also asserts that 'I persuaded the black devil to accompany me to the home of Prince Yusupov'.[25] In Yusupov's account, Lazovert stays in the car while Yusupov himself goes into the apartment alone.[26]

Back at the Yusupov Palace, in the downstairs dining room, Lazovert claims Rasputin spoke about plots he had been involved in and stated that the Germans will soon be in Petrograd.[27] None of this features in either the Yusupov or Purishkevich accounts.

Lazovert gives the impression that he is in the dining room when Rasputin consumes the poisoned cakes and wine: 'after a time [Rasputin] rose and walked to the door. We were afraid that our work had been in vain. Suddenly... someone shot at him... we left the room to let him die'. In the other accounts, Lazovert is upstairs and only comes down to examine Rasputin's body and declare him dead.[28]

Lazovert relates that, later, Purishkevich followed Rasputin 'into the gardens' and fired 'two shots swiftly into his retreating figure'.[29] Purishkevich himself refers to firing four shots.[30]

What Yusupov, Purishkevich and Lazovert do have in common is that their recollections fall into the general pattern of a good many post-crime accounts. After a crime is committed, the participants will often agree to tell the same story. However, while the basic narrative of their accounts will be very similar, it is in the fine detail that cracks begin to appear, for it is in the minutiae that they have not been able to collaborate or collude – it is here that the story starts to come apart at the seams.

All three accounts are equally irrational and self-serving. Apart from contradicting each other, they also contradict the evidence of witnesses and the evidence of the autopsy. Who and what should we believe? By a process of eliminating the most unlikely, implausible and impossible accounts and by applying the conclusions of new forensic evidence and testimony, we can at last begin to reconstruct the most likely solution to this nine-decade mystery.

ELEVEN

END OF THE ROAD

There seems no reason to disbelieve the story that Rasputin was collected from his apartment, after midnight, by Yusupov, and that both were driven to the Yusupov Palace by someone who could have been Lazovert. The 'canvas-topped' car, variously described as grey or khaki, sounds like Purishkevich's.

As to what happened next, the far-fetched stories of Yusupov and his servants and employees can be treated as suspicious, as can those of Purishkevich. That Rasputin was offered poisoned cakes and wine can again be taken as fact. However, according to Professor Kossorotov, who carried out the autopsy, 'the examination reveals no trace of poison'.[1] That is to say, if Rasputin took any poison, either he took in only the minutest trace of poison, or the cyanide was old and had lost its potency. Although Purishkevich and Yusupov contradict each other in detail, they concur in describing doses hefty enough to kill several horses. Had Rasputin ingested anything like the amount of unadulterated cyanide that they describe, he would have died at once. Maria, Rasputin's daughter, was 'positive that my father did not

eat the poisoned cakes, for he had a horror of sweet things...
Never since my childhood do I remember seeing him eat pas-
tries'.[2] Others, who believe Rasputin did eat the poisoned cakes,
have argued that the cyanide had no effect as it was 'neutralised
by the sugar in the cakes'.[3] In order to gain a definitive expert
appraisal of this and other crucial aspects surrounding Rasputin's
death, Professor Derrick Pounder, Head of Forensic Medicine
at Dundee University and a senior government pathologist, was
asked to undertake a review of the original Autopsy Report and
forensic evidence.

In considering the poisoning issue, Professor Pounder concluded that the sugar-as-an-antidote theory is just that – a
theory, which

> ...has no foundation in science. It is essentially a nonsense which
> has no support in forensic medical literature. If the cyanide had
> been cooked with the sugar in the cakes then there might be
> some potential for such a reaction. However, if cyanide is simply
> added to the cakes then the cyanide is not so intimately mixed
> with the sugar that such a reaction could occur. On contact with
> the stomach acid, potassium cyanide releases the cyanide which is
> absorbed into the body and kills rapidly by blocking the function
> of the chemical components of the body which enable us to use
> oxygen. In this way the victim is starved of oxygen despite an
> abundance of oxygen in the body. Immediately upon hitting the
> acid of the stomach the potassium cyanide would react with it
> to release cyanide before any more complex reaction with sugar
> could occur. The real proof that this theory has no substance in
> practice is the fact that we do not use glucose or fructose as an
> antidote to cyanide poisoning. The fact that Professor Kossorotov
> did not record a characteristic almond smell at autopsy does not
> discount the possibility of Rasputin having taken cyanide. Firstly,
> about 10% of people cannot detect the almond smell of cyanide
> and we do not know if Professor Kossorotov had inherited this
> inability to smell cyanide. Finally, if Professor Kossorotov was
> capable of detecting the smell of cyanide and had specifically

sought it out but had not smelt it, this still does not exclude the possibility that Rasputin had taken a dose of cyanide insufficient to kill him.

If Rasputin was indeed poisoned by cyanide but did not die as a result, then the only logical conclusion is that he did not ingest sufficient cyanide. The renaissance founder of modern toxicology, Paracelsus, said that 'the poison is in the dose'. If insufficient cyanide to kill but sufficient to produce symptoms had been taken, then this might be explained by an insufficient quantity of cyanide of good quality or alternatively a sufficient quantity of cyanide of poor quality.

If the poisoners thought that they had given a sufficient quantity of cyanide to kill then either they were mistaken and administered too little or alternatively, they administered what should have been sufficient but proved not to be because the quality of the poison was insufficient inasmuch as there was only a small component of active ingredient relative to the bulk. The lethal dose of cyanide is sufficiently small that the former possibility seems unlikely and the latter much more likely. If the quality of the poison was poor then that may be either because it was intrinsically of poor quality with a low content of potassium cyanide and a high content of inert material (somewhat akin to the heroin that can be purchased on the street today) or the poison was originally of high quality but deteriorated due to long term storage.[4]

Poisoning was, of course, the ideal murder method. With a whole troop of policemen within sight and sound of the crime scene, it was quiet and there would be no blood. So the question arises: when it didn't work, why didn't Dr Lazovert drive quickly to the dispensary of the hospital train and bring back a syringe and a lethal dose of, say, diamorphine? Even Purishkevich could have laid his hands on something. An irate 'diary' entry for 5 December reads 'I alone am responsible for supplying medicines, linens, boots, tobacco and books to the trenches'.[5] It was the dispensary in his train that carried those medicines.

The next 'fact' we may be inclined to accept is that at least one or two shots were heard around half-past two or three o'clock in the morning If we accept that the original idea was to poison Rasputin, and that a shot or shots were fired in the middle of the night, then we have to examine the circumstances. The story of Rasputin facing a kind of kangaroo court and being expected to shoot himself in front of those assembled is highly unlikely to say the least. Purishkevich thought Rasputin was a scoundrel, and Yusupov thought he was superhuman. However drunk they were, it is hard to believe that any of the protagonists would have risked putting a gun in his hand.

Questioned by police almost immediately, Byzhinski the butler was able to indicate 'the broken window on the ground floor overlooking the forecourt of the adjoining house'. Nobody reported finding any glass outside or hearing it shatter, but in the photographs taken next day, the study window on the courtyard side does look different from the rest; it seems to have some sort of frame, possibly masking tape, around it, and a square of paper on the inside over a hole about 10cm across. The hole is neat, as if broken from the inside at close range. Had there been a man standing in the courtyard, the hole in the window would have been about half a metre above his head.

It is unlikely that either of the two fatal shots hit Rasputin in the middle of the night. According to the Autopsy Report, 'the victim must rapidly have been weakened by haemorrhaging arising from a wound to the liver (bullet wound 1) and a wound to the kidney (bullet wound 2). Death would have been inevitable within 10 to 20 minutes.'[6]

There was more firing hours later, recorded by a whole bevy of police about an hour after their change of shift at six o'clock – firing for which there would have been no need at all had Rasputin received both wounds by three o'clock in the morning.

Shortly after the shot or shots had been heard, four men allegedly turned up in a car that sped off. Tikhomirov, the Okhrana man 'detailed to watch Rasputin', saw them and alerted the head of the Okhrana by telephone. This begs the question of what Tikhomirov was doing there in the first place. Nowhere are we told that he followed Rasputin from Gorokhovaya Street. He does not appear to have a car at his disposal – although there was one on standby at the Ministry of the Interior opposite. We do not know where he was watching from.

It seems likely that Tikhomirov was a late arrival, sent by Protopopov. When the Extraordinary Commission sat in 1917, Protopopov admitted that he had visited Rasputin just after midnight for about ten minutes.[7] Yusupov wrote that Rasputin had told him Protopopov had been there that night, and had warned him against visiting the Yusupov Palace. There was allegedly an arrangement whereby, if Rasputin failed to telephone Simanovich by two o'clock in the morning, Simanovich would be concerned and inform the authorities. This is, on balance, quite probable. If Protopopov received a phone call from Simanovich, whom he knew well, he would have sent Tikhomirov to Yusupov's palace.

If four men did turn up in a car, who were they and why were they there? According to Tikhomirov, they entered by the side door of number 92, which leads us to assume they were arriving by invitation. Princess Irina's brothers, Princes Andrew, Fyodor and Nikolai are three possibilities whose names had been linked with the murder almost from the beginning.

Assuming that Rasputin had survived an attempt to poison him, the next resort may well have been something just as quiet and bloodless as poisoning, but also fatal: a severe beating.

Given that the protagonists included Dmitri Pavlovich, Yusupov (who would certainly have shrunk from physical violence of that kind, despite the claims he was to make later),[8] and Lazovert (who was already physically ill as a result of the tension),[9] one might imagine that a tough peasant with a reputation for getting fighting drunk might well have seemed a daunting prospect. Whether, in light of Tikhomirov's observations, Yusupov subsequently called in extra hands must therefore be considered as a possibility. In any eventuality, the Autopsy

Report certainly indicates a range of severe wounds indicative of a major physical assault:

> The right eye has come out of its orbital cavity and fallen onto the face. At the corner of the right eye, the skin is torn.
>
> The right ear is torn and partially detached.
>
> The neck has a wound caused by a blunt object.
>
> The victim's face and body bear the signs of blows inflicted by some flexible but hard object.
>
> The genitals have been crushed.
>
> The left hand side of the back has a gaping wound, inflicted by some sharp object.

In 1993, a team led by Russia's leading forensic expert, Dr Vladimir Zharov, carried out a thorough review of the autopsy materials. In their report, which was never made public (but was made available to this author), they concur with this view:

> The mechanical injuries (the ones not caused by gunshots) in the region of the head were caused by a succession of blows inflicted by heavy, blunt objects. These injuries could not have been caused by the body hitting the pylon of the bridge from which it was thrown off.[10]

Furthermore, Zharov's team listed other wounds not referred to in the Autopsy Report, such as a 'squashed and deformed' nose and numerous 'scratches of irregular shape'. One such irregular shape was the Russian letter G, the fourth letter of the Cyrillic alphabet, which was scratched on the right jaw, possibly by a sword or knife. The most probable explanation is that Rasputin was beaten up by a number of assailants before he was shot, and that one was armed with a truncheon. Zharov and his colleagues further speculate that 'the gaping wound' on the left hand side of the back may have been made by a sword or a knife. Had a sword or knife been plunged into his left side, Rasputin might have been left for dead in the basement dining room.

Following the beating, the participants no doubt retired upstairs to the study to relieve the night's tension and to toast their success with a bout of drinking.

In their books, Purishkevich and Yusupov have Rasputin climbing the stairs unaided and escaping into the yard, whereupon he sprints for the gate (i.e. a thirty-metre dash through snow, part of it in the shadow of the building). Purishkevich allegedly fires four times and hits him twice. The courtyard is unlit. Purishkevich is short-sighted.

According to the Autopsy Report, two bullets were fired from a distance of 20cm and one with the gun pressed to his forehead. We can discount Purishkevich's entire confection; Rasputin was not hit by bullets when he was on the run. But he could have staggered out, drunk and wounded. And another drunken person, who knew he had escaped, could have shot wildly from the study into the courtyard – the hole in the window is quite neat, as if fired at close range, and it is on the side of the window that a person would fire from if they were aiming towards the snow-heap and the fence. A bullet or two overhead would have made Rasputin fall to the ground, and he would not have been clearly visible from beyond the fence because of the snow-heaps.

There were bloodstains, which Yusupov wanted to disguise, leading from the outer door along the wall and along the fence. There is a police scene of crime photograph that purports to show blood traces in the snow. It is possible that Rasputin somehow escaped, and, dripping blood, collapsed in the yard and was left there, with nobody quite daring to brave the watching police and approach him.

It was this shot or shots from the window that resulted in the first visit by the police. It was as a result of this occurrence that Yusupov invented the shot-dog story. According to Yusupov, he knew there were bloodstains in the snow, and, in order to confuse forensic analysis, he decided to have a dog shot and drag its body over the bloodstains. This is frankly ludicrous. Blood does not stain snow. Even in sub-zero temperatures, blood in snow can be shovelled into buckets and flushed down the nearest drain. It is more likely that Yusupov was making excuses for the presence of a dark shape near the snow-heaps by the fence. Either that, or he was too drunk to think straight. Furthermore, his claim that, on his instructions, a servant then shot a dog makes little sense either. No one in the vicinity claims or recalls hearing this shot, which would, according to Yusupov's story, have occurred sometime after the shot or shots heard at half-past two or three o'clock, but a good while before the shots heard just after six o'clock.

There is a hiatus of at least two hours, possibly three, between the original shot or shots in the courtyard, which had brought police to the palace, and their six o'clock roll call which was interrupted by the ejection of the women. The roll call is the only reliable timing we have between the departure of Rasputin from Gorokhovaya Street and the finding of the body. At the police station, the night shift was going off duty and the much bigger day shift was coming on. There were policemen to spare, and they saw what happened: two women, drunk, were forcibly bundled out. The most likely explanation is that these women knew the men were going to commit murder and they wanted either to stop them or to participate. And the men wanted them out of the way. Another, and not a contradictory, explanation, is that they were deliberately distracting the police from a rumpus in the courtyard.

Somebody had to have the nerve to go out and drag Rasputin back in. Daylight was approaching and he had to be got away from the building and finally disposed of. Shooting was the only way to finish him off properly, but it would cause damage in a confined space like the stairwell.

An unspecified time later, four shots were heard 'in rapid succession from the forecourt'. This does not necessarily mean that the shooting took place *on* the forecourt, but it is most likely. And we can treat 'rapid succession' with scepticism too. Had the reports alleged that the shots rang out over a five- or ten-minute period, or in the course of the women's departure, they would have seemed incompetent. But by this stage they did not *want* to see anything. A diligent policeman or Okhrana agent getting mixed up with Romanovs and Princes was likely to offend the wrong person and find his career at an end.

The group of early-morning shots, fired with a brief interval between them, came from different revolvers, according to the Autopsy Report. This view is backed up by the 1993 review led by Dr Vladimir Zharov. In 2004, Zharov told BBC Timewatch that microscopic measurements of the entry wounds proved that the three bullet-holes were of different sizes.[11] The report considered that the chest wound was most likely caused by a 6.35mm Browning handgun, the type used by Yusupov and Dmitri Pavlovich. The right-hand back wound was slightly larger, therefore consistent with Purishkevich's 7.65mm Savage pistol. These two shots were, the Autopsy Report says, fired from a distance of about 20cm, when Rasputin was *standing up*.[12] One bullet 'penetrated the left-hand side of his chest and passed through his stomach and liver' and the other 'entered the right-hand part of his back and passed through his kidneys'. Had these shots been fired simultaneously while Rasputin was sitting or standing, the assassins would have been at risk of wounding each other, diagonally through Rasputin's body.

There must have been an interval between shots. But how would Rasputin have remained standing? It seems most likely that he was carried out with his wrists bound and propped in a sitting position against a snow-heap; two people fired at him, and one bullet hit him as he fell forwards. Both these wounds would have, in themselves, been fatal within twenty minutes.

The Autopsy Report is equally adamant that the third bullet, which was immediately fatal, was fired at point-blank range while the body was supine. The most likely scenario is that, having shot Rasputin twice, the conspirators wrapped his body in cloth and carried it across the courtyard to the waiting car. This is consistent with the scene of crime photograph taken by the police showing a straight line of blood from the doorway across the courtyard. Had Rasputin staggered across the courtyard, as claimed by Yusupov and Purishkevich, one would expect to see an irregular trail of blood. As the killers approached the gate, either a spasm or a sound from the body indicated that he was still alive, if only barely. It is at this point that the body was then put down, and someone, with a handgun of a different calibre to the ones that had fired the first and second shots, delivered the *coup de grâce* that ended Rasputin's life.[13] The third shot is therefore the most crucial in determining the identity of Rasputin's killer. Professor Derrick Pounder, in his review of the ballistics evidence, observed that,

> At the centre of the forehead there is a gunshot wound of entry comprising a central defect and a very prominent abraded margin with two lines of radiating accentuation at 8 o'clock and 10 o'clock which likely represent radiating lacerations. The presence of the lacerations would allow for the opening up of the central defect and the passage of a much larger bullet than might be anticipated from the size of the central defect alone. The abraded margin reflects the grazing of the stretched skin by the bullet at the moment of bullet entry.[14]

Turning his attention to identifying the bullet, Professor Pounder calculated that

> the central defect of the wound is about 6mm true diameter and the abraded margin between about 12 and 15mm true diameter. The overall size of the wound and prominence of the abraded margin suggests a large lead non-jacketed bullet.[15]

Full metal-jacketed bullets for handguns were the norm by the outbreak of the First World War. These were completely encased in a hard metal jacket to prevent expansion upon impact. In fact, the use of expanding, unjacketed bullets in small arms ammunition had been limited and proscribed by The Hague Accords of 1899 and 1907. Britain, however, was unique in using unjacketed bullets for its standard-issue officer's revolver, the .455-inch (11.56mm) Webley, arguing that the design was compliant with the Accords.

In considering which handgun out of the range available at the time of the murder was the one compatible with the ballistics evidence, Professor Pounder concluded that, based upon calibre,

> the Webley is the likely culprit... the Webley was a revolver firing non-jacketed lead bullets while the other weapons [used by Dmitri Pavlovich, Purishkevich and Yusupov] were pistols firing jacketed ammunition, a contrast which would also favour the Webley since lead non-jacketed bullets produce the more prominent abraded margin.[16]

Dr Zharov's 1993 review supported Professor Kossorotov's opinion that the third bullet went straight through the head, exiting from the back, although they point out that there are no photographs of the back of the head, so this cannot be established with absolute certainty. A tell-tale clue, however, is a pool of blood in the snow which is evident in the police scene of crime photograph, close to the second courtyard gate. This is consistent with an exit wound to the back of the head while the body is lying on the ground. Dr Zharov's team also agree with Professor Kossorotov's view that, although Rasputin's body was removed from the courtyard and thrown in the river, he was already dead and did not, therefore, drown.

> The cause of death was not drowning... the lungs were not swollen and there was no water in the respiratory organs.[17]

Although the lungs contained a small amount of water, Professor Derrick Pounder also agreed that,

> since the diagnosis of drowning is one of exclusion based upon all of the evidence it is clear that he did not drown, given the presence of a prior lethal injury. The fluid on the lungs is a

common non-specific autopsy finding which is not a diagnosis of drowning.[18]

The above reconstruction of events is based upon a best-fit scenario taking into account the timings, reports and statements made in contemporary documents.

Whether the shots were indeed fired inside the building or outside in the courtyard, at whatever time of the night, it is clear beyond doubt from the forensic evidence that the following is true:

The first and second shots were fired at close range in quick succession to each other,[19] by guns of different calibre.

The third shot, fired at point-blank range to the forehead, was the fatal shot that killed Rasputin.

None of the shots was fired from a distance, which completely negates Purishkevich's story. His claim to have fired the fatal shot is further discredited by the fact that his gun, a Savage, fired jacketed bullets which do not match the ballistics evidence for the fatal wound.

The wound made by the fatal third shot is compatible with an unjacketed .455 bullet from a British officer's .455-inch Webley revolver.

Rasputin did not drown – he was dead before he was thrown in the river.

With these facts in mind, we now need to establish who was actually present at the scene of the murder and, more significantly, who fired the third and fatal shot that ended Rasputin's life.

It seems clear that Rasputin was tempted to the Yusupov Palace on the Moika by the prospect of female company – specifically, a young and beautiful Romanov married to a well-known homosexual transvestite. The implication is that he was enticed by a possible seduction. He may have seen her photograph, but he had never met her. Invited, as he was, to meet her after midnight on a Friday, he could reasonably have expected to find a private party, and indeed to meet her in the company of others; but she was not there.

Yusupov told General Popov that two women had left with Dmitri Pavlovich. But by the time he related his account to Stopford on 6 June 1917, it was already coherent from repetition, and the women were left out. He contradicts Purishkevich's 'diary' published the following year by denying that any women were present at all. But the police saw two. Madame Derfelden was held under house arrest for forty-eight hours after the murder, and Okhrana snoopers reported on Vera Koralli's stay at her hotel. Early correspondence between Yusupov and Irina – who at one point fully intended to be present – refers to other women being invited.

At least two women were there.

There is also some confusion about Yusupov's servants. He had a batman and a house steward. His batman could have been wearing military uniform, but Purishkevich had seen Yusupov's servants before, and knew that only two of them were going to be on duty; and he is adamant that the two men on duty that night, the one who let him into the palace and the other 'dressed in a soldier's uniform' sitting on the bench, were 'soldiers', not identifiable by rank. He is equally clear in calling Pavlovich's batman a 'servant' and voicing strong disapproval of his having been let in on the secret. Frankly, Purishkevich didn't approve of servants at all; 'impudent', he thought a chauffeur would look, and they were all a security risk as far as he was concerned. *He did not think that the two men who opened the door to him and helped with the general clearing-up were servants.* The Okhrana agent Tikhomirov witnessed a 'man in military field uniform' in the courtyard earlier in the evening. Yusupov, in his statement to Major Popov, uses the same description as if prompted. This could not have been Nefedev (Yusupov's batman) or Byzhinski (the butler) or Yusupov, Purishkevich or Sukhotin, who would have been wearing tunics, i.e. formal uniform. Field uniform was worn on active service.

Yusupov says they took a soldier with them to help dispose of the body. Had Yusupov's servant gone with them, he would have reported back to Yusupov on his return. But it was not until lunchtime the following day that Yusupov knew for sure from Dmitri Pavlovich where and how the corpse had been dumped. This implies that the 'soldier' was not Nefedev or Byzhinski. It is possible that there were two other people in military uniform. British officers in Petrograd wore Russian army greatcoats over their tunics as they considered their own coats inappropriate for the extreme cold of the Russian winter.

Oswald Rayner was in the palace that night. He was part of Yusupov's intimate circle. A reticent man, he nevertheless confided in later life to his cousin Rose Jones that he had been in the palace on the night of the murder.[20] He had, like John Scale, been 'involved in the planning'. We know this because the diary of William Compton, Rayner and Scale's chauffeur, records visits to the Yusupov Palace by Rayner and Scale on (British dates) 26 and 29 October, 3, 4, 9, 16 and 28 November and 2 December. (The corresponding Russian dates are 13, 16, 21, 22 and 27 October and 3, 15 and 19 November – five days before Purishkevich made his electrifying speech in the Duma.) The only date for which there is no entry in the diary is the day of the murder.[21]

Scale left Petrograd for Romania on 11 November (24 November in the British calendar), so he cannot have been present for the last two meetings, or on the night of the murder. There is no doubt about this: his written record of the journey, and of his actions when in Romania, is vivid and indubitably true. The blown-up factories and burning oil fields that met the German invaders bear witness to the success of his dangerous mission. He received a DSO.

Captain Stephen Alley was also involved in the planning of Rasputin's murder. As we have already noted, he and his family had a close and longstanding personal relationship with the Yusupov family. Like Rayner, Alley was a fluent Russian speaker. Did he accompany Rayner (with whom he shared an apartment) to the Yusupov Palace that night? Speaking fluent Russian and wearing Russian field coats, the pair would have been indistinguishable from any other Russian soldiers so far as Purishkevich, or indeed anyone else who might have met them that night, was concerned.

A British presence was, if anything, originally intended to be a token one, to discreetly observe that the job had been satisfactorily carried out. It is highly unlikely there was ever any anticipation that an active part would be taken in the proceedings. Further evidence of Alley and Rayner's complicity is found in a letter Alley wrote to Scale eight days after the murder. Scale, who had just been ordered to return to Petrograd from Romania, had voiced the opinion that merely blowing up oil fields was not sufficient. He therefore proposed that RFC planes should follow up the sabotage with regular raids to ensure that the Germans were unable to get the wells back in production.[22] London, it seemed, was a little apprehensive about the idea.

> 7th January, 1917
> Dear Scale,
> No response has thus far been received from London in respect to your oilfields proposal.
>
> Although matters here have not proceeded entirely to plan, our objective has clearly been achieved. Reaction to the demise of 'Dark Forces' has been well received by all, although a few awkward questions have already been asked about wider involvement.
>
> Rayner is attending to loose ends and will no doubt brief you on your return.
> Yours,
> Stephen Alley, Capt.[23]

There is also reason to believe that Rasputin's body was photographed at some point in the night, as evidence that he was indeed dead, prior to the disposal of the body (which it was hoped would never be discovered). Two months after the murder, these photographs were apparently discovered by the police and referred to in a report.

SECRET

To the Chief of the Public Security Department
Petrograd
        February 22nd, 1917

No 5698
Fifth Section

By order of the Chief of the Counter-Intelligence Department
of the Petrograd Military District Headquarters dated February
18th, Ref 3641, a search was made on February 19th at the apartment of Prince Yusupov Count Sumarokov-Elston's secretary,
Lieutenant of the 308th Petrograd druzhina, Leonid Rambur,
residing at Ofitserskaya 36. As a result of the search, two photographs have been discovered of Grigori Rasputin's dead body
along with a key to deposit box No 912 at the Azovsko-Donskoy
Bank. Rambur, who is not registered in our records as politically
disloyal, has been released.[24]

This is one of a number of police and Okhrana documents that
raise more questions than answers concerning an investigation
which can retrospectively be seen as inept and ineffective. While
appreciating that the investigation was still in its infancy when
word came from on high to close it down, the omissions are astonishing. The bloodstains that were seen, and have been marked on
the police scene of crime photographs, seem to have trailed from
the door to a snow-heap by the second gate. The Police Report
does not say the body was wrapped up or that the car drove into
the courtyard. It seems that the body was picked up in the courtyard and carried across the pavement to the car.

According to the plan, this was supposed to be Dmitri
Pavlovich's car, with Dmitri driving, accompanied by Lazovert,
Sukhotin, and Purishkevich.

The other omission has an internal political cause. Stepan
Beletski later testified to the Extraordinary Commission that,

because Protopopov was unwilling to have it known that he visited Rasputin, he had 'ordered the external surveillance agents removed after 10.00p.m.'[25] He told the Tsarina and Rasputin that the guard was on, but (Beletski said) 'it was stationed not by the gate but across the street out of sight'. In other words, there was no Okhrana man stationed within sight of whoever visited. Popov may have heard from the yard superintendent in Gorokhovaya Street that Protopopov himself had dropped by late on the night of Rasputin's death. If he did, either he judged it wiser to leave the information out, or he was told to. A number of writers and researchers, including Oleg Shishkin[26] and Phil Tomaselli,[27] have implied that Rasputin's bodyguard was somehow withdrawn by a sinister hidden hand acting on behalf of the conspirators. In fact, all that was necessary for the assassination plans to progress was the acquisition of the knowledge that the guard was withdrawn at ten o'clock.

Building on the fault lines of the haphazard and incomplete contemporary investigations, Purishkevich, Yusupov and Lazovert published their own accounts with ulterior motives. Purishkevich was used to the adulation of the crowd, and in 1918, after the revolution, he wanted to regain popular attention. By 1927, Yusupov needed the money. He had also remained in touch with Oswald Rayner. Lazovert, too, used his short 1923 account to boost his own modest role in events and was no doubt well paid for his trouble.

The three stories are similar in key respects: the poison failed; Rasputin did not die of the first lethal gunshot wound; he got out of the house and ran across the yard; he was hit by two more bullets; he was kicked in the head and he was beaten frenziedly by Yusupov. In that order.

The details vary. The poison is crystals or shavings; it's in either the chocolate cakes or the pink ones; the gang stay upstairs or don't... Neither of them has Rasputin wearing a blue embroidered silk smock – in both accounts it is white, and embroidered. It is odd that a scene that would have been imprinted on most minds was wrong in this respect. They both get the colour of the cord right.

The major difference between the accounts is the key protagonist. The eager reader of Purishkevich finds that he was the dynamic one: some kind of supernatural force flooded through him and he saved the day by shooting Rasputin. In Yusupov's story, he tries to be the hero, but ends up the victim of Rasputin's superhuman powers. Lazovert, too, casts himself in a central, proactive role.

Yusupov does not claim to have delivered the final shot and Purishkevich's story does not match the forensic evidence. Many at the time expected Dmitri Pavlovich to take the blame. Within thirty-six hours it became apparent that he was not going to admit a thing. Lazovert and Sukhotin are equally improbable candidates. So who did kill Rasputin?

He was strong and healthy, and harder to kill than they had expected. The poison failed. He was stabbed with a sword and left for dead. He escaped when the others were upstairs and they heard him opening the door. One of the party fired at him through the window, maybe another went out into the yard to have a look. Further firing was impossible. Reinforcements arrived.

As soon as the police had gone away, they dragged him back into the house. They did not want to shoot him because of the police. They tied him up and waited for him to die before taking him out to the Petrovski Bridge. But he did not die.

In desperation, two of them shot him outside in the yard. As they were carrying him out to the car, a third man checked, found that he still had a pulse, and put a bullet through his brain.

With the exception of Oswald Rayner's involvement with the production of Yusupov's Rasputin book in 1927, no one else in British circles wrote an account about Rasputin's murder. Sir Samuel Hoare and Sir George Buchanan wrote memoirs which included brief references to background events. Albert Stopford's diary likewise gives a commentator's account rather than a participant's.

However, a rich seam of oral history has survived through the children and grandchildren of the British officers who were involved in the planning of Rasputin's death. The family of William Compton, the chauffeur, have recollections of stories about his time in Petrograd, the terrible conditions, the Red Cross Hospital and the murder of Rasputin. According to Compton, it was 'a little known fact' that Rasputin had been shot not by a Russian but by 'an Englishman' whom he had known in Russia.[28] He said nothing more about the man other than that he was a lawyer and was from the same part of the country as Compton himself. This story was never taken seriously by Compton's family, who assumed that it was nothing more than a tale the old man told to add some colour to an otherwise uneventful and bleak period in his life.

According to the Compton family, William had been born not far from Birmingham. A search for his birth records reveals that he was born on 27 January 1881 in Kempsey, Worcestershire, some ten miles from where Oswald Rayner had been born and brought up.[29] On all official documents, right up to his death in 1961, Rayner described himself as a 'Barrister at Law'.[30] He had not only confided in his cousin, Rose Jones, that he had been at the Yusupov Palace when the murder took place, but he also showed close members of the family a bullet which he claimed he had acquired from the murder scene.[31] We also know that Rayner carried a .455 Webley service revolver, which, according to Professor Derrick Pounder, is the handgun that corresponds to the bullet that caused the fatal forehead wound.

The mysterious Englishman that the Tsar referred to during his conversation with Sir George Buchanan, whom he suspected of involvement in the murder, was certainly not Sir Samuel Hoare, who, as we have already seen, was not a college contemporary of Yusupov. Rayner was clearly the man whose identity Buchanan so carefully shielded when he came to relate the story in his memoirs.

On the afternoon following the murder, Yusupov met Rayner at the palace of his father-in-law, Grand Duke Alexander

Mikhailovich.[32] Together they had dinner with Irina's three elder brothers, Prince Andrew, Prince Fyodor and Prince Nikita, their tutor Mr Stuart and Mlle Evreinova, a lady-in-waiting to Irina's mother. Following the meal, Rayner, Yusupov, his three brothers-in-law and Mr Stuart took a car to the railway station in order to catch the nine o'clock train to the Crimea. At the station they found a large force of Palace Police on the steps of the main entrance. On getting out of the car, Yusupov was informed by a colonel that on the orders of the Tsarina he was forbidden to leave Petrograd and was to be placed under house arrest. Prince Nikita decided to proceed to the Crimea with Mr Stuart. Everyone else got back into the car and returned to the palace. Rayner, we are told, remained there with Yusupov. Although his escape had been foiled, Yusupov would survive to tell his story. After a brief appearance in the limelight of Yusupov's book, Rayner melted back into the milieu as unobtrusively as he had made his entrance.

TWELVE

AFTERMATH

O ut of the chaos, an aim was achieved: Rasputin died. Nobody was arrested for the crime and no charges were ever brought. When the Tsar realised the extent of his own family's involvement, the investigations were effectively closed. Despite Dmitri Pavlovich's request to be tried before a court-martial, Nicholas decided to exile Yusupov to his Rakitnoe estate near Kursk and exile Dmitri Pavlovich to Persia. No action was taken against anyone else allegedly involved in the murder. A court-martial would have made Dmitri a hero and given him a public platform. Nicholas's response was therefore a reluctantly practical one while at the same time typically weak and lenient.

Rasputin's body did not lie in peace for very long. In March 1917, a group of soldiers guarding the palace apparently dug up the body, soaked it in petrol and set fire to it in a nearby forest. This story is not wholly substantiated, however, and other evidence suggests that the body was exhumed on the orders of Alexander Kerenski and taken away to be secretly cremated.[1]

Many Rasputin biographers have, over the years, maintained
that he foresaw his own death, alluding to a letter Rasputin
apparently wrote to the Tsar, the contents of which Simanovich
made public.

> Russian Tsar! I have a presentiment that I shall leave this world
> by 1st January. If I am killed by hired assassins, then you Tsar
> will have no one to fear. Remain on your throne and rule. But
> if the murder is carried out by your own kinsmen, then not one
> member of your family will survive more than two years.[2]

However, the original copy of this letter in Rasputin's own
handwriting has never been found (if indeed it ever existed).
Those who have, in recent years, made a study of Rasputin's
writings have concluded that the construction of the prose has
no similarity with Rasputin's own uneducated but highly poetic
written style and grammatical conventions.[3]

The language in the passage bears all the hallmarks of
Simanovich himself, who published it after the execution of the
Tsar and his family, adding further to the myths surrounding
Rasputin.

Authentic or not, within months of Rasputin's murder, the
Romanov dynasty that had ruled Russia for over 300 years did
indeed fall. On 3 March 1917, the Putilov workforce in Petrograd
went on strike, and this developed into a general strike on 9
March. On the night of 11 March, units of the troops that had
been mobilised by the Tsar allied themselves with the strikers.
On 15 March, Nicholas, under pressure from all sides, abdicated.
On the day after the abdication, the Executive Committee of the
fourth Duma formed a Provisional Government under Prince
Lvov. It proclaimed civil rights, made a commitment to convene
a constituent assembly and declared its intention to continue the
war against Germany.

This was not the course of events that Dmitri Pavlovich,
Yusupov, Purishkevich and the others associated with the
plot had envisaged or predicted. They had hoped that the Tsar

would somehow exile his wife and lead Russia to victory with a united Duma behind him. Instead, the Tsar was banished, and the Tsarina with him, and the Duma proved incapable of taking control.

The Provisional Government kept Russia in the war on the Allied side until October 1917, when the Bolshevik coup took place. In this sense, time had worked in the Allies' favour, as the Americans had entered the war in April and were finally beginning to make their mark. Initially, their standing army was tiny and it took nearly a year for them to recruit and train a large army. By the time Lenin declared an armistice in December 1917, American soldiers were flooding onto the Western Front. By March 1918, when Russia finally signed the Treaty of Brest-Litovsk with Germany, a million Americans were in the field.

The peace treaty Germany forced on Lenin was a much harsher one than that offered to the Tsar in the summer of 1916. By this time, however, it was too late to prevent an Allied victory in the west, although the Germans did launch a massive last-ditch offensive on 21 March 1918 in a desperate attempt to score a decisive victory. Although the offensive achieved spectacular results early on, it gradually lost momentum, finally succumbing to an Allied counter-attack in July.

In a very real sense, being exiled probably saved the lives of Yusupov and Dmitri Pavlovich. Dmitri's father, like the Tsar and his family, was shot by the Bolsheviks. Those who survived headed south to Ukraine, which was still nominally in the hands of anti-Bolshevik forces now battling Lenin's new government in a fierce civil war. By early 1919, however, the Bolsheviks were advancing on the Crimea. In London, George V, no doubt regretting his earlier refusal to grant the Tsar and his family asylum in England, resolved to rescue his aunt, the Dowager Empress Marie. The battleship HMS *Marlborough* was therefore despatched in March 1919 to the Black Sea to take Marie and other surviving members of the Romanov family to safety. The ship's Captain, C.D. Johnson, carried with him a letter from George's mother, Queen Alexandra, imploring her sister to place herself under Captain Johnson's protection. In scenes that must have resembled the departure of Noah's Ark, Dowager Empress Marie, Grand Duchess Xenia, her sons Princes Andrew, Fyodor and Nikita, Grand Duke Nicholas, Grand Duke Peter, Felix and Irina Yusupov were among those who hastily boarded the *Marlborough* from a small cove on the Crimean coast at Koreiz on 7 April 1919. According to Rayner's family, he was present at Koreiz and accompanied Yusupov,[4] who was carrying as much of the family treasure as he could onto the ship.

John Scale, on the other hand, barely escaped in the clothes he was wearing following the Bolsheviks' seizure of power. He eventually made his way back to London, where he reported to C at SIS Headquarters at Whitehall Court. C had decided to appoint him Head of the ST Station in Stockholm, with the task of covertly sending a new cadre of British agents into Russia to report back on Bolshevik policy and intentions. On 15 March 1918, Scale, now known as ST0, introduced C to one Sidney Reilly, who would later find fame as the 'Ace of Spies'. Reilly became agent ST1. Scale recruited some thirty other ST agents, who included Oswald Rayner, Sir Paul Dukes, Arthur Ransome,[5] and Augustus Agar.[6] He stood down from intelligence work in 1922 due to ill health and finally retired from the army in May 1927. However, right up to his death in 1949[7] he kept in close touch with many of his former agents. Scale's daughters remember in particular the numerous visits Sir Paul Dukes made to their home in the inter-war years. When Felix Yusupov was in desperate financial straits in the early 1930s, it was Dukes who went out to France and saved him from ruin.[8] At whose behest Dukes performed this service is unknown.

Yusupov's finances were ultimately rescued by a stroke of good fortune. In 1932, MGM produced a big-budget epic, *Rasputin and the Empress*, starring John, Lionel and Ethel Barrymore, which was released in Britain the following year under the title *Rasputin, the Mad Monk*. While characters already dead were portrayed under their real names, others central to the plot who were still very much alive were given fictional names. For example, Rasputin's assassin is named Prince Chegodiev, and the character most resembling that of Princess Irina Yusupova is called Princess Natasha. In March 1933, Irina was introduced to American lawyer Fanny Holtzman, who was convinced that MGM had committed libel against her. In Holtzman's view, the film contained 'pictures and words which were understood to mean that Princess Natasha had been seduced by Rasputin'.[9]

In a landmark legal case at the High Court in London, which began on 28 February 1934, the Yusupovs' contention that Princess Natasha was indeed Princess Irina, who had, by implication, been libelled by MGM, was upheld by the jury.[10] Irina was awarded £25,000 and later received a further £75,000 from MGM in settlement of other actions the Yusupovs had initiated in the USA and against the film's distributors.

Further drama entered the Yusupovs' lives in 1940, when the German army swept through France. German officers apparently tracked them down to their Sarcells villa and informed them that they could return to Paris, where they would be lodged in a mansion of their choosing. In return, they would be asked to act as official hosts for important guests, throwing parties and dinners. To their credit, the Yusupovs rejected the offer. However, in 1941 they received a more profound offer, when Hitler dispatched his personal envoy to meet them.[11] Following the German invasion of Russia, the Nazis were clearly thinking about the possibility of an imperial puppet regime in a defeated Russia, and it was suggested to Yusupov by the envoy that he might be a suitable candidate for the throne. Again, he tactfully declined by suggesting that there were surviving members of the Romanov family in Paris the Germans could approach. Indeed, he would gladly provide their names and addresses if required.[12]

Yusupov was to die in Paris in September 1967, aged eighty, far outliving the other four declared assassins. Purishkevich had died of typhus in 1920 while fleeing from the Bolsheviks during the Russian Civil War. Sergei Sukhotin died in Paris in June 1939,[13] while Dmitri Pavlovich died of kidney disease in Davos, Switzerland in September 1942. Following his exile in Persia, Dmitri was given a commission in the British Army and served as a captain with the British Expeditionary Force in Mesopotamia. Most intriguingly of all, Stanislaus Lazovert, according to his son, apparently retracted his claim to have put poison in the cakes and wine on his death bed.[14] He also died in Paris in 1934.

In being considered a possible collaborator by the Nazis, Yusupov was unknowingly in the same company as former Head of the British Intelligence Mission Sir Samuel Hoare. Returning to active politics after the war, Hoare became Secretary of State for Air under Stanley Baldwin and Secretary of State for India in Ramsey MacDonald's national government. He reached the high-water mark of his career in June 1935, when Baldwin appointed him Foreign Secretary. Later that year, Hoare joined with Pierre Laval, the French Prime Minister, in an effort to resolve the crisis created by the Italian invasion of Ethiopia. A secret agreement, known as the Hoare-Laval Pact, proposed that Italy would receive two-thirds of the territory it conquered as well as permission to enlarge the existing colonies in East Africa. In return, Ethiopia was to receive a narrow strip of territory and access to the sea. Details of the pact were leaked to the press on 19 December 1935. The scheme was widely denounced as appeasement of Italian aggression. Baldwin's cabinet rejected the plan and Hoare was forced to resign.

Hoare returned to the government as First Lord of the Admiralty in June 1936. His appeasement views were popular with Neville Chamberlain, and in 1937 he was promoted to Home Secretary. On the outbreak of the Second World War he joined the War Cabinet as Lord Privy Seal. When Churchill became Prime Minister in 1940, Hoare was one of a number of ministers weeded out for their pro-appeasement views. In the opinion of Sir Alexander Cadogan, at that time Permanent Secretary of the Foreign Office, Hoare was an obvious candidate to head a puppet government in the event of a German occupation of Britain.[15] 'He'll be the Quisling of England', Cadogan confided in his diary shortly after Hoare's removal from the cabinet.[16] In October 2004, a newly released MI5 file on Albrecht Haushofer, described by the Service as 'the greatest expert in Germany on the British Empire', shed new light on Cadogan's suspicions. In a 1941 memo to Hitler entitled 'English Connections and the Possibility of their Employment', Haushofer listed a number of 'younger Conservatives' who, he believed, would collaborate – the names included the Duke of Hamilton, Lord Astor, Sir Samuel Hoare and R.A.B. Butler.[17]

Shortly after Rasputin's murder, it seems clear that London was actively considering replacing Hoare as Head of the British Intelligence Mission. On 29 January 1917 he cabled London:

> My health has been so bad during the last year that from every personal consideration I should welcome the opportunity of giving up my present work. I came out here a year ago as medically unfit to go abroad (with my yeomanry) and during that time I do not suppose that I have been well a single day. If, therefore, it is decided to discontinue my work in Russia, no one will be more delighted than myself.[18]

Soon after writing the letter, he was removed and sent on a new posting to Rome. Bearing in mind that he had been ill throughout his stint in Petrograd and that he was no worse in January 1917 than at any other time during his tenure, it seems unlikely that he was removed for purely health reasons. Neither does it seem likely that he was replaced because of any involvement in the Rasputin episode. If anything, he seems throughout to have been blissfully ignorant of what was going on around him. It is certainly possible that at some point in late 1916 London had taken the decision to actively sideline him and wait for an opportune moment to recall him. Equally, if he was considered in any way tainted by association with the events surrounding Rasputin's death, it seemed highly unlikely that London would opt for Stephen Alley as his successor, who, after all, seemed to have been in the thick of the plot.

It was, however, Alley that London turned to. Throughout the chaotic days of the Provisional Government, he, John Scale and the rest of his team struggled to do everything they could to help the new government hold on to the reins of power. When they were overthrown by the Bolsheviks, Alley did all he could to liaise with Lenin's commissars. During the months preceding the Treaty of Brest-Litovsk, he was secretly meeting with those on the Central Committee who would ultimately have to approve the treaty.[19] The objective was clearly to bring about a rejection of its terms and a consequent delay in the transfer of German troops to the Western Front. Trotsky, the Commissar for External Affairs, initially opposed ratification, pursuing a policy of 'neither peace nor war' in the hope that revolution would shortly erupt in Germany and Austria. Stalin, throughout, was in favour of the treaty. Trotsky eventually decided to back Lenin's appeal for ratification, so as to avert Germany's threat to resume its attack on Russia if there was a further delay in accepting the terms of the treaty. Ultimately, on 23 February 1918, the Central Committee of fifteen members gave its assent by seven votes to four, with four abstentions. While the majority were still unwilling to vote in favour of the treaty, Trotsky's change of mind and the four abstentions enabled its approval.

It was during the course of his secret meetings with Central Committee members in the weeks leading up to 23 February that Alley recalled:

> One telegram I got was that I had to liquidate Stalin. Seeing that I was negotiating with them at the time, it did not seem to be quite a good idea as it would have meant liquidating myself and him at the same time.
>
> When I got back to London… I was told that somebody had been put in my job and he happened to be E T Boyce, who had been one of my men in Russia. I believe the reason for my summary dismissal was that I had not killed Stalin, who, history tells, became the leader of the Bolsheviks in Russia. [20]

Apart from the enormity of Alley's statement concerning Stalin, and the consequent issues it raises in relation to British policy, significant questions about Rasputin's murder are also revived. While one might conclude, on the balance of the evidence so far considered, that Alley, Rayner and Scale were involved in a rogue operation[21] against Rasputin, conducted without London's knowledge, the Stalin claim raises some significant doubts.

Admissions made in the House of Commons in October 1920[22] revealed that Lloyd George's government was not adverse to authorising the use of murder and 'direct action' as policy in quelling the troubles in Ireland. If these tactics could be utilised in Ireland, so close to home, how much greater the possibility that they could be employed further afield in circumstances that raised a far more serious threat to the national interest than the IRA?

In his book *MI6: Fifty Years of Special Operations*, intelligence historian Stephen Dorril considers the *modus operandi* of MI6 in the context of assassination. Although dwelling on the post-war period, Dorril's analysis is particularly relevant to MI6 methods in the first half of the twentieth century.

In particular, he identifies 'a philosophy that is central to such operations and was a particular hallmark of MI6 planning – plausible deniability', concluding that, 'the use of third parties lessens the threat of any operation unravelling to reveal the hand of the sponsoring organisation'.[23] He also observes that, 'in times of war, constraints on such operations are not so tight and are more easily justified'.[24] The murder of Rasputin and Alley's order to assassinate Stalin both occurred during the First World War, and in this sense could well be viewed as actions necessary to achieve military objectives.

Subsequent history provides examples of situations where politicians have sought to sideline senior intelligence officers by dealing directly with those on the ground,[25] and indeed circumstances where intelligence officers have sanctioned operations without the knowledge or consent of politicians.[26] In light of the wealth of evidence, we know the Secretary of State for War and senior intelligence officers had known about Rasputin and the prospects of a separate peace, and it is difficult to believe that those in possession of such intelligence sat idly by knowing that Britain's fate rested on Russia remaining in the war. In a scenario where the thin margin between defeat and victory depended upon the thwarting of a separate peace, it is this author's belief that Rasputin's murder, effected through a third party, was officially sanctioned, either by Lloyd George, who as Secretary of State for War had political responsibility for the Secret Service, or by senior officers of the Service itself.

Under either scenario, Sir Samuel Hoare was outside the loop for reasons discussed earlier in this book. It is equally likely that any paper trail leading back to the authoriser of such an action has long since vanished, if indeed such a trail ever existed. As Professor John Lewis Gaddis reminds us, 'human relations, particularly in and between secret agencies, cannot always be reconstructed from documents'.[27] Whether documents exist or not, are closed or available in archives, the fact remains that, 'conversations occurring in corridors or over the telephone or at cocktail parties can at times shape events more decisively than whole stacks of official memoranda that find their way into the archives'.[28]

Precisely what the circumstances were behind Alley's replacement by Ernest Boyce is not entirely clear. It would seem, however, that he was involved in another critical mission shortly after Brest-Litovsk, which ultimately ended in failure.[29] In terms of the evidence currently available, it is not possible to determine the extent to which this may or may not have played a part in his dismissal.

Despite this unfortunate turn of events, Alley was to continue working in intelligence, in the service of MI5, until the end of the Second World War. He died on 6 April 1969 at the age of ninety-three, with the papers and souvenirs of his long intelligence career safely stored away in a trunk.

Rayner, too, kept his mementoes. The bullet from the night of Rasputin's murder he apparently had set in a ring.[30] He was awarded the Order of St Stanislaus in 1917 and remained in Petrograd until March 1918, when he was posted to the Intelligence Mission in Stockholm under John Scale. It was his task, in July of that year, to report the murder of the imperial Russian family to the King and Queen in London.[31] He later returned to Russia in 1922 as part of the British Trade Mission. While in Moscow, he married Tatiana Alexeievna Glubokovskia-Marek, whom he took back to England. They had three children and eventually divorced in August 1940.[32] During the Second World War, Rayner was again involved in intelligence work as a Liaison Officer in Canada. In 1943 he was sent to Spain, a hotbed of German activity, where he remained until the end of the war.

In 1947 he married his former secretary, Margaret Huntingford. When he was diagnosed with terminal cancer shortly before his death in 1961,[33] he burned all the papers connected with his time in Russia. Thankfully, he seems to have been the exception.

APPENDIX 1

SUPREME COURT- NEW YORK

SERGIUS MICHAILOW TRUFANOFF, being duly sworn deposes and says:

I reside in the Borough of Bronx, City, County and State of New York.

The defendant is a domestic corporation and engaged in the publication of a magazine known as the Metropolitan at 432 4th Avenue, Borough of Manhattan, New York City.

Annexed hereto is the complaint in this action which I herewith make part of this affidavit as if herein fully set forth.

I arrived in the United States of America on June 18th, 1916. On or about the 19th day of June, 1916 I called at the office of the Metropolitan magazine and met Mr. H. J. Wigham, whom I am informed, is the President of the defendant. At this conversation was present Mr. Herman Bernstein, myself, Mr. Tobenkin and a Stenographer. Tobenkin is a well known writer who is employed by the Metropolitan Magazine. I do not speak English. The conversation between me and Mr Wigham was interpreted by Bernstein. I was then told in the presence of Mr. Wigham by Mr. Bernstein in Russia that I was to give interviews to Mr. Tobenkin regularly and the information which I was to furnish him would be written into five articles or stories. These articles would be published once a month commencing with the issue of October, 1916.

While no definite amount was mentioned in this conversation, I received on May 13, 1916 a telegram from Mr Bernstein who was the go-between the defendant and myself as follows:

Communicated arrangement for manuscript, $5000. Entire sum will be paid before August 1st in several instalments; sending money now. Please send immediately rzsevsky chapter, also originals of letters or photographs. Copies in Bergen cable reply

BERNSTEIN
1781 Clay Avenue

I understood at this conversation that $5000 was to be paid to me by August 1st, 1916. From time to time I talked with Mr. Tobenkin in accordance with this agreement and gave him the data and material out of which he was to write the English story for the defendant. I did not keep dates of my conversations with him. These interviews were taken away by Mr. Tobenkin and were given by me about two or three times a week. This work started some time in June 1916 and continued right up to the latter part of September 1916. These interviews or stories of what I said are still in the possession of the defendant.

In the early part of September, I believe it was around the 9th, the Archbishop Evdokin and one Michael Oustinoff called to see me at my residence in the Borough of Bronx. My wife who was then looking out of the window told me that they were there and I went down to meet them. They took me into an automobile and we drove through Bronx Park. They told me that they had read in the Metropolitan that I was going to write some articles on Rasputin and the Czarina of Russia. They begged me not to publish the articles. They said it would hurt Russia very much and they offered to give me $25,000 and a full pardon so that I could return to Russia if I did not publish them. They also told me that if I refuse the offer the articles would not be published in the Metropolitan Magazine as the owner of the Company was their best friend. They also stated that they had enough influence with the magazine that the slightest wish regarding publication would be respected. They further stated that the only reason for their trying to buy the article was to prevent my publishing same in some other paper or magazine. I told them that I would refrain from publishing this article; that I believed it was necessary for the good of Russia and that the destruction of the influence of Rasputin would not be an injury to Russia but the best help in the world to that Country. I have been in prison for eleven months in Russia for my patriotism and my desire to save Russia. They continued to insist that I should not publish this article and solely for the purpose of seeing to what extent they would go and to learn whether or not they had any official authority, I pretended to take up these negotiations. I told them that I had already given the articles to the Metropolitan Magazine and even if I would agree not to publish it, the defendants might publish it themselves, and they told me that they would arrange with the magazine to get these articles back. I asked them if they would consent to the return of the articles and would also consent to the cancellation of my agreements with them, and if they would pay $25,000 within three days.

An affirmative answer would have shown me they were acting without communicating with Rasputin. They asked time to communicate with Petrograd in order to arrange for my pardon and for the money and I granted time so that I might definitely learn if said Rasputin was carrying on these negotiations and what he would try to do.

On or about the 14th day of September, 1916 they again called at my house. They told me that they had arranged a pardon for me and they had the money in their possessions. They asked me to call at the Consul's office for the money on the following day. Next day I called at the office of the Russian Consul, 22 Washington Square. I saw the Consul-General Oustinoff and the Consul Rutsky. I spoke to both of them. The Consul-General then told me that he had arranged with the Metropolitan that they were not to publish the articles, but nevertheless he said he ordered the Consul to pay me $1000 and he gave me the $1000 and I signed a receipt in Russian for the same. This receipt I left with the Consul-General. In this conversation I was given to understand that they would send word to Petrograd that they had arranged to stop the publication and would pay me the balance of the money as soon as they had heard from Petrograd. They also gave me to understand that they had made this arrange-ment with the consent of the defendant herein and that they would obtain from the magazine the articles that were written by Tobenkin and the written interviews, which I gave them. At that time I began to believe that said Rasputin was in charge of this matter and I was extremely desirous of having a tender of monies made thereunder.

On the 19th I received a telephone message from consul Rutsky and he said to me that he was sorry to say that they were all through with this subject and would drop the whole matter.

The Consul-General also talked to me at the same time asking me to call at the office for a friendly call. I went there on the 20th and he told me that they received word from Petrograd that I was not to receive the money. The Consul-General told me that he had talked to a Mr Whitney, the largest stockholder of the defendant and had induced him to agree not to publish the articles, and he asked me what I was going to do and I told him that I did not know. He then advised me to be very careful as to what I was doing as it may keep me away from Russia for the rest of my life.

The day before, the 19th, Mr Wigham telephoned and asked me to call. I went to see him and he told me that the articles would possibly never be published, but might be published after the war or within one year; he would give no definite date. He said he was very sorry for me but he would pay an additional $2,000. Up to this time I had received $2,000 from the defendant. This money I refused.

Subsequently I again saw Mr. Wigham and he repeated that he would not publish them at all.

During all my conversations with the defendant it was agreed that the article was to be published commencing October, 1916 and be continued thereafter and there would be five articles at $5,000. The money was to be paid me on August 1st. I only received $2,000.

It seems now and with the connivance of the Russian government, the Metropolitan Magazine refused to publish these articles and is willing to pay me in order to suppress them. I would never agree to suppress my articles. My intention was to publish them and my agreement with the defendant was for the publication of the articles and not for their suppression. My object in coming to this Country and giving this information to the Metropolitan Magazine was to have published in a neutral country this information of such great interest to Russia and my people. I have suffered imprisonment in my opposition to Rasputin, and would not permit this defendant or anybody else to silence my voice in this matter. The money I received is only small compensation for my expenses and the money is the least of my objects in this matter. The suppression of this article by this magazine, the copyrighting of the subject matter in part at least, prevent other magazines from publishing it and thereby the exposure which I desire to have it made is completely suppressed.

The defendant claims that they are the owners of the said articles written from the data which I gave them, and they consider it their property to do with what they please, and that they publish what they please concerning the same and that they will enjoin me from publishing the same, and will interfere with any other publication of this matter.

That in the November issue, the defendant published on the cover my picture or a picture, which was supposed to be of myself, but the article itself did not appear.

Since that time the defendant has repeatedly attempted to have me accept the $2000 but I refused to do so.

The defendant has committed a breach of its contract in that it failed to pay the money by August 1st, 1916 and has failed to carry out its agreement to publish the said articles and in violation thereof has intended and does intend to suppress the same.

I intend to use the material which I gave to them and the other material which I gave to them and the other material which I have concerning the Russian Emperor, the Czarina and the Russian Court in my own way and I desire an injunction order restraining the defendant from publishing or using the said manuscripts or any information which I gave them or from making the same public or from showing the same to any person, persons or corporation whatsoever until the trial of this action, and from interfering with my publication through other channels.

Russia in conjunction with the allies is now at war with Germany and its allies. The information which I have obtained in my close connection at Russian courts and with the Russian government has a peculiar importance at this time, during the war. It is a problem just how much value this information may have after the war. Russian court life and anything that pertains to the Russian government are now an interesting topic for literature, magazines and newspapers and it is possible that this interest may not exist after the war. Further, and more important, the suppression of this information at this time when it may weaken or destroy the Rasputin influence and intrigues may work an incalculable injury to Russia, and will defeat the purpose for which I am working and have suffered imprisonment.

As appears in the complaint herein I have graduated from the Imperial Sacred College of Petrograd and have been ordained a priest and also a monk priest. I was also a monk priest. I was also a professor of oratory and sermons. I was also a preacher of wide fame throughout Russia. I was also an Abbott at Tsaritsin Convent. I was prominently identified with the revolutions of 1905. I was strongly identified with the suppression of same and throughout Russia have been given the credit of being instrumental in their overthrow.

I was a confidential friend and advisor of Rasputin an illiterate and uneducated peasant who is known as a Pilgrim possessing certain supernatural gifts and he now dominates the Russian Court and the Empress Czarina and the Czar to a certain extent. My relations with Rasputin have been so intimate and friendly that I am acquainted with the secrets of the Russian Court and the wild orgies of the Russian Courtiers headed by the Empress.

This Rasputin is strongly pro-German and has such influence over the Czarina through his personal relations with her as to obtain her influence against the allies and in favour of Germany. This has recently resulted in a change of ministry of the Russian government. Rasputin is now engaged in a conspiracy to bring about a separate peace with the Russian government to apply for a loan of three million roubles from the English government with the threat that in case the money is not forthcoming a separate peace will be signed this winter. I am also informed that there is now a Russian officer, a relative of Rasputin, sent specially to spy upon me, from Russia.

All this information furnished and was to furnish the basis for the articles to appear in the Metropolitan and all of which are now suppressed by it.

Mr. Wigham, the president of the defendant, stated that he considered this article and information the property of the magazine, the defendant, and that in the event that I intend to make any arrangements with any other publication, to publish these articles or give the substance or interviews to anybody concerning Rasputin and the Russian Court, they would consider that an interference of their title to said manuscripts and they would prevent the publication thereof and would impair and impede my rights to publish the same in any way that they could. They also claim that they had copyrighted the said articles and that I have no right to publish the same.

They may also publish the information that I gave them to detriment of any arrangements that I may make with any magazine for the publication of these articles.

No application for this has been made. I therefore ask for an injunction restraining the said Metropolitan Magazine from interfering with me in the publication of my articles and giving out any information concerning them, from showing any articles or anything written as a result of my conversations with them to any person or corporations and from making the same public and from doing any other thing that might interfere with the publication thereof by me.

Sworn to by me this 17th day of October 1916

SERGIUS MICHAILOW TRUFANOFF.

Appendix 2

Police Report – December 17th 1916

To-day at about 2.30 in the morning, the policeman who stands on guard at the house of the Home Office situated on the Morskaia heard a detonation from the palace of Prince Yusupov situated on the opposite side of the Moika. As this post is a special one and the policeman on duty is forbidden to leave it, he went into the Home Office premises and communicated by telephone with the sergeant on duty at the adjoining station. Then the news of the shooting was passed on to the Kasan police district in which the palace is situated. The chief police officer, Colonel Rogov, with a detachment of men, proceeded to the spot. Examination of the dvornik on duty at the adjoining house elicited the fact that the shot had been fired from the young Prince's side of the palace. In order to ascertain the causes of the shooting in the palace, the assistant police officer, Captain Krylov, was ordered to enter the building, and he was informed by the butler that a reception was proceeding inside, and that one of the guests, while practising at a target, had missed his aim and fired into the window, in proof whereof Captain Krylov was shown the broken window on the ground floor overlooking the forecourt of the adjoining house. The data obtained through the investigations were communicated by Colonel Rogov the same night to the Police Master of the second division, Major-General Grigoriev, and to M.Chaplygin, the official on duty at the Prefecture.

Scarcely had the police officers left the palace when a motor-car drove up along Moika Canal quay and stopped near a small foot-bridge almost facing the palace. Four men were seen to alight from the car. The moment they had left it the chauffeur extinguished the lights, and, putting on full speed, made off along the canal. This scene was witnessed by a detective belonging to the Okhrana, named Tihomirov, who had been detailed by the police department to look after Rasputin. Tihomirov – presuming that the men who entered the palace, not by the main entrance, but from a door situated on the side of the palace and opening into the forecourt of the adjoining house, were robbers hurried across the canal to the police station, and thence telephoned a report of what was observed to the Chief of the Secret Police.

Colonel Rogov had no sooner returned to his home than he was notified from the Ochrana that information had been received relative to an attack on the palace of Prince Yusupov. A number of police officers were again dispatched there. The butler came out and explained to them that some very highly placed guests had just arrived from the environs of Petrograd. A report about this was made during the course of the night to the Prefect, General Balk.

Shortly after 6a.m., at the police station beside the palace, while the police officers who had come off duty were being questioned in the ordinary course as to the events of the night, the sound of several police whistles was heard from the street. This drew the police constables and police ser-geants to the windows, whence they perceived that from the main entrance of the Prince's palace two women were being helped out, and that they were offering resistance to their ejection and refusing to enter a motor-car, and doing their best to force a way back into the palace. In response to their protestations the detectives stationed along the canal had sounded the alarm. By the time the police rushed out of the police station the motor-car was already whirling off along the quay. Hastening out after his men, the police inspector, Colonel Borozdin, hailed the motor-car belonging to the Secret Police, which was permanently on duty at the Home Office building, and started off in pursuit. At the same time his men were hurried to the palace. It was impossible to overtake the fugitive car on account of its superior speed; moreover, it carried neither number nor lights. To the police who came to inquire at the palace the explanation was offered that two ladies belonging to the *demi-monde* had been misconducting themselves and been invited to leave the palace.

On the nocturnal adventures on the Moika a joint personal report was made to the Prefect in the morning by Colonel Rogov and Colonel Borozdin. The whole affair seemed to be at an end when suddenly from the forecourt alongside the palace four shots were heard in succession. Once more the alarm was sounded in both police stations, and again detachments of police appeared at the palace. This time an official wearing colonel's uniform came out to them and announced categorically that within the Prince's palace there was present a Grand Duke, and that H.I.H. would make in person to the proper quarters any explanations that might be necessary. After such a declaration, the police inspector, unable to obtain any enlightenment whatsoever, returned to his official's duties, leaving a patrol on the opposite side of the Moika by way of precaution. About an hour had passed when suddenly from the direction of the Blue Bridge a motor-car drove up to the palace. The servants, assisted by the chauffeur, in the presence of an officer wearing a long fur cloak, carried out what looked like a human body and placed it in the car. The chauffeur jumped in, putting on full speed, made off along the canal side and promptly disappeared. Almost the same time General Grigoriev was informed from the Prefecture that Rasputin had been killed in the Yusupov Palace.

The police officials on arriving at the palace were met this time by Prince Felix Yusupov himself, who told them that it would be necessary to draw up a report as to the killing of Rasputin. At first this announcement was not accepted seriously in view of all the strange occurrences of the night. But the police officials were invited to come into the dining-room in the basement, and were there shown the spot where the body had been lying. They saw on the floor a pool of congealed blood, and traces of blood were also visible on the snow in the forecourt of the adjoining house. In answer to the question where the body was, the Prince replied that the body was where it should be, declining to give any further explanation.

Soon afterwards the palace was visited by the Director of the Police Department, the Chief of the Secret Police, and the whole of the Generals of Gendarmerie. The police patrols were then relegated to their various stations, and at the subsequent investigation sent over to the officials of the Police department. At 5 o'clock on the following afternoon with a view to ascertaining the itinerary of the motor-cars, which had come up to the Prince's palace during the night, and one of the one which had been removed Rasputin's body in the morning. At the same time numerous police patrols were dispatched to the islands in the Neva and to the suburban districts.

Appendix 3

The following three reports (CTG. 91, CTG. 95, and CTG. 119) sent by Sir Samuel Hoare to Mansfield Cumming, the Chief of the Secret Intelligence Service, are reproduced below in full:

CTG. 91

From: Lt Col Sir Samuel Hoare (Petrograd)
To: 'C' (London)
January 1st 1917

The Death of Rasputin

In the early morning of Saturday, December 30th, there was enacted in Petrograd one of those crimes that by their magnitude blur the well-defined rules of ethics, and by their results change the history of a generation.

Gregory Efemich Novikh – for Rasputin, 'the rake', was only the nickname that his excesses gained him in his village – had governed Russia since the day, four years ago, when first he showed in the Imperial palace in Poland his healing powers over the Tsarevich. To describe the influence that he possessed, the scandals that surrounded his life and the tragedies that followed in his path, is to rewrite a Dumas romance.

Three times he was within an inch of being murdered. Once, an outraged peasant girl from his native Siberia stabbed him – the wound did not prove fatal. Next the monk Heliodor seemed to have him at his mercy in the Petrograd cell of the Metropolitan of Kiev – Rasputin's great strength and the arrival of help saved his life. Again, only ten months ago in a reserved room of one of the best Petrograd restaurants, the Bear, certain officers of the Chevalier Gardes would have killed him, if his familiars of the secret police had not appeared in time. The papers said nothing of these things. Indeed, to mention his name brought a fine of three thousand roubles. Day and night, the secret police were near him. Because he withdrew them, Khvostov, the Minister of the Interior, was dismissed. Only from time to time the mujik's uncontrollable appetite for debauch left him defenceless before his enemies. There is in Moscow a former officer of the Guards, now relegated to the Gendarmes, who boasts that the achievement of his career was the beating he gave Rasputin during some wild orgy. There are others who have seen him madly drunk in the streets and public places. Of one of these incidents there is a photograph, and a photograph that is said to have been shown to the Emperor. True to his nickname, it was at an orgy that Rasputin met his death.

On December 29th, the Duma session was abruptly closed twenty-four hours before the appointed time. On November 14th the debates had begun with Milyukov's fierce attack upon the 'Dark Forces' that had become the synonym for Rasputin's activities, an attack in which for the first time a Member dared to mention Rasputin by name. They ended with another onslaught, less personal, less sensational, but hardly less effective. 'The atmosphere is charged with electricity,' so ran Milyukov's peroration, 'no one knows where or when the blow will fall (applause).' The following morning the blow, the effects of which cannot be gauged, had already fallen.

On Saturday afternoon I was at the Restriction of the Enemy Supplies Committee. Several times during the sitting individual members left the room and returned with whispered messages to their neighbours. At the time I paid no attention to these interruptions of business. When the Committee broke up, I went with the chairman and the secretary to another room for the purpose of discussing various points connected with the publication of the Russian Black List. Before we could go far with our discussion, a well-known official of the Ministry of Commerce entered with the news that Rasputin had been murdered that morning by the Grand Duke Dmitri Pavlovich and Prince Yusupov. Professor Struve, Chairman of the Committee, at once sent out for an evening paper. In a few minutes the *Bourse Gazette* was brought in with the news actually published in it. The *Bourse Gazette* is always a paper of headlines. In this case, the first heavy type was devoted to the peace proposals, the second to the fight in Romania. Then came a headline, 'Death of Gregory Rasputin in Petrograd.' In the body of the paper there was little more than a single line, and that on the second page. The announcement ran as follows: 'A six o'clock this morning Gregory Rasputin Novikh died after a party in one of the most aristocratic houses in the centre of Petrograd.'

To one who had only been in Russia a few months the news was almost overwhelming. To Russian public men like Professor Struve, a publicist whose name has for a generation been in the forefront of Russian political and economic life, it seemed almost incredible. As I had no wish to appear to meddle in Russian internal affairs, I did not attempt to discuss the situation nor, needless to say, could I continue our prosaic conversation about the Black List.

Since Saturday, I have made it my business to discover as many details as I can about the murder, and I have been in touch with various people representing different classes and sections of opinion.

The result of my inquiries is as follows: Rasputin has not been seen since the evening of Friday, the 29th December, when he left his flat in company with an officer in a motor car. Prince Yusupov had a party on the same evening that was attended by one or two of the Grand Dukes. On the evening following Rasputin's disappearance, the Grand Duke Dmitri Pavlovich had another party in his rooms in the Palace of the Grand Duchess Elizaveta Fyodorovna, the upper floors of which are used by the Anglo-Russian Hospital. The party seems to have been of a most riotous description and did not break up until 7.30 on Sunday morning.

The details of the story vary. Some people say that Rasputin was got into a room and told to kill himself. I have heard it said that he did kill himself. I have also heard it stated that he fired the revolver that was given him at 2 o'clock in the morning in self-defence. The generally accepted story, however, is that he was shot. A motor is supposed to have taken the body to the Islands, where it was thrown into the sea or one of the rivers. This story is generally supported in Petrograd.

There seems also general agreement that he was killed either by the Grand Duke Dmitri Pavlovich or by Prince Yusupov. Many people say that lots were drawn as to who should kill him and that the lot fell upon the Grand Duke Dmitri, but that Prince Yusupov undertook the duty.

The Grand Duke Dmitri was brought up by the Grand Duchess Elizaveta Fyodorovna in the palace in which he is now living on the Nevsky Prospekt. He has had a gay career, and not long ago was in disgrace for some escapade.

Prince Yusupov, who is also Count Sumarokov-Elston, is the Count Elston who had so great a success in London society a year or two before the war. It will be remembered that during one season he was regarded as the greatest catch in London. This view of his eligibility was certainly correct, as he is one of the richest men in Russia. He has since married the Grand Duchess Irene, who a fortnight ago signed the protest of Princess Vassilshchikova to the Empress against the 'Dark Forces.'

Whether it was the Grand Duke Dmitri Pavlovich or Prince Yusupov who actually did the deed, it seems certain that it was planned and carried out by some of the best known people in Petrograd society. I am informed that the Grand Duke Dmitri Pavlovich and Prince Yusupov were together all the afternoon of December 31st, and that, when asked, they make no secret of the fact that Rasputin has been killed. Perhaps the fact that Rasputin had recently been meddling more than usually in the domestic affairs of the Imperial family hastened the event.

There have often been rumours of Rasputin's death. As recently as March, the *Times*, for instance, published a telegram from Bucharest announcing his murder. It will, therefore, be suggested that this is another rumour, and that after a few weeks of retirement he will reappear.

What then is the evidence that differentiates this case from the groundless rumours of the past?

It should be stated at once that the story is officially denied. The denial, however, is half-hearted, and given with conflicting details. The official answer was at first that nothing had happened. It now seems to have been modified to the extent of admitting that something has happened, that Rasputin has been wounded, but that he is going on well.

I am informed that an inquiry at his flat in the English Prospekt brought the answer that on Friday evening, the 29th December, he left in a motor with an unknown officer and has not since been seen. In the meanwhile, interested people seem to be purposely spreading fantastic and impossible rumours with the object of discrediting the whole story. The fact that no one has seen Rasputin's body goes to support all these official denials and contradictions.

The following facts, however, seem to afford overwhelming proof for the fact of Rasputin's death.

In the first place, the whole of Russia regards it as established beyond doubt. The news published in the *Bourse Gazette* has already been circulated through the provinces. The mysterious telegrams that are already appearing in the Petrograd press show how widespread is the conviction of the truth of the announcement.

Secondly, Rasputin's entourage is in a state of deep depression and great anxiety. His flat is filled with commotion and lamentation. His principal supporter at Court, Madame Vyrubova, has refused to leave her rooms and the guard of secret police outside them has been trebled.

Far more conclusive, however, than this hearsay evidence is the attitude of the Petrograd press. The *Bourse Gazette* would never have risked its existence for a rumour. Even had it done so, a mere rumour would not account for the meeting that was held on the evening of the 30th December of representative of all the Petrograd press, at which they discussed the question as to what policy they should adopt with reference to the publication of the news. The matter was decided for them, for during the conference they received a notice from the censorship, forbidding any publication of the event. None the less, both on the 31st December and 1st January there have appeared numerous indirect and mysterious references to the murder in most of the Petrograd papers. For instance, in the *Novoe Vremya* in a remote corner and in small print there is the following paragraph:

On December 30th, at the Zeloti Concert, as a result of a unanimous request, in view of events that are taking place, the National Anthem was sung amidst tumultuous applause.

Still more marked in the *Ruskaya Volya* there are no less than four more remarkable references to the event. It should be remembered that the *Ruskaya Volya* is a new daily paper that has just appeared, and that it is supposed to have particularly close connections with the Government. In addition to a poem, the motif of which are the words 'rasputin' and 'novikh' (Rasputin's names, and also the word for 'rake' and the genitive plural of the work 'new'), there are two leading articles in which the clearest reference is made to the news. In the first of them, Alexander Amphiteatrov, the editor, ends with the following words:

'I wrote so far, and then there came the news of the *Bourse Gazette*! In its big type was announced the sensational news that there had passed from the scene of life the strangest and the most notorious embodiment of the present reactionary might.'

The second article, entitled 'Short Chronicle,' deals in detail with the great excitement in Petrograd and states that never had the city passed through so nervous a day; never had the telegraph worked so incessantly as on Saturday, December 30th.

'Yesterday was the great day. About it no one can say more.'

Again, on page 6, there is a paragraph of twenty lines, headed:

Shooting in the Street.

Yesterday about six o'clock near the house of Prince Yusupov, Count Sumarokov-Elston, Moika 94, several revolver shots in succession were heard in the neighbourhood of a motor car that was standing close by.

The shooting was heard by a constable of the 3rd Kazan District and other constables who were standing on the opposite side of the Moika in the direction of the Admiralty District police station. The Kazan police station constable hurried to the spot and as he approached, the motor car went off at great speed.

It is supposed that a number of young men, after a good supper, had shot into the air.

On January 1st these references became more explicit. The *Rech*, for instance, published in its 'Latest News' the following paragraphs:

At three o'clock on the night of December 30th, a constable standing at the point opposite the Kazan section of the Ofitsersky Street, heard cries and a noise issuing from the garden of No. 21. At the same time, constables standing on their points upon the Moika Quay, not far from the Prachashnaya Bridge, also heard the noise from the same garden, that looks out upon the Moika. The garden at 21, Ofitsersky Street, stretches almost to the bank of the Moika and is enclosed on the side of the quay by a two-storied house, No. 92, belonging to Prince Yusupov. The next house to No. 92 also belongs to the same owner.

The constable in the Ofitsersky Street, some time after hearing the cries, saw several men coming out of the garden gate of No. 21. He tried to find out what had happened, but did not succeed.

A short time after this a motor car was noticed to arrive at the garden and seen afterwards to leave it.

According to the statements of passers by, another motor car arrived at the same garden from the Moika side about 3 o'clock. An examination shows that there were bloodstains upon the snow in the garden. The manager of the house declared that this was the blood of a dog that went mad during the night and was shot. Samples of the snow with the blood have been taken for examination.

In the course of December 30th, the news arrived that a mysterious motor car had been seen at the Petrovsky Island during the night. On December 31st the river was examined in the neighbourhood of the Petrovsky Bridge. A freshly made hole in the ice was discovered and footsteps passing backwards and forwards to it in different directions. Divers were given the duty of examining the bed of the rivers.

Some men's galoshes were found in the snow on the bank with suspicious dark stains.

The *Bourse Gazette* of January 1st, in a remote corner of it pages and in very small print, publishes the same story under the heading of 'Mysterious Discovery.' The only additional detail that it gives is that the divers found nothing.

The *Novoe Vremya* has another small paragraph entitled 'Mysterious Crime.' Much the same details are given in it with the addition that the secret police are guarding the river, and that photographs have been taken.

The feeling in Petrograd is most remarkable. All classes speak and act as if some great weight had been taken from their shoulders. Servants, *isvostchiks*, working men, all freely discuss the event. Many say that it is better than the greatest Russian victory in the field.

What effect it will have in Government circles, it is difficult to say. My present view is that it will lead to immediate dismissal of Protopopov and of various directors of the Secret Police, whilst in the course of the next few weeks the most notorious of Rasputin's clientele will gradually retire into private life. I would suggest, for instance, that careful attention should be paid to any changes that take place in the Department of the Interior and the Holy Synod, where Rasputin's influence was always strongest.

It is certainly fortunate for the cause of liberalism in Russia that the crime cannot even be remotely identified with the democratic movement or any revolutionary plot.

Further evidence of his death will, I also suggest, be forthcoming in the developments of such *causes celebres* as those of Sukhomlinov and Manuilov. For the moment, owing to the pressure that Rasputin applied, both trials have been stopped. If the proceedings are restarted, the fact will provide confirming evidence of the removal of the guiding hand that had hitherto stopped them.

Nowhere will any regret be felt for the crime except amongst those over whom Rasputin exercised a hypnotic influence, and the unscrupulous intriguers whom he used for his own ends and rewarded with innumerable appointments in the Church and State.

Of such a man no one can honestly say 'de mortuis nil nisi bonum.'

If one cannot write good about the dead, one can at least say about the death 'nothing but good.'

CTG.95

From: Lt Col Sir Samuel Hoare (Petrograd)
To: 'C' (London)
Date: January 2nd 1917

Death of Rasputin – Report No 2

Since writing the above memorandum I have received definite information that the body of Rasputin has been discovered in the river Nevka, near the Petrovsky Bridge. I received this information in strict confidence from the Chief of the Department of Military Police in the General Staff. He has himself seen the body. It appears that traces were purposely left about the hole in the ice, into which the body was thrown, in order that it should be discovered. The chief officials of the Ministry of the Interior, the Petrograd Prefecture, the River Police and the Department of Public Prosecutions have held investigations upon the spot, and a rough map has already been published in the *Evening Times* under the heading of 'Mysterious Murder.'

It is also certain that Rasputin was actually killed in Prince Yusupov's house and not in the motor. During the evening there seems to have been a certain amount of promiscuous shooting, in which a dog was killed in the courtyard and a window broken. Early in the morning, six men appeared in the courtyard with a body dressed in a *shuba*, that they put in a motor that was waiting. I understand that these facts are stated in detail in the report of the four secret police, who were waiting for Rasputin in the courtyard. A very well-known Russian told me that one of his friends had seen this report, in which were stated all the details of the arrivals and departures to and from Prince Yusupov's house during the evening.

It is also said that the company did not assemble at the house until very late in the evening, as most of the people had previously been to a party at the house of Mme. Golovina.

I am also informed, upon absolutely reliable authority, that the Empress was informed of the crime whether late on Saturday night or early on Sunday morning. As late as six o'clock on Saturday afternoon, when the news had already been published in the *Bourse Gazette*, she appears to have known nothing of what had happened. On Sunday morning, however, she ordered that a Liturgy should be performed in the Imperial chapel at Tsarskoe, and that special prayers should be said for Rasputin.

I also hear, but on less reliable authority, that Her Majesty sent the following telegram to the Emperor, who was still at the Stavka:

"Our friend had been taken from us. Dmitri and Felix (Prince Yusupov) are parties to it."

A cousin of Yusupov told me that his intended departure to the Caucasus had been stopped, and that the Grand Duke Dmitri and he had both been placed under domiciliary arrest.

CTG.119

From: Lt Col Sir Samuel Hoare (Petrograd)
To: 'C' (London)
Date: February 5th 1917
Death of Rasputin – Report No 3

Further details obtained from the Examining Magistrates and other reliable sources.

The following particulars may be taken as quite accurate as they have been given by people directly connected with the affair.

For some days before his death, Rasputin had been nervous and unwell. He had received a shock from what appeared to be the attempted suicide of the Cossack officer who was engaged to his daughter. As he was always in fear of his life, he took the greatest precautions for keeping his movements secret. He, however, always made it a practice to tell his two confidants, Simonovich and Bishop Isidor, where he was and where he was going. Simonovich is an unbaptised Jew, a curiosity seller, and

Isidor a bishop who, for bad behaviour was compelled to retire from his see. They live together in the Nikolaevsky Street. It was Rasputin's habit to telephone to them, whenever he left his house, and to tell them where he was to be found. On the evening of the 29th December, he was at his flat at No. 64, Gorokhovaya, with his two daughters, a niece and a secretary, all of whom acted as servants for the flat. Late in the evening he sent away the detectives of the Secret Police, and told them that they were not wanted any more. Shortly afterwards, a motor with a cape cart hood arrived and someone came and knocked at the back door. This proved to be a boy who frequently visited Rasputin, and to whom Rasputin always opened the door himself. The boy said something to Rasputin, and Rasputin answered 'I will come with you.' The two then went off in the motor in the direction of the Fontanka, and at the Fontanka Bridge were seen to turn right. Nothing more can be heard of the motor. A motor shortly afterwards drove up to Prince Yusupov's house. This, however, was a closed motor, and not the motor that had been seen to leave 64, Gorokhovaya. The dvornik at Prince Yusupov's house seemed either very stupid or very clever, and very little could be got out of him. He, however, admitted that the driver of the motor was in uniform, and was a very simple-looking person. He is supposed to have been the Grand Duchess Irene's brother.

At 12.30 the *gorodovoi* (i.e. the policeman) outside the Ministry of the Interior in the Moika heard four shots. This fact he reported to the Criminal Investigation Department, this is situated close by. At 3.30 the *gorodovoi* standing outside Prince Yusupov's house was called into the house by a man in general's uniform. The unknown general said, 'Do you know me?' To which the *gorodovoi* replied, 'Not at all.' 'Are you a patriot?' was the next question. 'Certainly'. The general then said, 'Rasputin is destroyed, you can go.' Shortly afterwards a motor left the house and was not seen again. The *gorodovoi* seems to have taken some time to think about what had happened, but after a time went off, and reported the matter to the nearest police station.

In the early morning the Minister of Justice, Makarov, was rung up by an unknown voice that said 'Rasputin has been murdered, look for his body in the Islands.'

As a result of these incidents, two examining judges, Sereda and Zarvatsky, and the police, went round in the morning to Prince Yusupov's house. The only trace that they could find of the murder was some bloodstains on the snow outside the small door that leads into the bachelor rooms which Prince Yusupov used before he married. They carefully collected the snow for examination. When they were there, Prince Yusupov came out, and said that he could explain the whole incident, and that all that had happened was that the Grand Duke Dmitri Pavlovich had shot a dog that had attacked him. The examining judges then went off to the Minister of Justice and congratulated themselves on having escaped the risk of being taken in, when all that had happened was the shooting of a dog. Whey they were waiting in Makarov's ante-room, Prince Yusupov arrived and went into the Minister's room. Shortly afterwards Makarov came out and said to the judges, 'It is all right, Prince Yusupov has explained every-thing; it was only a dog, thank you, you can go.' At Gorokhovaya 64, Rasputin's flat, there was in the meanwhile great excitement. At seven in the morning Simonovich and Isidor arrived. They could not understand why Rasputin had not told them where he was to be found. Shortly afterwards, there entered Mlle. Golovina, Rasputin's friend, who said 'I know where he is, he is all right, I will telephone.' She then, for some reason, telephoned in English, and, having got an answer, said to them, 'He will be back soon.' However, she seemed dissatisfied, and went out to telephone again, this time at the public call office in the street, as she evidently did not wish Simonovich and Isidor to know what she was saying. She then came back and said, 'He has left the place where I thought he was and has gone away.'

In the meanwhile, in view of the mysterious telephone message and the reports of the police, a search had begun. When, therefore, a golosh was discovered near the Petrovsky Bridge, it was taken to 64 Gorokhovaya for recognition. The Rasputin family at once recognised it as Rasputin's. The river in the neighbourhood was carefully searched. The great cold made this difficult, as the divers were not at all anxious to work. Eventually on Monday morning, something was seen in the ice. After great difficulty it was pulled out, and found to be Rasputin's body, completely frozen into a block of ice. Both his hands were raised, and one side of his face was badly damaged by the fall into the river. The body was put into a motor lorry and ordered to be taken to the Vyborg Military Hospital. The whole party, examining judges, police and the rest, then went off to have luncheon with a German Jew who is known as Artmanov. They had not begun luncheon, when they received a telephone message from Protopopov saying that on no account must the body be taken to the Vyborg side, because it was a workman's quarter, and there might be demonstrations. They replied that it had already been sent there, but Protopopov said that it must be stopped. They asked how could it be stopped. He said that he did not mind how, but that stopped it must be. Accordingly, they informed all the police at the street corners along the route through which it was to pass that they were to stop the lorry, when they saw it approaching. The lorry was finally stopped, and was ordered to proceed instead to the Chestminsky Almshouse, a desolate institution on the road to Tsarskoe. The examining judges had previously arranged that the post mortem examination should take place after twenty-four hours, as the body was so frozen that it was impossible to make any examination before that time. Protopopov, however, telephoned to say that the examination must be finished by 8.00a.m. the next morning. The judges and the doctor declared that it was impossible. Protopopov, however, said that it was necessary, and that the body was to be returned to the relations at 8 next morning. The judges then asked, how were they to reach the almhouse, that was some distance from Petrograd, as they could not afford a motor that would cost 200 roubles. Protopopov said that it would be all right as far as payment went.

Accordingly Sereda, the examining judge, got hold of Kosorotov, the well- known surgeon, and went off with him in a motor to the almshouse.

Their difficulties were not ended. Although the almshouse was lighted with electric light, there was no light in it at all when they arrived, and no means of lighting it. The three *gorodovois*, who were there, said that no light was necessary, as 'dead men need no light.' The judge and the surgeon declared that they must have some light. Accordingly, they sent out, and obtained two small lamps to hang upon the wall, whilst one of the *gorodovois* held a lantern. After a while, the *gorodovoi* declared that he felt ill, and that he could not hold the lantern any more. The judge and the surgeon, therefore, were left alone in the partially lighted room.

They found that Rasputin, although 46 years of age, had the look of a man of only 36. He was dressed, as was his habit, like a Russian mujik. He was wearing, however, a pair of very expensive boots and a blue shirt with yellow cornflowers sewn upon it. This shirt had lately been given him by the Empress. It should also be noted in this connection that two days afterwards, when a small and periodical operation was being performed on the Tsarevich's knee, the blue shirt was noticed by the surgeon to be under the operating table.

The examination showed that there were three wounds, one in his back and two in his head, all showing signs that they have been made by shots at a very close range.

Whilst the examination was proceeding, one of the *gorodovois* announced that two ladies had come for the body. Sereda and Kosorotov declared that this was impossible. A message then came back that they must give up the clothes. This, they did.

At last the examination was finished, and Sereda and Kosorotov returned, frozen and dispirited, to Petrograd. Since then, Zarvastsky, the other examining judge, has resigned, and another judge, Staravitsky, has been appointed to replace him. The body was subsequently taken to Tsarskoe. Whilst it was being conveyed from the station to the church, the garrison was confined to barrack in order to avoid any demonstration. Bishop Isidor, and not the Metropolitan Pitirim, conducted the service in the church.

APPENDIX 4

The following document, found among the Scale Papers, lists the members of the British Intelligence Mission in Petrograd at the time of Rasputin's murder:

Lt-Col. Hoare	Lt Lee
Lt-Col. Benet	Lt Urmston
Lt Rayner	Lt L. Hodson
Capt. Scale	Lt A. Hodson
Capt. Alley	Mr H. Grant
Capt. Hicks	Mr F. Hayes
Capt. Schwabe	Mr F. Ball
Capt. Bromhead	Mr L. Read
Lt MacLaren RNVR	Mr L. Webster
Lt Garstin	Mr H. Anderson
Lt Steveni	

ABBREVIATIONS USED IN NOTES AND BIBLIOGRAPHY

CAB	Cabinet (UK)
CUL	Cambridge University Library
EGAF	Central Archive of the Russian Federation
FO	Foreign Office
GARF	State Archive of the Russian Federation
GATO	State Archive of the Province of Tyumen
HLRO	House of Lords Record Office
MI1c	Military Intelligence 1c (see SIS)
MI5	Military Intelligence 5 – the Security Service
MI6	Military Intelligence 6 (see SIS)
NYSC	New York Supreme Court
PRO	Public Record Office (now TNA)
SIS	Secret Intelligence Service (MI1c now MI6)
TFGATO	Tobolsk Branch of the State Archive of the Province of Tyumen
TNA	The National Archive
WO	War Office

NOTES

CHAPTER ONE: MANHUNT

1 *The Ochrana*, A.T.Vassilyev (Harrup, 1930), p.47.
2 The statement of Fyodor Antonov Korshynov, yardkeeper, to Lt-Col. Popel of the Detached Gendarme Corps, 18 December 1916, Fond 102, Schedule 314, Case 35, GARF, Moscow.
3 Statement of Maria Grigorievna Rasputina to General Popov of the Detached Gendarme Corps, 18 December 1916, Fond 102, Schedule 314, Case 35, GARF, Moscow.
4 Statement of Anna Nikolaevna Rasputina to Lt-Col. Popel of the Detached Gendarme Corps, 18 December 1916, Fond 102, Schedule 314, Case 35, GARF, Moscow.
5 Statement of Ivan Manasevich Manuilov to investigator G.P. Girchich of the Provisional Government Extraordinary Commission 1917, Fond 1467, Schedule 1, Case 567, Folios 191-4, GARF, Moscow.
6 Statement of Akim Ivanovich Zhuk to investigator I.V. Brykin of the Provisional Government Extraordinary Commission 1917,

Fond 1467, Schedule 1, Case 567, Folios 31-6, GARF, Moscow.

7 Telegram to Tsar Nicholas II from Okhrana, 17 December 1916, Fond 111, Schedule 1, Case 2981a, Page 1, GARF, Moscow.

8 Dmitri Pavlovich was the only son of the Tsar's great-uncle Grand Duke Paul, who, after the death of Dmitri's mother, had made a morganatic marriage and gone into exile, leaving Dmitri and his sister to be brought up by Grand Duchess Elizaveta and Grand Duke Sergei.

9 Statement of Yulia Dehn to investigator F.P. Simpson of the Provisional Government Extraordinary Commission 1917, Fond 1467, Schedule 1, Case 567, Folios 364-7, GARF, Moscow.

10 To General Voikov, Palace Superintendent, December 1916, from Head of Interior Ministry, Fond 102, Schedule 314, Case 35, GARF, Moscow.

11 The bridge is just as long nowadays but is no longer wide. It was two carriage-widths before and is now essentially a footbridge.

12 Statement number 1740 of Police Inspector Asonov, Station no.4, 17 December 1916, Fond 102, Schedule 314, Case 35, GARF, Moscow.

13 *Lost Splendour*, Prince Yusupov (Jonathan Cape Ltd, 1953), p.235.

14 Yusupov, *ibid*.

15 Statement of Ivan Nefedev to Lt-Col. Popel of the Detached Gendarme Corps, 17 December 1916 and statement of Mounya Golovina to Lt-Col. Popel of the Detached Gendarme Corps, 17 December 1916, Fond 102, Schedule 314, Case 35, GARF, Moscow.

16 *The Murder of Rasputin*, V.M. Purishkevich, translated from the original Russian by Bella Costello, ed. Michael Shaw (Ardis Publishers, Ann Arbor, 1985), p.4.

17 Purishkevich, *ibid.*, editor's introduction.

18 Purishkevich, *ibid*.

19 The full text is quoted in *The Ochrana,* A.T. Vassilyev (Harrap, 1930). Vassilyev was the last Director of the Department of Police.

20 Lt-Col. Sir Samuel Hoare was an officer of the SIS, which was founded in 1909, and at this time (1916) operated under the name MI1c. It had stations throughout Europe and around the world. The Petrograd MI1c Station, run by Hoare, is referred to here and

throughout this book as the British Intelligence Mission. SIS operates today under the name MI6.

21 Report 'The Death of Rasputin', from Lt-Col. Sir Samuel Hoare to C, 1 January 1917, Papers of the British Intelligence Mission, Petrograd, Templewood Papers, Part II, File 1, (16), CUL.

22 The news was in the 6.00p.m. edition.

23 *The Russian Diary of an Englishman,* Anon. (the Hon. Albert Stopford) (Heinemann, 1919), p.21.

24 Report on Vera Koralli by Major-General Globachev, Fond 111, Schedule 1, Case 2981 (b), List 12, GARF, Moscow.

25 Samuel Hoare claims that Makarov 'in the early morning... was rung up by an unknown voice that said 'Rasputin has been murdered. Look for his body in the Islands.' *The Fourth Seal,* Sir Samuel Hoare (Heinemann, 1930), p.151.

26 Diary of the Grand Duke Nikolai Mikhailovich, 17 December 1916, Fond 670, GARF, Moscow.

27 *Lost Splendour,* Prince Yusupov (Jonathan Cape Ltd, 1953), p.186.

28 The existence of this mysterious woman may be fiction. Yusupov included the story in *Lost Splendour* along with a similar one about threats to Pavlovich which is not independently verified. Golovina is supposed to have heard a group of people at Rasputin's flat swearing revenge.

29 Yusupov, 1953, *ibid.,* p.239; a similar account of the evening is in Yusupov, 1927, *ibid.,* p.203.

30 *Dissolution of an Empire,* Meriel Buchanan (John Murray, 1932), p.49.

31 *The Fourth Seal,* Sir Samuel Hoare, (Heinemann, 1930), p.139. Hoare has a story about Yusupov being at the party with Dmitri Pavlovich and being carried shoulder high, but it is not a first-hand account and Hoare is unreliable.

32 Sir Samuel Hoare, 1930, *ibid.*

Chapter Two: Finger of Suspicion

1 Statement of Prince Felix Yusupov, Count Sumarokov-Elston, to General Popov of the Detached Gendarme Corps dated 18

December 1916, Fond 102, Schedule 314, Case 35, GARF, Moscow.

2 *Rasputin i evrei*, Aaron Simanovich (National Reklama, 1923), p.45.

3 Quoted in *Rasputin, the Last Word*, Edvard Radzinski (Weidenfeld & Nicolson, 2000), p.476.

4 *Lost Splendour*, Prince Yusupov (Jonathan Cape Ltd, 1953), p.241.

5 Statement of Anna Nikolaevna Rasputina, to Lt-Col. Popel of the Detached Gendarme Corps dated 18 December 1916, Fond 102, Schedule 314, Case 35, GARF, Moscow.

6 *Ibid*.

7 Statement of Maria Vasilyevna Zhyravleva, to Lt-Col. Popel of the Detached Gendarme Corps dated 18 December 1916, Fond 102, Schedule 314, Case 35, GARF, Moscow.

8 Statement of Fyodor Antonov Korshynov, to Lt-Col. Popel of the Detached Gendarme Corps dated 18 December 1916, Fond 102, Schedule 314, Case 35, GARF, Moscow.

9 Statement of Flor Efimov Efimov, to Lt-Col. Popel of the Detached Gendarme Corps dated 18 December 1916, Fond 102, Schedule 314, Case 35, GARF, Moscow.

10 Statement of Stepan Fedoseev Vlasuk to Lt-Col. Popel of the Detached Gendarme Corps dated 18 December 1916, Fond 102, Schedule 314, Case 35, GARF, Moscow.

11 *The Forgotten Hospital*, Michael Harmer (Springwood Books, 1982), p.117.

12 *Rasputin,* Prince Yusupov (Jonathan Cape, 1927), p.212.

13 Department of Police Report, 17 December 1916, Papers of the British Intelligence Mission, Petrograd, Templewood Papers, Part II, File 1 (47), CUL. Also reproduced in Appendix III of *The Russian Diary of an Englishman,* Anon. (the Hon. Albert Stopford), (Heinemann, 1919).

14 *Ibid*.

15 Appendix II 'Memorandum privately circulated on December 31, 1916' in Stopford, 1919, *ibid*.

16 *Ibid*.

17 Telegram from Lt-Col. Sir Samuel Hoare to C, 31 December 1916, Papers of the British Intelligence Mission, Petrograd, Templewood Papers, Part II, File 1 (47), CUL.

18 *Ibid*.

19 Report on Vera Koralli by Major-General Globachev, Fond 111, Schedule 1, Case 2891 (b), List 12, GARF, Moscow.

20 *The Russian Diary of an Englishman*, Anon. (the Hon. Albert Stopford), (Heinemann, 1919), p.44.

21 *Ibid*.

22 Report 'The Death of Rasputin', from Lt-Col. Sir Samuel Hoare to C, 1 January 1917, Papers of the British Intelligence Mission, Petrograd, Templewood Papers, Part II, File 1 (16), CUL.

Chapter Three: Body of Evidence

1 *A Collection of Historical Materials*, Grigori Rasputin, Vol. 4 (Moscow, 1997), p.236/7.

2 *Ibid*.

3 The *Times*, Thursday 4 January 1917, p.7 col.f. ('From our own correspondent,' Petrograd 3 January 1917.) It is obvious from his earliest bulletin, which didn't reach London, that he had seen the Police Report that Stopford and Buchanan saw at the embassy on the Sunday afternoon, as had other journalists.

4 *Rasputin,* Prince Yusupov (Jonathan Cape, 1927), p.193ff.

5 *Ibid*., p.191.

6 *Thirteen years at the Russian Court*, Pierre Gilliard (Hutchinson, 1921), p.47.

7 Telegram from Lt-Col. Sir Samuel Hoare to C, 1 January 1917, Papers of the British Intelligence Mission, Petrograd, Templewood Papers, Part II, File 1 (48), CUL.

8 Report No.2, Death of Rasputin, Lt-Col. Sir Samuel Hoare to C, 2 January 1917, Papers of the British Intelligence Mission, Petrograd, Templewood Papers, Part II, File 1 (50), CUL.

9 *The Fourth Seal*, Sir Samuel Hoare (Heinemann, 1930), p.156.

10 Report No.3. Further details obtained from the Examining Magistrates and other reliable sources, Lt-Col. Sir Samuel Hoare to C, 5 February 1917, Papers of the British Intelligence Mission, Petrograd, Templewood Papers, Part II, File 1 (20), CUL.

11 *Tsaritsa i Rasputin,* I. Kovyl-Boybyl (Petrograd, 1917), interview

between Kossorotov and Kovyl-Boybyl, a Petrograd journalist.

12 See note 10 above.

13 Report of the Autopsy on the body of Grigori Rasputin by Professor Kossorotov, 20 December 1916 (Museum of Political History, St Petersburg). Also reproduced in *Raspoutine est innocent*, Alain Roullier (France Europe Editions Livres, 1998), p.514ff.

14 *The Fourth Seal*, Sir Samuel Hoare (Heinemann, 1930), p.156ff.

15 The *Times,* 3 January 1917, p.8, col.d.

16 *The Fourth Seal*, Sir Samuel Hoare (Heinemann, 1930), p.67ff.

17 *The Russian Diary of an Englishman*, Anon. (the Hon. Albert Stopford), (Heinemann, 1919), p.83.

18 Like her mother, a woman of many accomplishments. 'Among her close friends were the Churchills, Maurice Baring, Arthur Rubinstein, J.M. Barrie, Rose Macaulay, Greta Garbo, Noël Coward, Jean Cocteau, Vita and Eddy Sackville-West and Hilaire Belloc (who was so fond of her that he wrote silly poems lauding her virtues).' *The Maugham-Duff Letters,* Loren R. Rothschild, the letters of W. Somerset Maugham to Lady Juliet Duff (Rasselas Press, 1982).

19 See note 17 above.

20 *My Mission to Russia,* Vol. II, Rt Hon. Sir George Buchanan (Cassell & Co, 1923), p.43.

21 *Ibid.*

22 Rt Hon. Sir George Buchanan, *ibid.*, p.50ff. Also, The Buchanan Collection, GB 0159 Bu, University of Nottingham Library.

Chapter Four: The Spies Who Came into the Cold

1 *Memoirs of a British Agent,* R.H. Bruce Lockhart (Putnam, 1932), p.308ff.

2 *Ibid.*

3 He was a Foundation Scholar and Staffordshire County Scholar.

4 Letter from Oswald Rayner in Finland to parents, 19 February 1907 (Papers of Joyce Frankel, sister of Oswald Rayner).

5 *Ibid.*, 19 February 1907.

6 *Ibid.*, 18 April 1907.

7 Entry 186, Register of Births, Registration District of Paddington

in the County of London, John Felix Hamilton Rayner, born 1 February 1924.

8 Letter to O.T. Rayner from C.F. Mobley-Bell (editor of the *Times*), 19 September 1910, Letter Book 55, No.814, Times Newspapers Ltd Archives, London; Letter to O.T. Rayner from C.F. Mobley-Bell, 22 September 1910, Letter Book 55, No.837, Times Newspapers Ltd Archives, London.

9 Memorandum on Censorship by Lt-Col. H.Vere Benet, 25 February 1917, Papers of the British Intelligence Mission, Petrograd, Templewood Papers, Part II, File 1 (29), CUL.

10 College Register, Evening Classes No.3, 1877–1895, Archive of King's College, London.

11 www.steamindex.com has the origins of the firm.

12 Matriculation Record of Stephen Alley, Ref R8/5/15/1, academic year 1894/5, Glasgow University Archive.

13 Memorandum – Biographical Details of Stephen Alley (The Alley Papers).

14 *The Fourth Seal*, Sir Samuel Hoare (Heinemann, 1930), p3ff.

15 Sir Samuel Hoare, *ibid*., p.29.

16 *Rasputin,* Prince Yusupov (Jonathan Cape, 1927), p.11ff.

17 *The Mystery of Lord Kitchener's Death,* Donald MacCormick (Putman, 1959), p.91ff.

18 Source Records of the Great War, Vols I-VII, Charles F. Horne (editor), (National Alumni, 1923).

19 *The Russian Diary of an Englishman*, Anon. (the Hon. Albert Stopford), (Heinemann, 1919), p.45.

20 Anon. (the Hon. Albert Stopford), *ibid*., 28 August 1915, p.56.

21 Anon. (the Hon. Albert Stopford), *ibid*., Letter to Lady Ripon, 5 September 1915.

22 Anon. (the Hon. Albert Stopford), *ibid*., Letter to Lady Sarah Wilson at the Allied Forces Hospital, Boulogne, 22 August 1915.

23 *My Mission to Russia*, Vol. I, Rt Hon. Sir George Buchanan, p.250.

24 *Lost Splendour,* Prince Yusupov (Jonathan Cape Ltd, 1953), p.186.

25 *The Russian Diary of an Englishman*, Anon. (the Hon. Albert Stopford), (Heinemann, 1919), Letter to Lady Juliet Duff, 17 October 1915.

26 *My Mission to Russia,* Vol. I, Rt Hon. Sir George Buchanan, p.250.

27 *Petrograd, the City of Trouble,* Meriel Buchanan (Collins, 1919), p.78.

28 Telegram from the Tsarina to the Tsar, 3 November 1915, Fond 640, GARF, Moscow.

Chapter Five: Dark Forces

1 *Rasputin,* Prince Yusupov (Jonathan Cape, 1927), p.74ff.

2 *Petrograd, the City of Trouble,* Meriel Buchanan (Collins, 1919), p.67.

3 *The Story of ST25,* Sir Paul Dukes (Cassell & Co, 1938), p.16ff.

4 *Rasputin: The Man Behind the Myth,* Maria Rasputin & Patte Barham, p.10ff.

5 *Rasputin, the Last Word,* Edvard Radzinski (Weidenfeld & Nicolson, 2000), p.25ff.

6 Marriage of Efim Yakovlevich Rasputin and Anna Vasilievna, 21 January 1862, Register of the Church of the Mother of God, Pokrovskoe, Fond 205, GATO.

7 Birth Registers, Church of the Mother of God, Pokrovskoe, Fond 205, GATO.

8 *Ibid.*

9 Pokrovskoe Censuses, Fond 177, *State Archive of the Province of Tyumen* GATO.

10 See note 4 above.

11 File of the Tobolsk Ecclesiastical Consistory – Charge made against Grigori Rasputin concerning the spreading of false teachings similar to those of the Khlysti, Fond 156, Tobolsk Branch of the State Archive of the Province of Tyumen (TFGATO).

12 Investigation of the assassination attempt on Grigori Rasputin in 1914, Fond 164, Tobolsk Branch of the State Archive of the Province of Tyumen (TFGATO).

13 Fond 164, GARF, Moscow.

14 Provisional Government Extraordinary Commission 1917, Fond 1461, Schedule 1, Case 567, GARF, Moscow.

15 See note 9 above.

16 *Rasputin i evrei,* Aaron Simanovich (National Reklama, 1923), p.20.

17 *Ibid.*

18 See note 4 above.

19 *Ibid.*

20 *Ibid.*

21 Provisional Government Extraordinary Commission 1917, Fond 1467, Schedule 1, Case 567, GARF, Moscow.

22 *Ibid.*

23 *Ibid.*

24 *Ibid.*

25 See note 4 above.

26 *Ibid.*

27 *Thirteen Years at the Russian Court*, Pierre Gilliard (Hutchinson, 1921), p.79.

28 Provisional Government Extraordinary Commission 1917, Fond 1467, Schedule 1, Case 567, GARF, Moscow.

29 *Ibid.*

30 *The Life and Times of Grigori Rasputin*, Alex De Jonge (Coward, McCann & Geoghegan, 1982), p.51ff.

31 *Ibid.*

32 *Dissolution of an Empire*, Meriel Buchanan (John Murray, 1932), p.87.

33 *Ibid.*

34 Statement of Olga Lokhtina to investigator T.D. Rudnev, Provisional Government Extraordinary Commission 1917, Fond 1467, Schedule 1, Case 567, Folios 100-4, 109-12, GARF, Moscow.

35 *Ibid.*

36 *Ibid.*

37 Diary of Tsar Nicholas II, 16 October 1906, Fond 601, GARF, Moscow.

38 *Rasputin, the Last Word*, Edvard Radzinski (Weidenfeld & Nicolson, 2000), p.91.

39 Statement of Grigori Sazonov to investigator F.P. Simpson, Provisional Government Extraordinary Commission 1917, Fond 1467, Schedule 1, Case 567, Folios 298-300, GARF, Moscow.

40 *Rasputin, the Last Word*, Edvard Radzinski (Weidenfeld & Nicolson, 2000), p.134.

41 *Thirteen Years at the Russian Court*, Pierre Gilliard (Hutchinson, 1921), p.65.

42 *Rasputin, the Last Word*, Edvard Radzinski (Weidenfeld & Nicolson, 2000), p.206.

43 Statement of Alexei Khvostov to investigator F.P. Simpson, Provisional Government Extraordinary Commission 1917, Fond 1467, Schedule 1, Case 567, Folio 302-10, GARF, Moscow.

44 *The Life and Times of Grigori Rasputin*, Alex De Jonge (Coward, McCann & Geoghegan, 1982), p.204.

45 *Ibid.*, p.205.

46 *Ibid.*

47 Articles and Correspondence on Russia & Romania, J.D. Scale DSO, OBE (Scale Papers).

48 *The Life and Times of Grigori Rasputin*, Alex De Jonge (Coward, McCann & Geoghegan, 1982), p.226.

49 *Memoirs of a British Agent*, R.H. Bruce Lockhart (Putnam, 1932), p.60.

50 *Rasputin*, Prince Yusupov (Jonathan Cape, 1927), p.154.

51 *Memoirs of a British Agent*, R.H. Bruce Lockhart (Putnam, 1932), p.129.

52 Statement of Alexei Filippov to investigator F.P. Simpson, Provisional Government Extraordinary Commission 1917, Fond 1467, Schedule 1, Case 567, Folios 327-42, GARF, Moscow.

53 *The Life and Times of Grigori Rasputin*, Alex De Jonge (Coward, McCann & Geoghegan, 1982), p.237.

54 *Memoirs of a British Agent*, R.H. Bruce Lockhart (Putnam, 1932), p.128ff.

55 *Ibid.*

56 *Ibid.*

57 *Ibid.*

Chapter Six: On the Brink

1 *Source Records of the Great War*, Vol. IV, p.185ff.

2 *The Russian Diary of an Englishman,* Anon. (the Hon. Albert Stopford), (Heinemann, 1919), Monday 5 June 1916, Tuesday 6 June 1916.

3 *The War Memoirs of David Lloyd George,* Vol. I, David Lloyd George (Odhams, 1938), p.418ff.

4   *Ibid.*

5   *Ibid.*, Letter marked 'Secret', From H.H. Asquith to David Lloyd
     George.

6   Telegram from the Tsarina to the Tsar, 17 April 1915, Fond 640,
     GARF, Moscow. Edvard Radzinski also draws attention to docu-
     ments burnt by the Tsarina in February 1917 that were believed
     to be compromising in terms of contact with Germany; *Rasputin,
     the Last Word,* Edvard Radzinski (Weidenfeld & Nicolson, 2000),
     p.405ff.

7   Edvard Radzinski, *ibid.*, p.408.

8   *Ibid.*, p.409.

9   This section draws on *The Warburgs: The Twentieth-Century Odyssey
     of a Remarkable Jewish Family,* Ron Chernow (Random House
     Inc., New York, 1993), and *Jacob Schiff: a study in American Jewish
     Leadership,* Naomi W. Cohen (Brandeis University Press, 1999). The
     British (S.G. Warburg) bank did not start up until 1935.

10   Money from the American Warburgs saved the Hamburg bank
     from collapse post-war. See Chernow, *ibid.*

11   Chernow, *ibid.* The 'financial talks in London' must have been the
     trip accompanied by Scale.

12   Kuhn, Loeb collaborated with Cassel, Rockefeller & J.P. Morgan.
     See Cohen, 1999, *ibid.*

13   Cohen, *ibid.*

14   www.britannica.com; Jack P. Morgan.

15   The diary of Alexei Raivid, Soviet Consul in Berlin, 1927, 6 July
     1927: conversation with Baron Hochen Esten, Fond 612, Schedule
     1, Case 27, pp.4-6, GARF, Moscow.

Chapter Seven: War Games

1   Entry 358, Register of Births in the Registration District of
     Merthyr Tydfil in the County of Glamorgan, John Dymoke Scale,
     27 December 1882.

2   *The Ordeal of a Diplomat,* K.D. Nabokov (Duckworth, 1921). As
     chargé d'affaires in London between 1917 and the end of the war, he
     was the senior Russian representative in London – the Ambassador

having been sent home and no replacement supplied. Some of his papers on India were later published by Trotsky in pamphlet form.

3 Nabokov, *ibid*.

4 *Articles & Correspondence on Russia and Roumania 1915–1917*, J.D. Scale DSO, OBE (The Scale Papers).

5 Typed letter from Capt. J.D. Scale (Petrograd) to London headed 'Dear Cox', 7 November 1916, initialled (The Scale Papers).

6 Muriel Harding-Newman, Scale's eldest daughter, referred to his friendship with Felix Yusupov in her interview with the author. She recalls that he was often a guest at the Yusupov Palace (interview 28 May 2003, Easter Ross, Scotland). According to Betty Aikenhead, his younger daughter, Scale last saw Yusupov in 1948, a year before he died (interview 9 February 2004, Toronto, Canada).

7 *Lost Splendour,* Prince Yusupov (Jonathan Cape Ltd, 1953), p.29ff.

8 *Ibid*.

9 *Ibid*.

10 *Rasputin,* Prince Yusupov (Jonathan Cape, 1927), p.47.

11 *Lost Splendour*, Prince Yusupov (Jonathan Cape Ltd, 1953), p.95.

12 Telegram from the Tsarina to the Tsar, 7 September 1916, Fond 640, GARF, Moscow.

13 Letter from David Lloyd George to H.H. Asquith, Prime Minister, 'Confidential', 26 September 1916, The Lloyd George Papers, LG/E/223/5, House of Lords Record Office.

14 Telegrams from the Tsarina to the Tsar, 18 and 24 September 1916, Fond 640, GARF, Moscow.

15 Sworn Statement of Sergei Trufanov, Sergei Trufanov v. The *Metropolitan* Magazine Company, Supreme Court, New York County, sworn 17 October 1916 (reproduced in full in Appendix 1).

16 *New York Times*, 27 December 1916, p.4.

17 William Wiseman Papers, Group 666, f.260, Russia, [1917] 1, Sterling Library, Yale University.

18 War Memoirs of David Lloyd George, Vol. I, David Lloyd George, p.464.

19 From Switzerland, notes from a reliable source, 'Secret', 3 October 1916, The Lloyd George Papers, LG/E/3/27/2, House of Lords Record Office. Theodor Bethmann-Holweg was the German

Premier.

20 Statement of Anna Vyrubova to investigator F.P. Simpson of the Provisional Government Extraordinary Commission 1917, Fond 1467, Schedule 1, Case 567, Folios 347-63, GARF, Moscow.

Chapter Eight: Cards on the Table

1 *Lost Splendour,* Prince Yusupov (Jonathan Cape Ltd, 1953), p.185.

2 Author's interview with Betty Aikenhead, 9 February 2004, Toronto, Canada.

3 Author's interview with Muriel Harding-Newman, 28 May 2003, Easter Ross, Scotland.

4 *Rasputin, the Saint who sinned,* Brian Moynahan (Random House, 1997), p.320; Statement of Ioann Aronovich Simanovich (son of Rasputin's secretary Aron Simanovich) to investigator V.M. Rudnev of the Provisional Government Extraordinary Commission 1917, Fond 1467, Schedule 1, Case 567, Folios 182-3, GARF, Moscow.

5 *Rasputin*, Prince Yusupov (Jonathan Cape, 1927), p.60ff.

6 *Ibid.*

7 In *Rasputin,* Yusupov does not name this person but simply says he is too old to take action; in *Lost Splendour* he identifies Rodzyanko.

8 See note 5 above.

9 Stopford's diary (which, unlike Yusupov's account, was written within days or hours of the events) has Dmitri Pavlovich in Petrograd quite specifically on 6/19 and 7/20 December, on which latter day Pavlovich and Stopford had lunch together privately in the Sergei Palace, and Stopford had supper there at midnight. If both accounts are correct, Pavlovich (presumably briefly in town to celebrate the Tsar's name-day on 6/19 December) was to spend only about thirty-six hours back at the Stavka.

10 *Rasputin*, Prince Yusupov (Jonathan Cape, 1927), p.199.

11 This is one of many contradictory aspects of Yusupov's story. Yusupov had twice visited the Golovinas when Rasputin was there, and their house was right next door to that of his in-laws. Admittedly these were both large mansions, but it would seem he was taking rather a risk that his own parents would soon know all

about it. According to Yusupov, when Rasputin suggested mentioning Felix's name to Vyrubova they both agreed that this wouldn't be a good idea at all as it would get back to his family. Yusupov says that he knew Vyrubova would be suspicious.

12 *Rasputin*, Prince Yusupov (Jonathan Cape, 1927), p.112.

13 Yusupov, *ibid.*, p.115.

14 Letter from Princess Irina Yusupova to Prince Felix Yusupov, 25 November 1916, Fond 1290, Russian State Archive of Early Acts, (RGADA), Moscow.

15 Letter from Prince Felix Yusupov to Princess Irina Yusupova, 27 November 1916, Fond 411, State Historical Museum (GIM), Moscow.

16 *The Murder of Rasputin,* V.M. Purishkevich, translated from the original Russian by Bella Costello, ed. Michael Shaw (Ardis Publishers, Ann Arbor, 1985), annex: correspondence between Maklakov and Paris publisher of 1923.

17 A pood weighs about 36lbs, i.e., well over 16 kilos.

18 See note 16 above.

19 *Ibid.*

20 *Ibid.*

Chapter Nine: A Room in the Basement

1 Police Department Report, 17 December 1917, CUL.

2 The author of the memorandum is unknown, although Stopford is the most likely. His book, published in 1919, did not appear under his own name, and if he was the author of the memorandum, he would not want his name to link the two publications.

3 'The True and Authentic Story of the Murder of Grigori Rasputin, As Recounted to Me on 6th June 1917, At Yalta by the Perpetrator', *The Russian Diary of an Englishman,* Anon. (the Hon. Albert Stopford), (Heinemann, 1919), p.83.

4 Report of the Autopsy of Grigori Rasputin, Professor Kossorotov, 20 December 1916, Museum of Political History, St Petersburg.

5 *Rasputin, The Man Behind the Myth*, Maria Rasputina & Patte Barham, p.231ff. According to Barham, a servant of Yusupov's was

one of the sources for what happened in the basement dining room. In an interview with the author on 21 February 2005, Maria Rasputina's granddaughter, Laurence Huot-Soloviev, expressed the view that Barham had somewhat embellished her grandmother's account.

6 *Ibid.*

7 *Ibid.*, and *My Father*, Maria Rasputina (Cassell & Co, 1934), p.111.

8 *Ibid.*

9 See note 4 above.

10 *Rasputin, the Last Word*, Edvard Radzinski (Weidenfeld & Nicolson, 2000), p.477.

11 *Ibid.*, p.482.

12 *Ibid.*, p.480.

13 See note 4 above.

14 *Ibid.*

15 *Rasputin, the Last Word*, Edvard Radzinski (Weidenfeld & Nicolson, 2000), p.482.

16 Professor Derrick Pounder, Senior Home Office Pathologist and Head of Forensic Medicine, University of Dundee, was commissioned by the author in February 2005 to carry out a review of the ballistics evidence and concluded the forehead wound was caused by an unjacketed bullet. The Browning pistol fires only jacketed bullets.

17 A revised edition, *Rasputin: The History of the Crime*, was published by Yauza, Moscow, in 2004.

18 *Ibid.*, chapter 18.

19 *A Watchman Makes His Rounds*, Sir Samuel Hoare (unpublished 1959 memoir of Hoare's time in Russia), p.72, Templewood Papers, Part II, File 1 (34), CUL.

20 *The Fourth Seal*, Sir Samuel Hoare (Heinemann, 1930), p.156.

Chapter Ten: Once Upon a Time

1 *Dnevnik*, V.M. Purishkevich (National Reklama, 1923), p.62.

2 *Ibid.*, p.63.

3 *Ibid.*, p.65.

4 *Rasputin*, Prince Yusupov (Jonathan Cape, 1927), p.133.

5 *Ibid.*, p.134.

6 *Ibid.*, p.138ff.

7 *Dnevnik*, V.M. Purishkevich (National Reklama, 1923), p.80ff.

8 *Rasputin*, Prince Yusupov (Jonathan Cape, 1927), p.134/135.

9 *Dnevnik*, V.M. Purishkevich (National Reklama, 1923), p.62/63.

10 *Rasputin*, Prince Yusupov (Jonathan Cape, 1927), p.135.

11 *Dnevnik*, V.M. Purishkevich (National Reklama, 1923), p.65.

12 *Rasputin*, Prince Yusupov (Jonathan Cape, 1927), p.148.

13 *Ibid.*, p.149.

14 *Dnevnik*, V.M. Purishkevich (National Reklama, 1923), p.70–74.

15 *Rasputin*, Prince Yusupov (Jonathan Cape, 1927), p.149.

16 *Dnevnik*, V.M. Purishkevich (National Reklama, 1923), p.70–74.

17 *Ibid.*

18 *Rasputin*, Prince Yusupov (Jonathan Cape, 1927), p.150.

19 *Dnevnik*, V.M. Purishkevich (National Reklama, 1923), p.75.
For Yusupov's June 1917 account see *The Russian Diary of an Englishman*, Anon. (the Hon. Albert Stopford), (Heinemann, 1919), p.83.

20 *Rasputin*, Prince Yusupov (Jonathan Cape, 1927), p.153.

21 *Dnevnik*, V.M. Purishkevich (National Reklama, 1923), p.79.

22 *Ibid.*, p.81.

23 *Rasputin*, Prince Yusupov (Jonathan Cape, 1927), p.157/158.

24 Irina Yusupov v MGM 1933, Fanny Holtzman Papers, Series A, Sub-series 1, Box 16, Folders 5-10, American Jewish Archives, Cincinnati, Ohio; Felix Yusupov v CBS 1965, Series A, Sub-series 1, Box 15, Folders 5-12, American Jewish Archives, Cincinnati, Ohio. See also The *Times* Law Reports, Friday 17 August 1934, Vol. 1, p.581ff.

25 'The Assassination of Rasputin', *Source Records of the Great War*, Stanislaus Lazovert, Vol. V, ed. Charles F. Horne (National Alumni, 1923), p.86.

26 *Ibid.*

27 *Ibid.*, p.87.

28 *Lost Splendour*, Prince Yusupov (Jonathan Cape Ltd, 1953), p.228.

29 'The Assassination of Rasputin', Stanislaus Lazovert, p.88.

30 *Dnevnik*, V.M. Purishkevich (National Reklama, 1923), p.80ff.

Chapter Eleven: End of the Road

1 Report of Autopsy on the Body of Grigori Rasputin by Professor Kossorotov, 20 December 1916, Museum of Political History, St Petersburg.

2 *My Father*, Maria Rasputina (Cassell & Co, 1934), p.111.

3 *The Yusupov Palace*, Galina Sveshnikova, p.75.

4 Report by Professor Derrick Pounder, Senior Home Office Pathologist and Head of Forensic Medicine, University of Dundee, August 2004, commissioned by the author.

5 *Dnevnik*, V.M. Purishkevich (National Reklama, 1923), p.21.

6 See note 1 above.

7 Statement by Stepan Beletski to Provisional Government Extraordinary Commission 1917, Fond 1467, Schedule 1, Case 567, GARF, Moscow.

8 *Rasputin*, Prince Yusupov (Jonathan Cape, 1927), p.163.

9 *Dnevnik*, V.M. Purishkevich (National Reklama, 1923), p.70ff.

10 Report The Opinion of the Specialists, 18-30 June 1993, by V.V. Zharov, Igor Panov and Valery Vasilevsky of the Moscow Forensic Medical Analysis Bureau (unpublished review of the 1916 autopsy undertaken by Professor Kossorotov).

11 Interview of Vladimir Zharov by Richard Cullen and Ilya Gavrilov, *Who Killed Rasputin?*, Timewatch, broadcast BBC 2, Friday 1 October 2004, 8.00p.m.

12 See note 1 above.

13 This conclusion, articulated by Richard Cullen in the BBC Timewatch episode *Who Killed Rasputin?* (see broadcast details in note 11 above), is the most plausible explanation.

14 Report by Professor Derrick Pounder, Senior Home Office Pathologist and Head of Forensic Medicine, University of Dundee, February 2005, commissioned by the author.

15 *Ibid.*

16 *Ibid.*

17 *Ibid.*

18 *Ibid.*

19 See note 10 above.

20 On Rayner's death in 1961, Rose Jones gave a brief account of his life to the *Nuneaton Observer* (10 March 1961). The story was featured under the headline 'Was in Palace When Rasputin was Killed'.

21 Diary of William J. Compton, 1916; also, General Index of Personnel from World War 1, William John Compton #9440, Red Cross Archive, London.

22 Scale recalls the events surrounding the Romanian oil fields operation in a letter to General C. Ismay dated 19 September 1940 (Scale Papers).

23 Letter from Capt. Stephen Alley to Capt. J.D. Scale, 7 January 1917 (Alley Papers).

24 To the Chief of the Public Security Department, Petrograd, 22 February 1917, Fond 102, Schedule 357, Case 115, GARF, Moscow.

25 See note 7 above.

26 *Rasputin: A History of the Crime*, Oleg Shishkin, chapter 21ff.

27 'Britain "helped Rasputin's killers"' by Phil Tomaselli, *BBC History Magazine*, April 2003, p.6.

28 Interview with Mark Lane, grandson of William Compton, 5 February 2005.

29 Entry 148, Register of Births in the Registration District of Upton-on-Severn, in the Sub-district of Kempsey in the County of Worcester, William John Compton, 27 January 1881.

30 Entry 330, Register of Deaths in the Registration District of Abingdon in the County of Berkshire, 6 March 1961, Oswald Rayner, Barrister at Law (retired).

31 Interview with Gordon Rayner, nephew of Oswald Rayner, 13 March 2004, Birmingham; interview with Myra Whelch and Michael Winwood, first cousins of Oswald Rayner, 6 November 2004, Birmingham.

32 *Rasputin*, Prince Yusupov (Jonathan Cape, 1927), p.180ff.

Chapter Twelve: Aftermath

1 *Rasputin, the Last Word*, Edvard Radzinski (Weidenfeld & Nicolson, 2000), p.492ff

2   *Ibid.*, p.495

3   *Ibid.*

4   See note 31, chapter 11 notes.

5   Ransome is best known today for his bestselling children's book
    Swallows and Amazons. His MI5 file, # PF R.301 Vols 1 & 2,
    was released to the National Archive in February 2005, TNA
    KV2/1903–1904.

6   Augustus Agar won the VC for sinking the Soviet cruiser *Oleg* in
    June 1919. He was commanding a skimmer motor launch torpedo
    boat (CMB 4) that had been pioneered by SIS. For a full account of
    this mission see *Baltic Episode*, Augustus Agar, 1963.

7   Entry 263, Register of Deaths in the Registration District of Battle
    in the county of East Sussex, John Dymoke Scale, 22 April 1949.

8   *En Exil*, Prince Yusupov (Plon, 1954), p.76.

9   Irina Yusupov v MGM, see note 24 in chapter 10 notes.

10 *Ibid.*

11 *En Exil*, Prince Yusupov (Plon, 1954), p.102ff.

12 *Ibid.*

13 Little if anything has been known about Sukhotin. In Yusupov's
    book his Christian name is never mentioned. In the course of
    researching this book, the military service file for Sergei Sukhotin
    was found, and reveals he joined the 4th Life Guards in 1911 after
    graduating from the Naval Corps in 1906. Sukhotin was also a
    distant relative of the composer Tchaikovsky, whose great-niece
    Galina von Meck recalls that he was sentenced to ten years in
    a Soviet labour camp in 1919 (see *I Remember Them*, Galina von
    Meck, p.183ff). Fond 400, Schedule 9, Case 34159, Pages 644-646,
    Russian State Military History Archive (RGVIA), Moscow.

14 This seems unlikely, as although Rasputin was not fatally poisoned,
    he certainly showed symptoms of having consumed a non-fatal
    dose, i.e. hyper-salivation, irritated throat etc. (see notes 15/16,
    chapter 10). The story of Lazovert's death-bed confession is at best
    anecdotal and is more than likely motivated by his son wishing to
    dissociate him from the murder.

15 *If Britain Had Fallen*, Norman Longmate, p.117ff.

16 *Ibid.*

17 TNA KV 2/1684–1685.

18 Memorandum 'British Intelligence Mission' by Lt-Col. Sir Samuel Hoare to C, 29 January 1917, Papers of the British Intelligence Mission, Petrograd, Templewood Papers, Part II, File 1 (52), CUL. This document remains closed and will be reviewed again by the Cabinet Office in 2011.

19 Alley refers to these meetings in his notes for January/February 1918 (Alley Papers).

20 Typed aide memoire (Alley Papers).

21 Hoare was clearly unaware of what was going on, which is reflected in his communications with C, particularly one telegram dated 2 January 1917 where he effectively asks C if he knows any more than himself; Papers of the British Intelligence Mission, Petrograd, Part II, File I (50), CUL.

22 House of Commons Debates 1920 (Hansard), Vol. 133, col. 1008-13, 1048; Vol. 134, col. 542; Vol. 135, col. 518-24.

23 *MI6: Fifty Years of Special Operations*, Stephen Dorril (Fourth Estate, 2000), p.611.

24 *Ibid*.

25 In 1956, according to Foreign Office Minister of State Anthony Nutting, Prime Minister Sir Anthony Eden declared that he wanted Egyptian President Nasser murdered. Eden apparently approached MI6, not through the then 'C' Sir John Sinclair, but via Joint Intelligence Committee Chairman Patrick Dean and MI6's Middle East specialist George Young. *The Perfect English Spy: Sir Dick White and the Secret War*, Tom Bower (Heinemann, 1995), p.195; *Through the Looking Glass*, Anthony Verrier (Jonathan Cape, 1983), p.143 & 159.

26 In Dorril, p.611, SOE Operational Head Sir Colin Gubbins is quoted as telling a minister that there is 'really no need for him to know about such things' as assassination.

27 Professor John Lewis Gaddis, senior fellow of the Hoover Institution, as quoted in Dorril, p.xiii.

28 Alex Danchev, Professor of International Relations at the University of Nottingham, as quoted in Dorril, p.xiv.

29 Alley's second cousin, Michael Alley, expressed the view within

the family that he 'got into trouble in Murmansk' (interview with author, 15 March 2005). Alley's papers certainly give strong indications that he was involved in a special assignment in Murmansk at this time, which may ultimately have resulted in failure. This is an area the author intends to research further in due course.

30 See note 31, chapter 11 notes.

31 See note 20, chapter 11 notes.

32 Certificate of Decree Nisi Absolute (Divorce), No.18 of 1940, High Court of Justice, Principal Registry of the Family Division.

33 Entry 330, Register Deaths in the Registration District of Abingdon in the County of Berkshire, Oswald Theodore Rayner, 6 March 1961.

BIBLIOGRAPHY

R.J.Q. Adams, *Arms and the Wizard* (Texas University Press, 1978).

Christopher Andrew, *Secret Service* (Heinemann, 1985).

Edward J. Bing (editor), *The Secret Letters of the Last Tsar* (Longmans, 1938).

Gordon Brook-Shepherd, *Iron Maze* (Macmillan, 1998).

Alexander Bokhanov, *The Romanovs: Love, Power and Tragedy* (Leppi Publications, 1993).

Gleb Botkin, *The Real Romanovs* (Revell, 1933).

Sir George Buchanan, *My Mission to Russia* Vol. I (Cassell & Co, 1923).

—, *My Mission to Russia* Vol. II (Cassell & Co, 1923).

Meriel Buchanan, *Petrograd, the City of Trouble* (Collins, 1919).

—, *Dissolution of Empire* (John Murray, 1932).

Ron Chernow, *The Warburgs* (Random House, 1993).

William Clarke, *The Lost Fortune of the Tsars* (Weidenfeld & Nicolson, 1994).

Naomi W. Cohen, *Jacob Schiff* (Brandeis University Press, 1999).

Andrew Cook, *On His Majesty's Secret Service* (Tempus, 2002).

—, *Ace of Spies; The True Story of Sidney Reilly* (Tempus, 2004).

—, *M: MI5's First Spymaster* (Tempus, 2004).

Colin Cross (editor), *Life with Lloyd George; The Diary of A J Sylvester 1931/45* (Macmillan, 1975).

Richard Deacon, *A History of the British Secret Service* (Frederick Muller, 1969).

—, *A History of the Russian Secret Service* (Taplinger, 1972).

Alex De Jong, *The Life and Times of Grigorii Rasputin* (Coward, McCann & Geoghegan, 1982).

Lili Dehn, *The Real Tsarina* (Thornton Butterworth, 1922).

Isaac Deutscher, *Stalin* (Penguin, 1966).

Christopher Dobson, *Prince Felix Yusupov* (Harrap, 1989).

Sir Paul Dukes, *The Story of ST25* (Cassell & Co, 1938).

Michael G. Fry, *Lloyd George and Foreign Policy,* Vol. I (McGills – Queen's University Press, 1977).

Joseph T. Fuhrmann, *Rasputin: A Life* (Praeger, 1990).

Rene Fulop-Miller, *Rasputin, The Holy Devil* (Doubleday, 1928).

Alexandra Fyodorovna, *The Letters of the Tsar to the Tsarina, 1914–1917* (Duckworth, 1923).

Pierre Gilliard, *Thirteen Years at the Russian Court* (Hutchinson, 1921).

John Grigg, *Lloyd George; The People's Champion 1902–1911* (Penguin, 1997).

—, *Lloyd George; From Peace to War 1912–1916* (Penguin, 1997).

—, *Lloyd George; War Leader 1916–1918* (Penguin, 2003).

Sir John Hanbury-Williams, *The Emperor Nicholas II as I Knew Him* (Humphreys, 1922).

Michael Harmer, *The Forgotten Hospital* (Springwood Books, 1982).

Sir Samuel Hoare, *The Fourth Seal* (Heinemann, 1930).

—, *A Watchman Makes His Rounds* (Unpublished, 1959).

Richard Holmes, *The Western Front* (BBC, 1999).

Charles F. Horne (editor), *Source Records of the Great War,* Vol. I, Causes (National Alumni, 1923).

—, *Source Records of the Great War,* Vol. II, 1914 (National Alumni, 1923).

—, *Source Records of the Great War,* Vol. III, 1915 (National Alumni, 1923).

—, *Source Records of the Great War,* Vol. IV, 1916 (National Alumni, 1923).

—, *Source Records of the Great War,* Vol. V, 1917 (National Alumni, 1923).

—, *Source Records of the Great War*, Vol.VI, 1918 (National Alumni, 1923).

—, *Source Records of the Great War*, Vol.VII, 1919 (National Alumni, 1923).

Iliodor (Sergei Trufanov), *The Mad Monk of Russia* (Century, 1928).

Alan Judd, *The Quest for C* (Harper Collins, 1999).

Michael Kettle, *The Allies and the Russian Collapse*, Vol. I (Andrew Deutsch, 1981).

Greg King, *The Man Who Killed Rasputin* (Citadel Press, 1995).

Martin Kitchen, *The German Offensives of 1918* (Tempus, 2001).

Alfred Knox, *With the Russian Army* (Dutton, 1921).

Miriam Kochan, *The Last Days of Imperial Russia* (Macmillan, 1976).

David Lloyd George, *The War Memoirs of David Lloyd George*, Vol. I (Odhams, 1938).

—, *The War Memoirs of David Lloyd George*, Vol. II (Odhams, 1938).

Robert Bruce Lockhart, *Memoirs of a British Agent*, (Putman, 1932).

Norman Longmate, *If Britain Had Fallen* (Greenhill Books, 2004).

Donald MacCormick, *The Mystery of Lord Kitchener's Death* (Putman, 1959).

Giles MacDonogh, *The Last Kaiser* (Weidenfeld & Nicolson, 2000).

George Thomas Mayre, *Nearing the End in Imperial Russia* (Dorrance, 1929).

Shay McNeal, *Plots to Rescue the Tsar* (Century, 2001).

Alexander Mikhailovich, *Once a Grand Duke* (Doubleday, 1932).

Brian Moynahan, *Rasputin; The Saint Who Sinned* (Random House, 1997).

K.D. Nabokov, *The Ordeal of a Diplomat* (Duckworth, 1921).

Sir David Napley, *Rasputin in Hollywood* (Weidenfeld & Nicolson, 1989).

V.M. Purishkevich, translated by Bella Costello, ed. Michael Shaw, *The End of Rasputin* (Ardis Publishers, 1982).

—, *Dnevnik* (National Reklama, 1923).

Edvard Radzinski, *The Last Tsar* (Doubleday, 1992).

—, *Rasputin, the Last Word* (Weidenfeld & Nicolson, 2000).

Grigori Rasputin: A Collection of Historical Materials, Vols 1–4 (Moscow, 1997).

Maria Rasputina, *My Father* (Cassell, 1934).

Maria Rasputina and Patte Barham, *Rasputin* (Prentice-Hall, 1977).

John Reed, *Ten Days That Shook the World* (Sutton, 1997 edition).

Mikhail Rodzyanko, *The Reign of Rasputin* (Philpot, 1927).

Allain Roullier, *Raspoutin est Innocent* (France Europe Editions Livres, 1998).

Robert Service, *Lenin* (Macmillan, 2000).

—, *Stalin* (Macmillan, 2004).

Richard Shannon, *The Crisis of Imperialism 1865–1915* (Hart-Davis, McGibbon, 1974).

Oleg Shishkin, *Rasputin, The History of the Crime* (Yauza, 2004, revised edition, originally published 2000).

Aron Simanovich, *Rasputin i evrei* (National Reklama, 1923).

Richard B. Spence, *Trust No One* (Feral House, 2002).

Serita D. Stephens with Anne Klarner, *Deadly Doses: A Writer's Guide to Poisons* (Writers Digest Books, 1990).

Hon. Albert Stopford, *The Russian Diary of an Englishman*, Anon. (Heinemann, 1919).

Galina Sveshnikova, *The Yusupov Palace* (St Petersburg Star, 2003).

—, *The Yusupov Palace: A Room to Room Guide* (Art-Palaces Publishers 2004).

Norman G. Thwaites, *Velvet & Vinegar* (Grayson, 1932).

Leon Trotsky, *The Russian Revolution* (Victor Gollancz, 1934).

A. T. Vassilyev, *The Ochrana* (Harrup, 1930).

Galina Von Meck, *I Remember Them* (Dobson, 1973).

Emmanuel Victor Voska & Will Irwin, *Spy and Counter Spy* (Doubleday, 1940).

Nigel West & Oleg Tsarev, *The Crown Jewels* (Harper Collins, 1998).

Colin Wilson, *Rasputin and the Fall of the Romanovs* (Farrar Strauss, 1964).

Robert Wilton, *Russia's Agony* (Edward Arnold & Co., 1918).

Anthony Wood, *Great Britain 1900–1965* (Longman, 1978).

Prince Felix Yusupov (translated Oswald Rayner), *Rasputin* (Jonathan Cape, 1927).

Prince Felix Yusupov, *Lost Splendour* (Jonathan Cape Ltd, 1953).

—, *En Exil* (Plon, 1954).

LIST OF ILLUSTRATIONS

27 Police Scene of Crime Photograph – The door to the study and cellar is to the right; a temporary repair has been made to the bottom right-hand window (Museum of Political History, St Petersburg).

28 Police Scene of Crime Photograph – two individual pictures joined together; the police have marked the trail of blood with red ink dots (Museum of Political History, St Petersburg).

29 The door to the courtyard from the inside staircase in 2004 (Author).

30 The cellar of 92 Moika in 2004 – Rasputin's waxwork sits at the dining table (Author).

31 Police Scene of Crime Photograph – Rasputin's frozen corpse is removed from the rive; a close-up of his chest, head and shoulders (Museum of Political History, St Petersburg).

32 Police Scene of Crime Photograph – Rasputin's body is put on a sledge; wooden planks lead from the hole in the ice to the river bank (Museum of Political History, St Petersburg).

33 Police Scene of Crime Photograph – a close-up of the frozen body; while in the water the rope detached and the arms rose before the corpse froze (Museum of Political History, St Petersburg).

34 Police Scene of Crime Photograph – a close-up of the hole in the ice; Petrovski Bridge, from where Rasputin was thrown, can be seen in the background (Museum of Political History, St Petersburg).

35 Police Scene of Crime Photograph – Petrovski Bridge; the car tyre tracks are still visible in the snow (Museum of Political History, St Petersburg).

36 Police Scene of Crime Photograph – traces of blood are in evidence on the girders (Museum of Political History, St Petersburg).

37 Police Scene of Crime Photograph – investigators can be seen examining the spot on Petrovski Bridge from where the body was thrown into the water (Museum of Political History, St Petersburg).

38 Petrovski Bridge in 2004, now a pedestrian bridge (Author).

39 Autopsy Photograph – Rasputin's still-clothed corpse before the autopsy commenced (Museum of Political History, St Petersburg).

40 Autopsy Photograph – right-hand side of Rasputin's head; damage

INDEX

TEMPUS – REVEALING HISTORY

Britannia's Empire
A Short History of the British Empire
BILL NASSON

'Crisp, economical and witty' *TLS*
'An excellent introduction the subject' *THES*

£12.99   0 7524 3808 5

Madmen
A Social History of Madhouses,
Mad-Doctors & Lunatics
ROY PORTER

'Fascinating'
The Observer

£12.99   0 7524 3730 5

Born to be Gay
A History of Homosexuality
WILLIAM NAPHY

'Fascinating' *The Financial Times*
'Excellent' *Gay Times*

£9.99   0 7524 3694 5

William II
Rufus, the Red King
EMMA MASON

'A thoroughly new reappraisal of a much
maligned king. The dramatic story of his life is
told with great pace and insight'
John Gillingham

£25   0 7524 3528 0

To Kill Rasputin
The Life and Death of Grigori Rasputin
ANDREW COOK

'Andrew Cook is a brilliant investigative historian'
Andrew Roberts
'Astonishing' *The Daily Mail*

£9.99   0 7524 3906 5

The Unwritten Order
Hitler's Role in the Final Solution
PETER LONGERICH

'Compelling' *Richard Evans*
'The finest account to date of the many twists
and turns in Adolf Hitler's anti-semitic obsession'
Richard Overy

£12.99   0 7524 3328 8

Private 12768
Memoir of a Tommy
JOHN JACKSON
FOREWORD BY HEW STRACHAN

'A refreshing new perspective' *The Sunday Times*
'At last we have John Jackson's intensely
personal and heartfelt little book to remind us
there was a view of the Great War other than
Wilfred Owen's' *The Daily Mail*

£9.99   0 7524 3531 0

The Vikings
MAGNUS MAGNUSSON

'Serious, engaging history'
BBC History Magazine

£9.99   0 7524 2699 0

If you are interested in purchasing other books published by Tempus, or in case you have difficulty finding any
Tempus books in your local bookshop, you can also place orders directly through our website

www.tempus-publishing.com

TEMPUS – REVEALING HISTORY

D-Day The First 72 Hours
WILLIAM F. BUCKINGHAM

'A compelling narrative' *The Observer*
A *BBC History Magazine* Book of the Year 2004

£9.99   0 7524 2842 X

The London Monster
Terror on the Streets in 1790
JAN BONDESON

'Gripping' *The Guardian*
'Excellent... monster-mania brought a reign of
terror to the ill-lit streets of the capital'
The Independent

£9.99   0 7524 3327 X

London
A Historical Companion
KENNETH PANTON

'A readable and reliable work of reference that
deserves a place on every Londoner's bookshelf'
Stephen Inwood

£20   0 7524 3434 9

M: MI5's First Spymaster
ANDREW COOK

'Serious spook history' *Andrew Roberts*
'Groundbreaking' *The Sunday Telegraph*
'Brilliantly researched' *Dame Stella Rimington*

£20   0 7524 2896 9

Agincourt A New History
ANNE CURRY

'A highly distinguished and convincing account'
Christopher Hibbert
'A *tour de force*' *Alison Weir*
'*The* book on the battle' *Richard Holmes*
A *BBC History Magazine* Book of the Year 2005

£25   0 7524 2828 4

Battle of the Atlantic
MARC MILNER

'The most comprehensive short survey of the
U-boat battles' *Sir John Keegan*
'Some events are fortunate in their historian, none
more so than the Battle of the Atlantic. Marc
Milner is *the* historian of the Atlantic campaign... a
compelling narrative' *Andrew Lambert*

£12.99   0 7524 3332 6

The English Resistance
The Underground War Against the Normans
PETER REX

'An invaluable rehabilitation of an ignored
resistance movement' *The Sunday Times*
'Peter Rex's scholarship is remarkable'
The Sunday Express

£12.99   0 7524 3733 X

Elizabeth Wydeville: The Slandered Queen
ARLENE OKERLUND

'A penetrating, thorough and wholly convincing
vindication of this unlucky queen'
Sarah Gristwood
'A gripping tale of lust, loss and tragedy'
Alison Weir
A *BBC History Magazine* Book of the Year 2005

£18.99   0 7524 3384 9

If you are interested in purchasing other books published by Tempus, or in case you have difficulty finding any
Tempus books in your local bookshop, you can also place orders directly through our website

www.tempus-publishing.com

TEMPUS – REVEALING HISTORY

Quacks Fakers and Charlatans in Medicine
ROY PORTER

'A delightful book' *The Daily Telegraph*
'Hugely entertaining' *BBC History Magazine*

£12.99   0 7524 2590 0

The Tudors
RICHARD REX

'Up-to-date, readable and reliable. The best
introduction to England's most important
dynasty' *David Starkey*
'Vivid, entertaining... quite simply the best short
introduction' *Eamon Duffy*
'Told with enviable narrative skill... a delight for
any reader' *THES*

£9.99   0 7524 3333 4

The Kings & Queens of England
MARK ORMROD

'Of the numerous books on the kings and
queens of England, this is the best'
Alison Weir

£9.99   0 7524 2598 6

The Covent Garden Ladies
Pimp General Jack & the Extraordinary Story of Harris's List
HALLIE RUBENHOLD

'Sex toys, porn... forget Ann Summers, Miss
Love was at it 250 years ago' *The Times*
'Compelling' *The Independent on Sunday*
'Marvellous' *Leonie Frieda*
'Filthy' *The Guardian*

£9.99   0 7524 3739 9

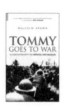

Okinawa 1945
GEORGE FEIFER

'A great book... Feifer's account of the three
sides and their experiences far surpasses most
books about war'
Stephen Ambrose

£17.99   0 7524 3324 5

Tommy Goes To War
MALCOLM BROWN

'A remarkably vivid and frank account of the
British soldier in the trenches'
Max Arthur
'The fury, fear, mud, blood, boredom and
bravery that made up life on the Western Front
are vividly presented and illustrated'
The Sunday Telegraph

£12.99   0 7524 2980 4

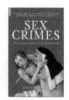

Ace of Spies The True Story of Sidney Reilly
ANDREW COOK

'The most definitive biography of the spying
ace yet written... both a compelling narrative
and a myth-shattering *tour de force*'
Simon Sebag Montefiore
'The absolute last word on the subject' *Nigel West*
'Makes poor 007 look like a bit of a wuss'
The Mail on Sunday

£12.99   0 7524 2959 0

Sex Crimes
From Renaissance to Enlightenment
W.M. NAPHY

'Wonderfully scandalous'
Diarmaid MacCulloch

£10.99   0 7524 2977 9

If you are interested in purchasing other books published by Tempus, or in case you have difficulty finding any
Tempus books in your local bookshop, you can also place orders directly through our website

www.tempus-publishing.com